I0191986

Race and War in the Lovecraft Mythos: A Philosophical Reflection

César Guarde Paz

"The past is *real*—it is *all there is*" (*SL* 3.31).

I. Introduction

In many places H. P. Lovecraft portrayed himself as a "mechanistic rationalist" (*SL* 4.383) in the line of Democritus, Epicurus, and Lucretius. In a letter to Bernard Austin Dwyer (in November 1927) he speaks of the latter as "still living though not personally known to us" (*SL* 2.193) and hence, not surprisingly, in another letter to Woodburn Harris (25 February 1929) he complains that Rome had "adopted this mawkish slave-religion" of "softness, justice, and universal brotherhood . . . of the long-decadent East" (*SL* 2.293)— the Hebrew slave-psychology (*SL* 4.207). Of course, the Semitic faith that he regarded as "an absurdity & an anomaly" (*SL* 3.341) of "erotic perversion" (*SL* 3.232) was the twilighted idol of Christianity, which he condemned for introducing into "our virile, ebullient Western stock" the burden of superstition and meekness (*SL* 3.45).

To some extent, this can be considered a Nietzschean justification of racism, and indeed a number of studies have been written to justify—or condemn—Lovecraft's bigotry and disdain. Nevertheless, our primary interest here will lie in the roots of his racist ideology and the changes it experienced over the years, and to address questions about how it was reflected in his fiction. I will argue that for Lovecraft racism is a substantive issue that needs to be addressed from a strictly materialistic viewpoint, as a Democritean force imbued with the constituent elements of classical civilization: the wisdom of Greece, the legal system of Rome, and the strength of the Nordic stock; three chemical fluids blending together in the blood of the British people.

Thus, my main thesis will be that Lovecraft's fiction and its capacity to dramatize human fear rest upon the *anxiety of genetic impurity* and the *slim chance of decay*, of evolutionary reversal. And though he remained a racist all his life, the object of this anxiety moved from merely race-based criticism to German culture to Asian cultures. Although I shall begin with a brief presentation of the "intellectual racist environment" that characterized Western culture in those years, in what follows I should not be understood as attempting to justify Lovecraft's race-prejudice, for he was fully aware of it:

> Nothing means anything, in the end, except with reference to that continuous immediate fabric of appearances and experiences of which one was originally a part. . . . Naturally, if a race wants to submit to the fantastic martrydom of mongrelisation for an agonising period of centuries, there will emerge a new composite race and culture whose members will have attained a new homogeneity—and therefore a new and satisfying equilibrium. But who cares to sacrifice himself for the sake of this hypothetical future race—a race as genuinely foreign and meaningless to him as the Peruvians would have been to the Greeks, or as the Thibetans are to ourselves? All that any living man normally wants—and all that any man worth calling such will stand for—is as stable and pure a perpetuation as possible of the set of forms and appearances to which his value-perceptions are, from the circumstances of moulding, instinctively attuned. That is all there is to life—the preservation of a framework which will render the experience of the individual apparently relevant and significant. Here we have the normal phenomenon of race-prejudice in a nutshell—the legitimate fight of every virile personality to live in a world where life shall seem to mean something. (*SL* 3.254)

II. Cultural and Atomistic Racism

Historically, the entire Western intellectual tradition offered a respectable wealth of evidence in support of the idea of white cultural supremacy and, more particularly, of the excellency of the "noble BRITISH race" ("New England Fallen," *AT* 392, l. 152).

THE LOVECRAFT ANNUAL

Edited by S. T. Joshi   No. 6 (2012)

Contents

Abbreviations used in the text and notes:

AT   *The Ancient Track* (Night Shade Books, 2001)
CE   *Collected Essays* (Hippocampus Press, 2004–06; 5 vols.)
D   *Dagon and Other Macabre Tales* (Arkham House, 1986)
DH   *The Dunwich Horror and Others* (Arkham House, 1984)
HM   *The Horror in the Museum and Other Revisions* (Arkham House, 1989)
LL   *Lovecraft's Library: A Catalogue*, 3rd rev. ed. (Hippocampus Press, 2012)
MM   *At the Mountains of Madness and Other Novels* (Arkham House, 1985)
MW   *Miscellaneous Writings* (Arkham House, 1995)
SL   *Selected Letters* (Arkham House, 1965–76; 5 vols.)

Copyright © 2012 by Hippocampus Press

Published by Hippocampus Press, P.O. Box 641, New York, NY 10156
http://www.hippocampuspress.com

Cover illustration by Allen Koszowski. Hippocampus Press logo designed by Anastasia Damianakos. Cover design by Barbara Briggs Silbert.

Lovecraft Annual is published once a year, in Fall. Articles and letters should be sent to the editor, S. T. Joshi, c/o Hippocampus Press, and must be accompanied by a self-addressed stamped envelope if return is desired. All reviews are assigned. Literary rights for articles and reviews will reside with *Lovecraft Annual* for one year after publication, whereupon they will revert to their respective authors. Payment is in contributor's copies.

ISSN 1935-6102
ISBN 978-1-61498-049-0

While this was never scientifically demonstrated, most scholars and philosophers proclaimed that no culture could be regarded as superior to the Christian Western civilization, and even if there was indeed widespread disdain for the dark-colored natives of the new discovered worlds, from America to Asia, the main thrust behind this discourse—its overriding concern—was that the West had never encountered a native civilization as developed as its own. This situation was soon to change, however, with the rediscovery of China and the first missions of the Jesuits in that country. The German philosopher Leibniz, disquieted by the Christian schisms, found in China an ethical and scientific model that could unify a decentralized Europe. He justified his Eurocentric vision with the following words, in a letter to Francesco M. Grimaldi, S.J. (1618/9–1663): "So far we have had numerous relations with the Indies and of various types; not yet, however, have we had scientific relations" (330, 3–5; Lach 29). And while the inhabitants of India were despised by the Jesuits as "brute beasts" who were "born to serve rather than to command" (Spence 41), the Chinese and the Japanese were called "gente bianca," "white people" (Schütte 130), an idea that the Japanese army would recover in the nineteenth century in order to keep themselves separated from the inferior yellow race, i.e. the Chinese (Berlinguez-Kono 20). David Hume, in 1753, was following the same path that Voltaire himself followed when he referred to the "negroes" as "naturally inferior to the whites. There never was a civilized nation of any other complexion than white" (629), and from his statement made in "Of the Rise and Progress of the Arts and Sciences" (Hume 123) we are compelled to assume that the Chinese were still included in this later group of white civilized people.

It was not before the second half of the eighteenth century, however, that Western literature, whether scientific or not, began to claim the existence of a separated "yellow race," usually referred to as "Mongoloid" by Kant and Schopenhauer. As a result of the dramatic rediscovery of the lost Roman cities of Herculaneum (1719) and Pompeii (1748), along with the forgotten temples of Paestum (1750) and the Indo-European roots of the West (1786), a shift from China or Eastern Asia to India and Classical Greece occurred in Western thought. Kant could therefore safely believe that not only "the yellow Indians do have a meagre talent," but also the Chinese and "the Negroes are far below them" (63). Schopenhauer, who on the other hand was fond of India, insists that "the highest civilization and culture, apart from the ancient Hindus and Egyptians, are found exclusively among the white races" (158). This, together with the immediate influence of authors like Huxley or writings like Spengler's *The Hour of Decision*, already studied in Lovecraft scholarship (Joshi, *Decline of the West* 74–80), constitutes an important and shining tradition of historical supremacy that could not be denied by someone devoted to the past glories of the British Empire.

With this, however, I do not wish to justify the unjustifiable racism of Lovecraft, but to enlighten the way we can approach his conception of racialism and its relation with the themes of war and mythology as present in his later fiction. Lovecraft's thesis was, in fact, entirely different from that emerging racism found in Western philosophy, with the exception of some faint echoes of Hume—who considered the Germans "the most rude and barbarous of the whites" (629)—and Kant, who also defined race decadence in relation to blood combinations (41). Lovecraft's explicit materialistic view is laid down with Democritean—or Epicurean—notes in a letter to Rheinhart Kleiner:

> Sometimes I think of racial combinations as chemical reactions; for instance, I believe that certain stocks have greater assimilative powers than others. The Gallo-Basque stock with Latin infusion, which constitutes the bulk of the French population, is much more receptive to alien blood than is our colder and more Teutonic stock. (*SL* 1.17–18)

That this was not an occasional thought but a long-meditated attempt to explain the glory of the noble British stock can be seen throughout his early poetry. In "Britannia Victura," Lovecraft defines the noble British race in the following terms:

> The mind of Greece, the law of Rome,
> > The strength of Northern climes remote
> On one fair Island made their home,
> > And in one race their virtues wrote:

> The blended glories of the past
> In England evermore shall last! (*AT* 405, ll. 7–12)

The Britons are then understood to be the legitimate "deathless heirs" ("1914," *AT* 398, l. 68) of classical antiquity, blending chemically dissimilar components into one single final stock: from the Greeks they received all knowledge, a legacy that was embodied in pagan literature and used to sustain Roman laws (cf. "On the Ruin of Rome," *AT* 12, ll. 1–9). This same idea can be extended to include other features such as literature and language and, tentatively, any other aspect of human culture. Not only has poetry and the metric sense "taken on different aspects among different races" (*CE* 2.11), but the English verse of Dryden and Pope was conceived by Lovecraft as the natural and superior blending of Greek and Roman verse with the British Teutonic versification style (see, for example, his essays "Metrical Regularity" and "The Allowable Rhyme"). The English language was also understood as the chemical interaction of various factors in the lexical environment: "our speech is probably the most forceful and expressive of modern tongues, combining as it does the vigour of the Teutonic with the precision of the Latin elements"--a precision marked by grammar, the *laws of the language*—and also possessing "the straightforwardness of its Teutonic skeleton and the exactness of its Latin vocabulary" (*CE* 1.59–60).

But the Romans were conquered by the barbarous Teutons, the Northern white tribes, sons of Odin, who added the strength necessary to create a new racial legacy: a complete human being with all the resources for the foundation of a real civilization. And they occupied a little island, sweeping from the land the poor Celts ("Ad Britannos—1918," *AT* 415, ll. 57–60). This legacy finally resurfaced in America, where a New England was built, and from where it sings for a lost Europe:

> Behold the Teuton, threat'ning in his guilt
> The laws and arts your matchless Athens built;
> Your laws and arts, by Roman prowess spread
> Thro' grateful Europe, and to Britain led;
> By British pow'r sent o'er the ocean crest
> Where young Columbia rules th' expansive West.
> ("To Greece, 1917," *AT* 410, ll. 31–6)

The idea of the chemical combination of these three elements clearly reflects a reading of the thesis of William Z. Ripley's *The Races of Europe: A Sociological Study*, and not necessarily a direct one (Joshi, *H. P. Lovecraft: A Life* 134): a year before Lovecraft's poem "Britannia Victura" appeared in 1917, Madison Grant published in his *The Passing of the Great Race* a map showing the distribution of the *three* European races, the Teutons in the north, the Alpines in Central Europe, but also in Greece, and the Mediterraneans in the Roman Empire. For Lovecraft Latin blood was more receptive and allowed the perfect mixture of Greek knowledge and Teutonic strength, but it was not the most important part of the complete human being. Latin Europe needed the strength of the Teuton in order to save itself from destruction, but the Teuton was also in need of Latin and Greek blood if they wished to control their own strength and, in the end, so that they will not become destroyers. So he says in "The Crime of the Century":

> As the power of the Roman Empire declined, the Teuton sent down into Italy, Gaul, and Spain the re-vivifying elements which saved those countries from complete destruction. Though now largely lost in the mixed population, the Teutons are the true founders of all the so-called Latin states. . . . After the native elements absorbed the Teutonic invaders, the Latin civilizations declined tremendously, so that the France, Italy, and Spain of today bear every mark of national degeneracy. (*CE* 5.13–14)

And later, in a letter to Kleiner:

> Teutonic blood snatched Britain from the Celt and made England the greatest force in all civilisation. Teutonic blood conquered the Western wilderness and gave America an instant place amongst the great nations of the globe. But this blood has become so extensively and tragically diluted, that the non-German Teutons may well look with concern to their future. . . . Germany herself has set a truer valuation on the importance of unmixed blood, but may yet come to grief through the absorption of Slavic elements. The course of Germany during the last half-century has been one of curiously mixed merit. Certain scientific and philosophical developments have been marvellous, yet they have been conjoined to a brutality and narrowness of vision which threaten the devel-

opment of civilization. The pan-Teutonic ideal, attainable only by a complete and amicable co-operation between Anglo-Saxon and Germanic races, has been fallaciously subordinated to a petty pan-Germanic ideal which is bringing about the virtual suicide of the Teutonic race, and driving the Anglo–Saxons and Germans into equally unnatural alliances with alien races. (*SL* 1.53)

What Lovecraft seems to imply here, if we try to explain his letter from the strict materialistic approach of chemical combinations, is that the Germanic Teutons have lost or betrayed the laws of Rome—cf. his poem "Germania—1918," in which he reinvokes the same idea—and, with some knowledge daubing their still remaining Greek veins, they have created advanced scientific and philosophical models to conform to their low ambitions: the pan-Germanic ideal, or the eradication of all law and education. It is, in the end, the Greek element in the Teutonic blood, "a Nordic-Mediterranean blend" (*SL* 4.249), is the one that allows civilization to flourish and prosper. This leads us directly to the causes of the Great War, as Lovecraft explained it from a racial perspective.

III. The Great War as Racial Decadence

Lovecraft's thoughts regarding the First World War are mainly collected in his essay "The Crime of the Century" (1915) and expressed in the early poetry of this period. Here I do not wish to discuss further his historical understanding and political ideas about the conflict, accounts of which can be found in several sources, but to draw attention to the way in which his racial representations found room for expansion. Briefly stated, there are two different immediate causes responsible for the Great War between brother nations: the increasing degeneration of the Germanic Teuton, and the effeminacy of Latin Europe, a situation that could only be solved through the intervention of the true Teutons, the holy race of England, paired with the United States of America, its natural descendant.

Lovecraft's insidious attacks against German culture and mentality are not uncommon, and his poems are abound in adjectives like "proud invader," "savage" ("1914," *AT* 397, l. 10) or "bestial" ("The Crime of Crimes," *AT* 398, l. 2), most of which have been reviewed by Phillip A. Ellis in a former number of this journal

(129). For Lovecraft, the German type was taken back to its early stage of human evolution, prior to the acquisition of the Roman and Greek spirits: the Germanic Teuton is no longer human, because "The laws of man! What laws can curb or sway / The Prussian wolf, with manhood cast away?" ("The Crime of Crimes," *AT* 399, ll. 13–14). In order to show this, Lovecraft resorts to calling them not only wolves, but also Goths, Vandals, and Huns ("To Greece, 1917," *AT* 409, l. 20, 28; 410, l. 37), that is to say, incomplete savage Teutons not yet blended with the knowledge of Greece and the laws of Rome.

This loathing for anything German was not, indeed, something alien to modern Western philosophical tradition. Hume, as we have seen, considered the Germans "the most rude and barbarous of the whites" (629), and Friedrich Nietzsche did not spare words in describing their sick soul full of Germanness, suspicious as he was of anything German, from music to language to education. In his late autobiography, *Ecce Homo*, the Prussian philosopher writes with Lovecraftian delight and satire: "It is quite enough to turn a genius into something mediocre, something 'German'. . . . I am— alien to everything German in my most profound instincts, so that even having a German near me slows down my digestion. . . . I shall never grant that a German could know what music is. . . . A German is almost like a woman in that you can never get to the bottom of him: *he doesn't have one.* . . . Should I not suggest the word 'German' as an international coinage for *this* psychological depravity?" (Nietzsche 22, 27, 29, 85). It is not clear whether Lovecraft did actually derive his inspiration for such Germanophobic ideas from the work of these philosophers, but they were by no means the exception: after the Franco-Prussian War of 1870–71, hostility toward German products and people rapidly increased in Britain, with fears that this little island was about to become Germany's next booty. This phenomenon reached its peak in the first decade of the twentieth century, only four years before the beginning of the Great War (Panayi 90–91; Massie 213ff.).

Even though Lovecraft could have stopped here and left Germany with this huge burden, his British eyes still perceived something else, something unearthly, crawling "from the pit below" ("Germania—1918," *AT* 418, l. 8): not only did the Germanic Teuton degenerate into its former, ruthless self, but also the Latin/Greek type was shrinking back to its un-Teutonic component, the same weakness that allowed Rome to fall into decay and perish miserably at the hands of the Ostrogoths: "Tacitus wrote an account of the German tribes, whose savage virility and rude virtue he held up in scornful contrast to the effeminate and decadent society of imperial Rome" ("The Literature of Rome," CE 2.30). Lovecraft blamed not only the blood in their veins, but also democracy and the "effeminate idealist" ("The Crime of the Century," CE 5.13):

> There is something the matter with the morale of the more polished nations—they need a little more brutality of the ancient Teutonic sort. No army can win without a certain savage lust of combat, and this spirit is being undermined with the current cant about democracy, idealism, and all that sort of rot. . . . Racial factors are also against us. For all our Roman civilisation, the enemy has the preponderance of superior blood. If all the Allied nations were as thoroughly Teutonic as Prussia, the end would be nearer and happier. . . . But this blood has become so extensively and tragically diluted, that the non-Germanic Teutons may well look with concern to their future. (SL 1.53)

And, as already quoted: "After the native elements absorbed the Teutonic invaders, the Latin civilizations declined tremendously, so that the France, Italy, and Spain of today bear every mark of national degeneracy (CE 5.13–14).

Lovecraft is referring here to the Dark Ages, when the Caliphs of Bagdad and Cordova were the true dominant civilization and the Teutonic blood had to recover the lost Southern Europe for the Caucasian race (SL 2.296). The culmination of the gradual decline of the West came from President Wilson, when in a May 1915 speech in Philadelphia he was willing to say in reference to the participation of the States in the Great War: "There is such a thing as a man being too proud to fight" (88). For someone like Lovecraft, the very fact that Europe and the United States were too proud to fight could only mean that they were too cowardly to fight, too un-Teutonic. This was, of course, not an isolated reaction: After the *Gunflight* (1 May 1915) and *Lusitania* (7 May) torpedoing incidents, and led by former president Theodore Roosevelt, many individuals and newspapers ridiculed President Woodrow Wilson on both sides of the Atlantic (Hecht 33). Lovecraft felt naturally compelled, not only to express his disapproval of the War as a fratricidal confrontation of blood, but also to plead for the recovery of the old Teutonic elements thus far kept away in the deep noble veins of the British people. His poem "Ad Britannos—1918" was written with all these considerations in mind: firstly, "the hot blood of pillagers ruthless and bold," "the blood of the past is raging within" the German (*AT* 414, ll. 21–22), while "we patiently stand in our honour and meekness" (l. 25), and we unfurl our banner, inscribed with the words "TOO PROUD TO FIGHT!" ("Pacifist War Song—1917," *AT* 224, ll. 3–4). But "our blood is the same the vandals are vaunting," for we "too are the stout sons of Woden and Thor" (*AT* 414, ll. 53–54), and so we must fight against the decline of the Great Race. This leads us to the final battle for Europe, which is ultimately the battle for the world's civilization, and which could bring us back to the Dark Ages (*SL* 1.54). No doubt he felt, like Spengler, that the end was near, and that the Great War was just another symptom of the growing genetic dysfunction that had infected the Great Race: "That Arabic Empire was the last of the great Semitic cultures, just as our Teutonic Western civilisation is the last of the Great Aryan cultures. Both branches of the white race are getting toward the final sunset" (*SL* 1.296). This future event was written down in poetical form as an answer to his historical and racial inquiries: "The Teuton's Battle-Song."

IV. "The Teuton's Battle–Song"

This poem was originally published in the *United Amateur* (February 1916), but since the title is mentioned once in a letter to Maurice W. Moe, dated in 17 December 1914, it was probably composed at least two years before its publication. The topic under consideration is thus explained by Lovecraft in his long "Author's Note," located after the poem's end (available in *AT* 510–11): "to trace the ruthless ferocity and incredible bravery of the modern Teutonic soldier to the hereditary influence of the ancient Northern Gods and Heroes." But this is clearly an emotivist reading with aesthetic intent, a poetical mechanism that Lovecraft liked to use to exemplify the rule of Nature and Beauty, far beyond his own atheism. As he explained some years later to Alfred Galpin, quoting John Keats: "Beauty is certainly the prime object; Truth is to be considered only when coincident with Beauty" (*Letters to Alfred Galpin* 21). As a poet, Lovecraft was less concerned with the real causes of the Great War than with the "aesthetical truth" behind it, and he beautified and adorned that "truth" with gods and heroes, either pagan, Nordic, or even Christian. "The Teuton's Battle–Song" relates, indeed, that Great War, the Doom of the Gods or *Ragnarok*, when blood brothers have committed themselves to kill each other, assisted by their natural enemies. Gods in Heaven observe the Teutonic soldier fighting and sacrificing his strength and vitality for the sake of Valhalla, obtaining both winners and sinners, a place among the Aesir Gods—but not those cowards too proud to fight. The day will come, as well, when those Gods have to fight one another and be killed, to see their land destroyed by Surtur's horde. But this final battle between Teutonic powers—Englishmen and Germans alike—will only be solved when Alfadur, the All-Father, enlists himself (*AT* 396, l. 29) and helps their old brothers make "his realm anew. / And Gods and men with purer life indue" (ll. 55–56). This Alfadur can be suggestively identified with the United States (note the image of the soaring eagle in the final verses), the poet's last hope to end the existing chaos in Teutonic blood.

But this poem is particularly important to us for two additional reasons. In the first place, Lovecraft shows once more his chemical reading of racial miscegenation when he sings, pointing at those hypocrites of the brotherhood of Man: "Could your shrill pipings in the race impair / The warlike impulse put by Nature there?" (ll. 9–10), and later, more explicitly, in his note to the poem:

> Despite the cant of the peace-advocate, we must realise that our present Christian civilisation, the product of an alien people, rest but lightly upon the Teuton when he is deeply aroused, and that in the heat of combat he is quite prone to revert to the mental type of his own Woden-worshipping progenitors. (*AT* 510)

Two points should be highlighted here: the alien component of our present Christian civilization, and the reverting to the original pagan and Teutonic type. What Lovecraft is stressing here is the un-Christian origin of Europe, the foundations of which had been built upon the ashes of previous cultures, namely, Greece and Rome, together with the victorious barbaric tribes that had conquered the Western Roman Empire. Penetration of (Christian) pacifism into the Teutonic blood allowed Europe to immerse itself in an ignominious alliance with alien people, fragmenting nations otherwise bound together by common ties of religion, literature, culture, or blood. But this chaotically mixed chemical solution still preserves some of the original Teutonic strength, and it can be reverted quickly with the natural heat of battle (note, again, the chemical metaphor). Lovecraft's truly cosmic fear was the already tainted ancestry of Man, and the ever-present possibility of reversal to the previous state of pacifism or total warfare—instead of the "middle way" ethos between the barbaric blood of the Teuton and the serene laws of Rome.

In the second place, Lovecraft himself specifically declares that this epic composition "is an attempt of the present critic to view the principles of human warfare without the hypocritical spectacles of sentimentality" (*AT* 511), that is to say, from the perspective of a trans-human entity beyond good and evil, emancipated from any human emotion or sensibility, which observes human war and destiny as an unimportant game of chance. This is, I believe, Lovecraft's first utterance of "cosmicism," written two years before his "The Poe-et's Nightmare" (1916)—if we assume "The Teuton's Battle-Song" was originally composed with that intention—and where he portrayed a similar view, as already pointed out by S. T. Joshi (*A Subtler Magick* 231):

> Alone in space, I view'd the feeble fleck
> Of silver light, marking the narrow ken
> Which mortals call the boundless universe.
> On ev'ry side, each as a tiny star,
> Shone more creations, vaster than our own,
> And teeming with unnumber'd forms of life;
> Tho' we as life would recognise it not,
> Being bound to earthly thoughts of human mould.
>
> (*AT* 22, ll. 152–59)

This idea, taken from his readings on astronomy and philosophy, was certainly decisive for the development of his later mythology, but it was the convergence of Lovecraft's whimsical approaches to war and race that left a profound impact on all his future writings. Indeed, the final battle of the *Ragnarok* represented here already sets out *in nuce* the essential features of his weird tales and the Lovecraft Mythos: not only do we find a cosmic trans-human view of mortal events and an imaginary New England (for example, in the country of Abundance mentioned in lines 57ff.), but also the important image of a non-Christian pantheon of gods recklessly indifferent to Earth and its human inhabitants. Of course, Lovecraft had to change the concept of benign pagan gods and his beautiful Promised Land in order to create a more suitable environment for his cosmic horror. We can still find, however, this same image in his beautiful "Poetry and the Gods" (1920), where he writes:

> *that the Gods were never dead*, but only sleeping the sleep and dreaming the dreams of Gods in lotos-filled Hesperian gardens beyond the golden sunset. And now draweth night the time of their awaking, when coldness and ugliness shall perish, and Zeus sit once more on Olympus. . . . The day now dawns when man must answer for centuries of denial, but in sleeping the Gods have grown kind, and will not hurl him to the gulf made for deniers of Gods. Instead will their vengeance smite the darkness, fallacy, and ugliness which have turned the mind of man; and under the sway of bearded Saturnus shall mortals, once more sacrificing unto him, dwell in beauty and delight. (*D* 352)

Indeed, this tale takes place "just after the close of the Great War" (*D* 349). Needless to say, this portrayal of the return of the Gods and the end of the modern degenerate aesthetics is essentially a mirrored image of his later horror tales. Compare, for instance, the "In his house at R'lyeh dead Cthulhu waits dreaming" ("The Call of Cthulhu," *DH* 139), already pointed out by George Wetzel (56); "*Man rules now where They ruled once; They shall soon rule where Man rules now. . . . They wait patient and potent, for here shall They reign again*" ("The Dunwich Horror," *DH* 170); "Soon from the sea a noxious birth began; / Forgotten lands with weedy spires of gold;

/ The ground was cleft, and mad auroras rolled / Down on the quaking citadels of man. / Then, crushing what he chanced to mould in play, / The idiot Chaos blew Earth's dust away" ("Nyarlathotep," *AT* 73, ll. 9–14; cf. "The Crawling Chaos," *HM* 15). The argument I want to turn to in the next section is that the catalyst for this conversion was Lovecraft's conception of racial combinations as chemical reactions, and especially his fear that the purity of Britain would revert completely to the ancient/modern German type—or even to the more effeminate pacifist.

V. Race, War, and Decadence in the Lovecraft Mythos

The importance of race in Lovecraft's cosmicism has been stressed a number of times. We may find traces of it in many important tales, such as "The Shadow over Innsmouth," where interbreeding occurs between humans and a race of fish–frogs; "The Dunwich Horror," between Yog-Sothoth and a mortal woman; or "Facts concerning the Late Arthur Jermyn and His Family" and "The Lurking Fear," and many more (Joshi, "Time, Space, and Natural Law" 195–97). It has been pointed out how Lovecraft's own experiences, from his deteriorating health and his father's illness to the economic decay of his family, predisposed him to embrace his well-known "horror of corruption and decay" (*D* xl). He was indeed concerned for the future of human civilization when he wrote that "the old culture with its idea of quality versus size is worth fighting for—perhaps the only thing on earth worth fighting for—*but I don't think it's going to win*" (*SL* 3.78). But the fundamental problem with this twofold affirmation is that it presents us with a Lovecraft who is sincerely concerned, not just with his own position in society, but with the position of the modern Western society as a whole in the history of world civilization: we should understand his "horror of corruption and decay" as a social rather than personal concern and obligation, a figment of his British imagination in which Britons hold a key position in the foundation and creation of laws, morals, and science. Certainly, the same idea of evolution was a real problem in Lovecraft's times, for evolution would mean that those same lofty Britons and their sublime civilization—and together with them, Greeks and Romans—

were preceded by inferior beings with a very much lower if not nonexistent culture: we either had in our veins the blood of a terrible mammal beast carried by our great ape ancestors, or the not less savage stock of ancient Africa. This debate between polygenists and monogenists was an issue Lovecraft himself could not avoid writing about:

> No line betwixt 'human' and 'non–human' organisms is possible. . . . There are many elephants more human than many Bantu niggers. . . . Many anthropologists have detected both negroid and gorilla resemblances in these 'dawn' skulls, and to my mind it's a safe bet that they were exceedingly low, hairy negroes existing perhaps 400,000 years ago and having perhaps the rudiments of a guttural language. Certainly, it is not extravagant to imagine the existence of a sort of sadistic cult amongst such beasts, which might later develop into a formal Satanism. . . . Indeed, I think that certain traits in many lower animals suggest, to the mind whose imagination is not dulled by scientific literalism, the beginnings of activities horrible to contemplate in evolved mankind. (*SL* 1.258; quoted in full in *Lord of a Visible World* 122)

Lovecraft's rhetoric is once again trying to trace an invisible but nevertheless broad line between civilization and barbarism in terms of race and culture, to advocate instead an aesthetic polygenist view—races seen as separate products with different origins—by separating the real humans from the less civilized dark-skinned people. He knew and believed that apes "preceded us ancestrally" (*SL* 3.43) and that "the negro, australoid, neanderthal, rhodesian" were all "human and humanoid types" (*SL* 3.277), with "the negro" representing "a vastly inferior biological variant which must under no circumstances taint our Aryan stock" (*SL* 4.195). We can trace this racist idea already in his first creations: "The Beast in the Cave" (1905), one of his earliest extant stories, is interesting to us in many ways, and not only because it tries to explain a folktale in terms of scientific evolutionary principles. This upbeat story tells us of a white hairy ape living in the Mammoth Cave in Kentucky that turns out to be a man, and it is his isolation from civilization that increased his physical degeneration, going back to the white apes human beings once were.

Later Lovecraft found this same idea in his esteemed Arthur

Machen, for he quoted a passage from "The Red Hand" as the epigraph for "The Horror at Red Hook" (1925): "It is possible that man may sometimes return on the track of evolution, and it is my belief that an awful lore is not yet dead." This idea became central to Lovecraft's cosmicism: we can find it in his Commonplace Book: "Individual, by some strange process, retraces the path of evolution & becomes amphibious" (*MW* 128), an obvious reference to his later "The Shadow over Innsmouth" (1931). Thus, this lonely instance in "The Beast in the Cave" could be read as a revelatory premonition of his later encounter with Machen, a natural development that can hardly be considered casual, for it has to be found in many tales before his reading of the "The Red Hand" in 1925 (*LL* 578) and of course, as we have seen, in his Great War essays and poetry.

Racism was his companion in verse as early as 1905, when he composed his "De Triumpho Naturae" after reading William Benjamin Smith's racist *The Colour Line*. The title of the poem refers to the will of Nature that "must in Time be done" to take the "savage black, the ape-resembling beast" back to its original state of vice and barbarism, destroying the same freedom they could not achieve by themselves (*AT* 13–14). This conviction continued unabated in the feverish opening days of the Great War, only to be combined with an active and passionate criticism of Germany and the German mind. In 1912 he wrote "On the Creation of Niggers," and just one year before "Dagon" (1917) he would still remember how the "nameless multitudes upon our shore / From the dim corners of creation pour, Whilst mongrel slaves crawl hither to partake / Of Saxon liberty they could not make" ("An American to Mother England," *AT* 400, ll. 15–18).

But the new conflict earned Lovecraft a new enemy: Germany. "Dagon" opens with a German sea-raider capturing an unnamed individual—the narrator himself—in a time when "the great war was then at its very beginning, and the ocean forces of the Hun had not completely sunk to their later degradation" (*D* 14). Degeneration is already present in "The Temple" (1920), where a German submarine finds again an unnamed seaman after filming the shooting of a British vessel and sinking their lifeboats. This is the first tale relating the progressive deterioration of the Prussian mind: commander Karl Heinrich witnesses how the crewmen begin to damage the ship until finally he is forced to kill them, only to suffer himself the last obnoxious call from the sunken temple—an Atlantean temple built by "fair Nordick bearded men [who] dwelt in my city, and spoke a polish'd tongue akin to Greek" (SL 1.287), which would imply that the vile Prussian was being purified or simply killed by the pure Greek element of human civilization. And we should not forget the prophetic ending of "Dagon": "I dream of a day when they may rise above the billows to drag down in their reeking talons the remnants of puny, *war-exhausted mankind*" (D 19; my emphasis).

Between these two stories Lovecraft wrote "Beyond the Wall of Sleep" (1919), which is of immediate interest here insofar as it depicts the inability of certain degenerate human brains to bear the weight of a superior intellect. The human here, Joe Slater (or Slaader), was "one of those strange, repellent scions of a primitive colonial peasant stock whose isolation for nearly three centuries in the hilly fastnesses of a little-travelled countryside has caused them to sink to a kind of barbaric degeneracy" (D 26). In other words, he is, both physically and mentally, a decadent specimen in the same way the inhabitants of Dunwich "have come to form a race by themselves, with the well–defined mental and physical stigmata of degeneracy and inbreeding" (DH 157). Physical stigmata leads to moral inability in both cases: compare, for instance, "the half-hidden murders, incests . . . [and] unnamable violence" in Dunwich with Slater's non-existent law and morals (D 26). He is, indeed, unable to bear the intellect that possessed him, for he "was too much of an animal, too little a man" (D 34). This theme of degeneracy and the unfitness of some humans for certain elements designed for superior white individuals reappears in his serialized tale "Herbert West—Reanimator" (1921–22): the *chemical* solution prepared "from experience with white specimens" cannot properly work with other races and, more specifically, with black people, ultimately suggesting that they are a separate species (D 146–47). The cases of Joe Slater and the occasional black boxer are parallel if we accept Lovecraft's theory of genetics and race differentiation as chemical compounds: Slater's ancestry, being isolated, has become an animal, a monster, a beast like the Beast in the

Cave or the Martense family in "The Lurking Fear" (1922). And when we read of the resurrected black boxer with the small figure of a missing kid in his mouth, we cannot help but remember the final horror in "The Rats in the Walls" (1923), those "activities horrible to contemplate in evolved mankind" (*SL* 1.258), when the narrator is found in the blackest pit with the "plump, half-eaten body of Capt. Norrys, with my own cat leaping and tearing at my throat" (*DH* 45).This idea of reversion due to a tainted ancestry present in "The Rats in the Walls" is a curious one. Joshi has correctly traced it back to Irvin S. Cobb's "The Unbroken Chain," a short story Lovecraft read in the same year (note in *The Call of Cthulhu* 382), but we should specify that it is the way this regression happens, and not the regression itself, that Cobb's tale triggered Lovecraft's imagination—as it was not Machen's "The Red Hand" the true catalyst for "The Horror at Red Hook." Indeed, the narrator discovers mysteries lurking far back in his family tree, and it is his discovery of such facts—the mental apprehension of them—that transforms him physically. Lovecraft is clearly suggesting that mental processes are as physical as any other chemical reaction (see, for example, *SL* 4.135–36), and that a taint in the line can be brought back just by *knowing of* its existence—a theme already present before his reading of Cobb. Thus, when the narrator finally confronts this knowledge, he begins to change in a way similar to Cobb's Frenchman—speaking archaic English, Middle English, Latin, Gaelic, and pre-human grunts (note that he doesn't seem to have pre-German or Greek blood).

A similar idea can be found in "The Picture in the House" (1920). The narrator, looking for "certain genealogical data," creeps into the old isolated house of a blue-eyed Puritan, one of those exiled from their kind who "in their isolation . . . came to them dark furtive traits from the prehistoric depths of their cold Northern heritage." If this was not sufficient warning of lurking fears to come, the narrator remarks that "in my genealogical researches I had encountered legends of a century before which biased me against places of this kind" (*DH* 117–18). The traveler in the house marvels with morbid curiosity at Pigafetta's *Regnum Congo* and its engravings depicting "negroes with white skins and Caucasian features" (*DH* 119). This is of course racist rhetoric at its best, but what

Lovecraft may be suggesting here is the existence of a prehistoric white Congolese civilization and a connection between them and the modern Englishmen (as happens with Arthur Jermyn). The story would have safely worked out without any reference to this picture by the De Bry brothers: the book persistently opens itself at Plate XII, showing the gruesome butcher's shop of the cannibal Anziques, and the old blue-eyed host is revealed to be also a cannibal who has been influenced by the morbid picture. But if we assume that Lovecraft was trying to convey something with the white Congolese engraving, apparently not related to the cannibalism of Anziques, a new insight can be added to this story: what the old blue-eyed man discovered in his lonely reading of the *Regnum Congo* was a taint in the line, the existence of a prehistoric white Congolese race of cannibals who were the ancestors of the white race. And *that knowledge* led to a change in his behavior, bringing him back to his ancestors' prehistoric state of cannibalism.

One of the best examples of how miscegenation was understood as a process of tempering and eventually eradicating the purity of the white race is described in "The Lurking Fear" (1922). The original builder of the Martense mansion, Gerrit Martense, was a Teuton who hated English civilization. He settled down in Tempest Mountain, merging with the "mongrel population" and "intermarrying with the numerous menial class about the state." Such behavior against civilization marked the family with "a peculiar inherited dissimilarity of eyes; one generally being blue and the other brown" (*D* 191). When the narrator finally discovers the secret behind the destiny of the Martense progeny, the resulting inbred beasts are described in the recurrent terms of a terrible mammal ("The Beast in the Cave") or a gorilla-like ("Herbert West—Reanimator") entity: a "nauseous; a filthy whitish gorilla thing with sharp yellow fangs and matted fur. It was the ultimate product of mammalian degeneration" (*D* 199).

This answers an interesting question if we read it carefully: What is, in fact, the "lurking fear" we see in many Lovecraftian tales, that "embodiment of all the snarling chaos and grinning fear that lurk behind life" (*D* 199), those "mysteries which evidently lurked far back in my family tree" (*DH* 28), that *colour* "lurking under there" in "The Colour out of Space" (*DH* 77), and also "the ceaseless fear of the dark, windowless elder ruins," that "curious fear" of the Great Race in "The Shadow out of Time" (*DH* 397, 400), and the "shadowy fear about which [the Old Ones] did not like to speak" (*MM* 66)? Lovecraft provides a very interesting answer in his essay "Supernatural Horror in Literature" (1925):

> There is here [in the supernatural tale] involved a psychological pattern or tradition as real and as deeply grounded in mental experience as any other pattern or tradition of mankind; coeval with the religious feeling and closely related to many aspects of it, and *too much a part of our inmost biological heritage to lose keen potency over a very important, though not numerically great, minority of our species.* (*D* 366; my emphasis)

That Lovecraft identified himself with the narrator a number of times is no secret, since he believed that "no first-rate story can ever be written without the author's actually experiencing the moods & visions concerned in a sort of oneiroscopic way" (*SL* 3.213; Joshi, "Autobiography in Lovecraft" 51–63). In "The Rats in the Walls" the raconteur, Delapore, is clearly Lovecraft himself, owning a cat called Nigger-Man. In "The Dunwich Horror" (1928), another tale about inbreeding and miscegenation, Lovecraft found himself "psychologically identifying with one of the characters (an aged scholar who finally combats the menace) toward the end" (letter to August Derleth, September 1928, quoted in Joshi, *A Dreamer and a Visionary* 273). And something similar awaits the reader in "Facts concerning the Late Arthur Jermyn and His Family," which I shall take into consideration later. That "lurking fear" was, in fact, Lovecraft's own "lurking fear," the fear of a *colour* taint in his white Great Race, the fear of a regression to the monsters of the past:

> My hair and eyes are dark, though—I suppose there is something of the Cymric elder Briton in me . . . at times I have liked to think that I am part Roman (*SL* 1.299). My interest grows languid and academic as names recede toward the Domesday Book or pre-Renaissance oblivion, since the amount of any one strain of blood I may inherit from such a date is virtually negligible. So long as it isn´t Negro or australoid, I don´t kick. (*SL* 4.143)

But with the Great War, this monster had become the German

Teuton. Besides "Dagon" and "The Temple," such tales as "Pickman's Model" and "Cool Air" (1926), "The Dunwich Horror" ("In 1917 the war came . . .": *DH* 165) and "The Thing on the Doorstep" ("When the war came . . .": *DH* 279) present brief references to this event. The single most important tale directly related to the Great War and its horrible effects upon mankind and society is "Herbert West—Reanimator." The main character, we are told a number of times, had "yellow hair, pale blue eyes," a feature Lovecraft repeated in the introduction to every chapter. He was, then, a pure Teuton, playing with the scientific discoveries of his time in order to improve society. But with the horrors of the Great War—"Some of these things have made me faint, they have convulsed me with devastating nausea, while still others have made me tremble" (*D* 153), says his companion—Herbert West *changed*. He had served then, together with his only friend and unnamed narrator of the story, as a surgeon in Flanders, but his experiments had finally become so morally depraved and reprehensible that his own friend considers him "fiendishly disgusting" (*D* 159):

> I speak of West's decadence, but must add that it was a purely mental and intangible thing. Outwardly he was the same to the last—calm, cold, slight, and yellow–haired, with spectacled blue eyes and a general aspect of youth which years and fears seemed never to change. He seemed calm even when he thought of that clawed grave and looked over his shoulder; even when he thought of the carnivorous thing that gnawed and pawed at Sefton bars. (*D* 161)

It could be safely said that "Herbert West—Reanimator" is the story of the decadence and "the end of Herbert West" (*D* 161), and we must ask ourselves if Lovecraft was not making a clear reference to *West*ern civilization in general and, more clearly, to German science. Let us not forget his letter to Kleiner, already quoted: "Certain scientific and philosophical developments have been marvellous, yet they have been conjoined to a brutality and narrowness of vision which threaten the development of civilization" (*SL* 1.53).

Finally, I shall now succinctly consider some of the constituent aspects of other remaining stories and their relation to Lovecraft's materialistic theory of racial miscegenation, trying to remark how his strategy appears to focus on the idea of an ancient, but not yet diluted, chemical pollution threatening the integrity of (white) civilization.

"From Beyond" (1920) tells the story of a scientist who invents a machine that "will generate waves acting on unrecognized sense-organs that exist in us as atrophied or rudimentary vestiges," and thus, it will awaken the sleeping past conscience still living inside us. This process provokes the mental and physical degradation of Crawford Tillinghast, the scientist. The scenario is similar to but not identical with what we will witness in "He" (1925). If in "From Beyond" we are led to a hidden world surrounding our present time through the activation of our ancient senses, in "He" we observe with our normal senses the world that existed around us in the past—and then, that ancestral past lurks in the shadows of our present, haunting us. But the main idea behind "He" is, of course, the decadence of the city, the society and, ultimately, the final and never reversing degeneration of all civilization. In "He" the narrator may be Lovecraft himself, claiming that his coming to New York had been a mistake, but the real leading role here is for Anglo-Saxon culture:

> My coming to New York had been a mistake . . . I had found instead only a sense of horror and oppression which threatened to master, paralyse, and annihilate me . . . swarthy strangers with hardened faces and narrow eyes, shrewd strangers without dreams and without kinship to the scenes about them, who could never mean aught to a blue-eyed man of the old folk, with the love of fair green lanes and white New England village steeples in his heart. (D 267)

If inbreeding and miscegenation were previously understood as the degenerative process of an individual or a small group of isolated citizens, with "He" and his previous short story, "The Street" (1920), we experience the first stage of Lovecraft's Copernican shift toward "The Colour out of Space" (another chemical alien intrusion): cities may have a soul, refined and polished over the years, but when in contact with another culture—an alien element that may or may not be harmless—that same soul could stand in jeopardy or even pass away:

[New York] is in fact quite dead, its sprawling body imperfectly embalmed and infested with queer animate things which have nothing to do with it as it was in life. (*D* 267)

New York is dead, and the brilliancy which so impresses one from outside is the phosphorescence of a maggoty corpse. (*SL* 2.101)

That embalmed and yet maggoty corpse was, of course, not only New York but the future America and Western civilization. Immigration, that "twisted ratlike vermin from the ghetto" (*SL* 2.101), was responsible for bringing back the "hellish black city" with "strange flying things" that existed around us thousands or millions of years ago.

The horrors of war and the "slow decadence of the ancient stock, coupled with a growing ferocity toward the outside world" (*D* 106), reenter Lovecraft's prose with "The Nameless City" (1921), where an ancient ruined metropolis with frescoed walls and ceilings recounts ancient wars and the exodus of their reptilian "death-hating race" (*D* 108) for a new paradise. It is tempting to identify, or at least connect, this evil crawling race with the war-exhausted, scientifically depraved German nation of the Great War.

We have learned some interesting approaches to the question of how knowledge of that lurking fear from the past may lead us to physically experience that very fear—the final transformation into something pre-human. Both "The Quest of Iranon" and "The Moon-Bog" (1921) deal with this issue in opposite but complementary ways: Iranon, a young yellow-haired traveler who sings the glories of his father's kingdom Aira, finally acknowledges that he was in fact "a beggar's boy given to strange dreams" (*D* 117). Thus, the ever young Iranon ages suddenly and takes his own life walking into the lethal quicksands: "That night something of youth and beauty died in the elder world." On the other side, Denys Barry is, like Iranon, another avatar for Lovecraft himself, for both wanted to buy back their ancestor's home in the Old World (Joshi & Schultz, *An H. P. Lovecraft Encyclopedia* 17). Like Iranon, Barry must travel to Ireland to confront his past—this journey being a requirement of the Hub Club (*SL* 1.128)—but he is already *affected* by America and chooses to drain the bog near his castle: "he hated the beautiful wasted space" (*D* 119), we are told. Knowledge killing beauty results in the aging of Iranon, and the killing of beauty leading to some nameless horror of past naiads in the bog transforms the transgressor into "a nauseous, unbelievable caricature—a blasphemous effigy of him who had been Denys Barry" (*D* 126).

Another tale of human decadence is the short novel *The Case of Charles Dexter Ward* (1927). We find the same transformation through knowledge we have seen in previous tales, culminating in "the horrible and uncanny alienation of 1928" (*MM* 111) of Charles Dexter Ward, who is once more a self-portrayed Lovecraft. Ward's mental and physical corruption begins when he discovers "among his maternal ancestors a certain very long–lived man named Joseph Curwen" (*MM* 116), "a learned and cultivated Englishman . . . [but] for some reason or other Curwen did not care for society" (*MM* 120). Similar ideas can be found in Pickman's "four-times-great-grandmother" (*DH* 15) and the suggestion of his sardonic linkage with the dog-things, and in Arthur Jermyn's "great-great-great-grandfather" who marries the "daughter of a Portuguese trader whom he had met in Africa; and did not like English ways" (*D* 74).

"Facts concerning the Late Arthur Jermyn and His Family" (1920) presents most of the problems we have encountered in Lovecraft's racial narrative. Arthur Jermyn not only discovers a taint in *his* line, but the ultimate horror is the striking truth that all white civilization comes from Africa (Joshi, "What Happens" 160–61). This Darwinian horror is strengthened by the fact that Sir Wade Jermyn married an ape-goddess; but this we are not yet told. For the moment we are content to know that Sir Wade married an unseen Portuguese woman, whose "Latin blood must be shewing itself" in the mental inclinations of young Jermyn (*D* 77–78). This chemical Latin element that Jermyn carries is still reinforced with the gypsy wife of Sir Philip. Hence, we are meant to believe, the physical and mental stigmata of the Jermyn line is the result of the inbreeding between noble Englishmen and low women of Latin or gypsy extraction. It is only afterwards that we learn of the Darwinian truth behind the origin of our species: the Portuguese woman was, in fact, the ape-goddess delivered at Jermyn House, and it is only when Jermyn opens the box that he finally confronts the horror of knowing that the arms and face of the ape were, in fact, *his own arms and face*. He naturally commits suicide.

Jermyn's conclusion predates "The Shadow over Innsmouth" (1931), an expansion of the former with some elements obviously related to Lovecraft's racism, rather than reversion to a primitive savage state. The theme is, once more, the inexorable call of heredity (Joshi, *H. P. Lovecraft* 38): Robert Olmstead—again, Lovecraft himself—goes on a genealogical excursion to Newburyport, only to be attracted by the rumors of a strange city named Innsmouth, whose "folks here and hereabouts always try to cover up any Innsmouth blood they have in 'em" (*DH* 306). The city was ravaged by a foreign plague that killed half its population, taking off "the best blood in the place" (*DH* 309) and leaving only those with an exaggerated case of civic or biological degeneration (*DH* 310, 314). Like Arthur Jermyn, Olmstead is about to discover that his ancestry was not human, but the result of an intermarriage between Obed Marsh and a monstrous amphibious mother—a fish-frog. Of course, after full realization of his hereditary taint, he acquires the Innsmouth look, and we are left to wonder whether it was time or knowledge that brought him to the final transformation—since he already "had the true Marsh eyes" (*DH* 363). Would Olmstead have ever acquired that Innsmouth look if he had never trod on Innsmouth's shores?

The Innsmouth look or transformation can still endure another philosophical reading, and a very materialistic one: babies born from this curious inbreeding go back, after some years, to the salty waters that corrupted them, only to live there forever as immortals. Is Lovecraft suggesting that, after the decadence and fall of Western civilization resulting from breeding with foreign cultures, there is no coming back and we will lose ourselves into a new— and final—Dark Age? The same can be said about "The Shunned House" (1924). Here we have what I would read as a reference to those nameless multitudes of immigrants whom he calls "mongrel slaves crawl hither to partake / Of Saxon liberty they could not make" ("An American to Mother England," *AT* 400, ll. 15–18):

> One might easily imagine an alien nucleus of substance or energy, formless or otherwise, kept alive by imperceptible or immaterial

subtractions from the life-force or bodily tissues and fluid of other and more palpably living things *into which it penetrates* and *with whose fabric it sometimes completely merges itself.* It might be actively hostile, or it might be dictated merely by blind motives of self–preservation. (*MM* 252; my emphasis)

This anthropomorphic horror inhabiting the Shunned House is later described as "half-human and half-monstrous," "all eyes"—suggesting rather the nameless multitudes of immigrants than the democratic mass of ignorant population—"a vaporous corpse-light" (*MM* 257) that reveals itself with the features of the Harris line (*MM* 258). And the reader should not forget "The Thing on the Doorstep" (1933) and its "tales of horrible bargains about the year 1850, and of a *strange element* 'not quite human' in the ancient families of the run-down fishing port" (*DH* 280; my emphasis).

VI. Lovecraft's "Coming Race"

Let us walk several miles back to our previous encounter with "The Shadow over Innsmouth." Not only were the city and its inhabitants described as decadent, both physically and mentally: even the church decayed, "given over to a degraded cult" (*DH* 318). This connects the story with one of Lovecraft's most representative themes that served as the core around which "The Festival" (1923) was composed: the existence of a satanic underground witch-cult in white Western lands that would trace back its origins to a pre-Aryan race (*SL* 4.297). This fanciful thought was in some ways already anticipated even before Lovecraft was born, with the science fiction novel *The Coming Race*, written in 1871 by Edward Bulwer-Lytton. In this story, the narrator finds a highly advanced civilization that exists beneath the surface of the planet. He soon discovers that the Vril-ya are descendants of an antediluvian culture; they have linguistic Aryan roots, but they are biologically different from us, having evolved from some sort of frog-like creature. Eventually, when their utopia runs out of resources, they will reclaim the surface, destroying mankind if necessary.

This all sounds too familiar, but Lovecraft does not mention Bulwer-Lytton's novel until 1933, in a letter to Carl Ferdinand Strauch (*LL* 132) dated July 8 ("Letters to Carl Ferdinand Strauch"

115). However, we should be aware that the way Lovecraft speaks of *The Coming Race* seems to imply he knew of this novel—it was, after all, a well-known Utopia in the late nineteenth century—and, given the familiarity of those themes, Lovecraft would surely have announced it in a way similar to his discovery of Dunsany and Machen. Between November 1925 and May 1927 he wrote in his celebrated essay "Supernatural Horror in Literature":

> Much of the power of Western horror-lore was undoubtedly due to the hidden but often suspected presence of a hideous cult of nocturnal worshippers whose strange customs—descended from pre-Aryan and pre-agricultural times when a squat race of Mongoloids roved over Europe with their flocks and herds. (*D* 370)

This conception goes back to Margaret Alice Murray's *The Witch-Cult in Western Europe* (1921), a book Lovecraft read around 1923. Its importance derives from the fact that by reading this essay Lovecraft could change his orientation toward human degeneration and miscegenation: while in "Arthur Jermyn" or "The Rats in the Walls" we are confronted with the evolutionary legacy of our own cannibalistic past, later stories like "The Call of Cthulhu" (1926), "The Dunwich Horror," or "The Shadow over Innsmouth" embody a displacement of focus from where the "true horror" lies. There may be—indeed, most probably there will be—a taint in the line, yet it was not part of our noble Teuton race, but introduced later, in recent times, as a contaminant agent preserved by a corrupted pre-Aryan race through an evil cult lost in time and space. Thus, in "The Call of Cthulhu" we heard of an

> indescribable horde of human abnormality . . . void of clothing, this hybrid spawn were braying . . . men of a very low mixed-blooded, and mentally aberrant type. Most were seamen, and a sprinkling of negroes and mulattoes. . . . Degraded and ignorant as they were, the creatures held with surprising consistency to the central idea of their loathsome faith. (*DH* 138–89)

These are the scions of the evil cult discovered by the late Professor George Gammell Angell, a creed that calls for the destruction of noble human beings: "The time would be easy to know, for then mankind would have become as the Great Old Ones, free and wild and beyond good and evil, with laws and morals thrown aside and all men shouting and killing and reveling in joy" (*DH* 141).

Lovecraft had conceived the existence of this sadistic worship years before as part of our ancestry "which might later develop into a formal Satanism" (*SL* 1.258). With the reading of Murray's book and the identification of Satanism and the witch-cult, he related it to "some of the squat Mongoloids now represented by the Lapps" (*SL* 3.162). Lovecraft hence accepted that the creatures of the Celtic myth-cycle—fairies, gnomes, and little people, in contrast to the Aryan fauns, satyrs, and dryads—were vague memories of an old Asian tribe, "essentially *repulsive* and *monstrous*, subterraneous in their habits of dwelling, and given to a queer kind of hissing discourse" (this certainly echoes the reptilian race in "The Nameless City"). In modern times, this "degenerate cult gained strength, struck back, and increased in malignancy, until it seemed to be almost beyond control" (*SL* 3.181), penetrating southern Germany and threatening the foundations of civilization (Lovecraft goes so far as to compare the Vehmic court with the modern Ku Klux Klan). These lessons were incorporated into a number of stories—"The Horror at Red Hook," "Pickman's Model," and "The Very Old Folk" (1927), to name a few— connecting "the gangs of young loafers & herds of evil-looking foreigners that one sees everywhere in New York" with those medieval "hellish antique rites [that] still exist in obscurity" (*SL* 2.27). Furthermore, relations between the figure of Nyarlathotep in *The Dream-Quest of Unknown Kadath* (1926–27) or "The Dreams in the Witch House" and the witch-cult have been pointed out earlier (Price 18). However, it is also likely to have influenced the war fragments in "The Shadow out of Time" (1934–35):

> Warfare, largely civil for the last few millennia though sometimes waged against reptilian and octopodic invaders, or against the winged, star-headed Old Ones who centred in the Antarctic, was infrequent though infinitely devastating. An enormous army, using camera-like weapons which produced tremendous electrical effects, was kept on hand for purposes seldom mentioned, but obviously connected with the ceaseless fear of the dark, windowless elder ruins and of the great sealed trap-doors in the lowest

subterranean levels. . . . The basis of the fear was a horrible elder race of half-polypous, utterly alien entities which had come through space from immeasurably distant universes and had dominated the earth and three other solar planets about six hundred million years ago. They were only partly material—as we understand matter—and their type of consciousness and media of perception differed wholly from those of terrestrial organisms. (*DH* 400–401)

These hissing subterranean beings were so alien to any normal configuration of time and space that their minds could not be affected by the Great Race, for their texture made them invulnerable to mind exchange. This suggests some sort of chemical or physiological condition that Lovecraft had previously related to degeneracy from isolation (Joe Slater in "Beyond the Wall of Sleep") and, two years later, to other races (Herbert West's solution based on white specimens). The elder race of half-polypous entities represents the ultimate representation of Lovecraft's lurking fear—from our evolutionary past to the existence of a pre-Aryan race of unnamable evil awaiting "patient and potent, for here shall They reign again" (*DH* 170).

VII. Conclusion

This article barely exhausts the interpretation of Lovecraft's fiction in terms of racial conflict, whether viewed as the fear of reverting to our previous savage state or the discovery of a taint in the line. Lovecraft's theory of racism underwent several fundamental changes, but regardless of its profound modifications, the central idea of the preservation of distinctive unmiscible races and, more specifically, the anxiety of losing an important part of the British civilization into a Dark Age of evil cult remained constant. His first creations, in the form of essay and verse, were mainly oriented against black people. The Great War, however, attracted Lovecraft's patriotic attention and allowed him to develop his racial theory in terms of chemical compounds: the white and supreme race was the result of the conjunction of the wise Greek and Latin blood with the cold and courageous German people. None of them could survive long without each other, for German blood would need of the laws and wisdom of Rome and

Greece so as not to destroy itself. Likewise, Latin blood on its own would lead to a feeble effeminate mass of useless citizens waiting to be annihilated by a greater, more aggressive force. After some time, and especially with his readings of Machen's pagan stories and Murray's *Witch-Cult*, Lovecraft's lurking fear to find a taint in the line and be reduce to again being the savage Hun was partially replaced by a new thought: the existence of a subterranean race of abnormal size, the "little people" of Celtic legends, who possessed no Aryan blood in their veins. Evil and hideous, these degenerated cultists still gather outside our cities, planning how to take back or destroy those once desert lands they inhabited.

The unabashed racism and xenophobia that permeated his works may also help us to understand the reasons for Lovecraft's propriety in sexual matters. The superior races he created had no sex and reproduced through seeds or spores—i. e., the Old Ones and the Great Race of Yith (*MM* 64, *DH* 399). As he himself explains in his letters, sexual or erotic impulses were an irrational part of humans that accounted for the unspeakable truth behind evolution: that we are still tainted by our *animal* ancestry.

> Eroticism belongs to a lower order of instincts, and is an animal rather than nobly human quality. For evolved man—the apex of organic progress on the earth—what branch of reflection is more fitting than that which occupies only his higher and exclusively human faculties? The primal savage or ape merely looks about his native forest to find a mate; the exalted Aryan should lift his eyes to the worlds of space and consider his relation to infinity!! . . . When I contemplate man, I wish to contemplate those characteristicks that elevate him to a human state, and those adornments which lend to his actions the symmetry of creative beauty. 'Tis not that I wish false pompous thoughts and motives imputed to him in the Victorian manner, but that I wish his composition justly apprais'd, with stress lay'd upon those qualities which are peculiarly his, and without the silly praise of such beastly things as he holds in common with any hog or stray goat. (*SL* 1.106, 283)

And more succinctly:

I have opposed eroticism for several reasons, (a) because of the acknowledged repulsiveness of direct erotic manifestations, as felt by all races and cultures and expressed in reticence to a greater or less degree, (b) because of the obvious kinship of erotic instincts to the crudest and earliest neural phenomena of organic nature, rather than to the phenomena resulting from complex and advanced development (i.e., purely intellectual phenomena), (c) because of the apparent connexion betwixt ages of erotic interest and national decadence, and (d) because so far as I could judge erotic interests are overrated; being in truth mere trifles which engross crude minds. (*SL* 1.29–30)

But this is neither the place nor the time in which to extend ourselves beyond the limits of our discourse. Lovecraft's idea of race miscegenation as chemical combinations of intellectual elements remains one of the most important ideas in the whole of his philosophy. His own supernatural creations were the result of one of those combinations, for he embraced the preternatural tale and still tried to be as rational as possible. And thus he wrote in "Supernatural Horror in Literature":

Wherever the mystic Northern blood was strongest, the atmosphere of the popular tale became most intense; for in the Latin races there is a touch of basic rationality which denies to even their strangest superstitions many of the overtones of glamour so characteristic of our own forest-born and ice-fostered whisperings. (*D* 371)

Works Cited

Berlinguez-Kono, N. "Debates on Naichi Zakkyo in Japan (1879–99): The Influence of Spencerian Social Evolutionism on the Japanese Perception of the West." In *The Japanese and Europe: Images and Perceptions*, ed. Bert Edström. London; Routledge, 2000.

Ellis, Phillip A. "The Construction of Race in the Early Poetry of H. P. Lovecraft." *Lovecraft Annual* No. 4 (2010): 124–35.

Hecht, Marie B. *Beyond the Presidency: The Residues of Power.* New York: Macmillan, 1976.

Hume, David. *Essays, Moral, Political, and Literary.* Ed. Eugene F. Miller. Indianapolis: Liberty Classics, 1987.

Joshi, S. T. "Autobiography in Lovecraft." In Joshi's *Primal Sources: Essays on H. P. Lovecraft.* New York: Hippocampus Press, 2003.

———. *A Dreamer and a Visionary: H. P. Lovecraft in His Time.* Liverpool: Liverpool University Press, 2001.

———. *H. P. Lovecraft.* Mercer Island, WA: Starmont House, 1982.

———. *H. P. Lovecraft: A Life.* West Warwick, RI: Necronomicon Press, 1996.

———. *H. P. Lovecraft: The Decline of the West.* Mercer Island, WA: Starmont House, 1990.

———. *A Subtler Magick: The Writings and Philosophy of H. P. Lovecraft.* San Bernardino, CA: Borgo Press, 1996.

———. "Time, Space, and Natural Law: Science and Pseudo–Science in Lovecraft." *Lovecraft Annual* No. 4 (2010): 171–201.

———. "What Happens in 'Arthur Jermyn.'" In Joshi's *Primal Sources: Essays on H. P. Lovecraft.* New York: Hippocampus Press, 2003.

Joshi, S. T., and David E. Schultz. *An H. P. Lovecraft Encyclopedia.* Westport, CT: Greenwood Press, 2001.

Kant, Immanuel. "On the Different Races of Man." In *Race and the Enlightenment. A Reader,* ed. Emmanuel Chukwudi Eze. Cambridge, MA: Blackwell, 2001.

Lach, D. F. *The Preface to Leibniz' Novissima Sinica: Commentary, Translation, Text.* Honolulu: University of Hawai'i Press, 1957.

Leibniz, G. W. *Briefwechsel.* Hanover: Niedersächsische Landesbibliothek, 1846.

Lovecraft, H. P. *The Call of Cthulhu and Other Weird Stories.* Ed. S. T. Joshi. New York: Penguin, 1999.

———. *Letters to Alfred Galpin.* Ed. S. T. Joshi and David E. Schultz. New York: Hippocampus Press, 2003.

———. "Letters to Carl Ferdinand Strauch." *Lovecraft Annual* No. 4 (2010): 46–123.

———. *Lord of a Visible World: An Autobiography in Letters.* Ed. S. T. Joshi and David E. Schultz. Athens: Ohio University Press, 2000.

Massie, Robert K. *Dreadnought: Britain, Germany, and the Coming of the Great War.* New York: Random House, 1991.

Nietzsche, Friedrich. *Ecce Homo: How to Become What You Are.* Ed. Duncan Large. Oxford: World's Classics, 2007.

Panayi, P. "German Immigrants in Britain, 1815–1914." In *Germans in Britain Since 1500*, ed. Panikos Panayi. London: Hambledon Press, 1996.

Price, Robert M., ed. *The Nyarlathotep Cycle.* Hayward, CA: Chaosium, 2006.

Schopenhauer, Arthur. *Parerga and Paralipomena: Short Philosophical Essays*, 2. Ed. E. F. J. Payne. Oxford: Oxford University Press, 2000.

Schütte, J. F. *Valignano's Mission Principles for Japan: Volume I, From His Appointment as Visitor Until His First Departure from Japan (1573–1582).* St. Louis: Institute of Jesuit Sources, 1985.

Spence, J. D. *The Memory Palace of Matteo Ricci.* London: Penguin, 1984.

Wetzel, George. "Genesis of the Cthulhu Mythos." In *Discovering H. P. Lovecraft*, ed. Darrell Schweitzer. Holicong, PA: Wildside Press, 2001.

Wilson, Woodrow. *Selected Addresses and Public Papers of Woodrow Wilson.* Ed. Albert Bushnell Hart. Honolulu: University Press of the Pacific, 2002.

Briefly Noted

Film adaptations of Lovecraft's work are ongoing, but one in particular—the German film *Die Farbe* (2010)—should be singled out for especial praise. This superb adaptation of "The Colour out of Space" is without question the finest and most evocative full-length film adaptation of a Lovecraft story ever made, and all interested Lovecraftians are urged to see it. Written and directed by Huan Vu, this 86-minute film stars Michael Kausch as "Armin Pierske" (i.e., Ammi Pierce) and Olaf Krätke in the role of the narrator/protagonist, "Mr. Danforth" (!). A black-and-white film (except at the end, when the "colour" manifests itself), it is terrifying in its own right and a brilliantly faithful adaptation.

Of Regner Lodbrog, Hugh Blair, and Mistranslations

Martin Andersson

The story of Lovecraft's poem "Regner Lodbrog's Epicedium" starts in the ninth century with the mythical Viking chieftain Ragnar Lodbrok or Lodbrog ("Ragnar Hairy-Breeks"). He got his nickname from killing a dragon; as protection against the venom of the dragon he was wearing breeches of fur that had been dipped in pitch and rolled in sand. He may be based in part on a historical person, a Danish Viking chieftain named Ragnar, who is famous for sacking Paris in 845 C.E. There are various conflicting accounts of Lodbrok's demise; according to the most widely spread version, he was captured by the Northumbrian king Aella and executed by being thrown into a pit filled with vipers.

In the snake pit, Ragnar is said to have composed a death-song in 29 stanzas, reminiscing over a life filled with heroic deeds. However, this death-song, known as *Krákumál* (The Lay of Kraka; after Ragnar's second wife, Aslaug, who was also known as Kraka), was most likely composed in the twelfth century, probably in the Scottish islands, but Iceland is also possible.

The poem was translated into Latin by the Icelandic priest Magnús Ólafsson of Laufás in the early seventeenth century, a translation that was published along with the original text by the Danish scholar Olaus Wormius in his book *Runir seu Danica antiquissima* (1636), also known as *De Literatura Runica*—hence the misapprehension, by Lovecraft and others, that Wormius was the translator. In 1761 the Latin text was translated into English by Thomas Percy and later published in *Five Pieces of Runic Poetry Translated from the Icelandic Language* (1763), thus making it one of the first complete Norse poems to appear in English. Some mistakes were made in the translation; among other things, Conrad Hjalmar Nordby points out that

> The negative contractions in Icelandic were as yet unfamiliar, and so, as Walter Scott pointed out (in *Edin. Rev.*, Oct., 1806), Percy made Regner Lodbrog say, "The pleasure of that day (of battle, p. 34 in this *Five Pieces*) was like having a fair virgin placed beside one in the bed," and "The pleasure of that day was like kissing a young widow at the highest seat of the table," when the poet really made the contrary statement. (13f)

Another problem with many early translations is the translators' ignorance of the Norse poetical device of the *kenning*. This may be best described as a sort of poetical euphemism, in which a compound using figurative language replaced a more concrete single-word noun. Thus, for example, Percy's translation has Ragnar say: "Soon, in the splendid hall of Oden, we shall drink beer out of the skulls of our enemies" (40). However, the original has "ór bjúgviðum hausa," which means simply "from the curved branches of heads," i.e., horns. The kennings are still a problem for translators of Norse literature: Should they be retained for poetical flavor at the expense of intelligibility, or should they be changed to plain language?

In the early 1760s, Dr. Hugh Blair, minister of the Church of Scotland and Regius Professor of Rhetoric and Belles Lettres at the University of Edinburgh, enters the history of *Krákumál*. Blair was a friend of James Macpherson and published *A Critical Dissertation on the Poems of Ossian, the Son of Fingal* in 1763. The purpose of this essay was to prove the authenticity of the Ossian poems, and it was included in every publication of *The Works of Ossian* after 1765, where presumably Lovecraft read it (he owned a copy of *Ossian:* item #541 in *Lovecraft's Library*). In the essay, Blair includes the entire text of Ólafsson's Latin translation (misattributing it to Wormius) and provides his own partial English translation in prose. When compared to the commonly available original text of *Krákumál* found online, it will be seen that stanzas 7 and 8 have switched places in Oláfsson's Latin text, a reading that is then carried over into the English translations of Percy, Blair, and Lovecraft; however, several sources for the original text have the stanzas in this particular order, so this cannot be considered a genuine error (Rafn 88).

Lovecraft wrote his version of the poem in late 1914. In a letter to Maurice W. Moe, dated 17 December 1914, he writes:

I recently tried the "Hiawatha" type of blank verse in translating a curious bit of primitive Teutonic martial poetry which Dr. Blair quotes in his "Critical Dissertation on the Poems of Ossian." This fragment is a funeral song composed in Runes by the old Danish monarch Regner Lodbrok (eighth century A.D.). In the Middle Ages Olaus Wormius made the rather incoherent Latin version which Blair uses. It is in stanzas, each headed by the words "Pugnavimus ensibus." In translating, I end each stanza with a rhyming couplet. (quoted in Joshi 145)

Lovecraft's misdating of Wormius to the Middle Ages has already been ably covered by Joshi in "Lovecraft, Regner Lodbrog, and Olaus Wormius," so I will not go into that here. I should, however, point out that in the original, the last stanza is an exception to the others and does not start with "Hjoggum vér með hjörvi" ("Pugnavimus ensibus" = we fought with swords).

Lovecraft's translation covers stanzas 1 through 6, stanza 8, lines 1–3 of stanza 7, and line 9 of stanza 10 of the original as published on the Heimskringla website. There are several gaps in the text, as well as lines surrounded by parentheses. As Joshi points out, these presumably indicate passages where Lovecraft cannot make sense of the Latin text; in fact, his version is much dependent on Blair's English text.

The various names in the poem are interesting enough to warrant a closer examination and comparison side by side:

Original	*Ólafsson*	*Percy*	*Blair*	*Lovecraft*
Gautlandi	Gotlandia	Gothland	—	Gothland's

This does not refer to the island of Gotland off the east coast of Sweden, but rather to Götaland, the land of the Götar in the south of Sweden. Blair did not translate the first stanza.

| Þóru | Thoram | Thora | — | Thor |

Thora was Ragnar's first wife, whom he won by killing the dragon/serpent. Percy correctly has "my reward was the beauteous Thora"; Lovecraft the erroneous "We have gain'd from Thor" followed by a gap and an empty line. He had no translation by Blair to rely on for this stanza.

Eyrasundi	Oreonico freto	straights of freto	bay of Oreon	channel of Oreon

Öresund is the strait between the Danish island Sjælland (Zealand) and the Swedish province of Skåne (Scania).

Dínu mynni	Dimini portum	mouth of the Danube	port of Dominum	the harbour

This is the River Daugava or Western Dvina, flowing through Russia, Belarus, and Latvia, draining into the Gulf of Riga in the Baltic Sea.

Ívu	Vistulae	the Vistula	the Vistula	the Vistula

The Íva ("Ívu" is the accusative singular feminine) is a river that has not been identified. Its identification with the Vistula is doubtful. Rafn relates several theories, the most plausible of which is that the name refers to a river in Sweden or somewhere along the northern coasts of the Baltic (101f).

heimsala Óðins	aulum Odini	habitation of the gods	hall of Odin	hall of Woden

Oden/Odin/Woden is of course the Norse patron god of those who died in battle. Percy, who has translated the original quite freely, explains in a footnote that the literal meaning of the original is "the hall of Odin."

Helsingja	Helsingianos	inhabitants of Helsing	Helsingians	Helsingian foemen

The Helsings were the inhabitants of Hälsingland (Helsingia), on the coast of the Baltic Sea in the north of Sweden.

Herrøðr	Heraudus	Herauder	Heraudus	Heraudus

Herröd was a legendary king of Gautland; he was the father of Ragnar's first wife Thora.

Skarpa-skerjum	Scarforum cautes	the very rocks	the Scarfian rocks	Scarfian rocks

The original name means "the sharp rocks" or "the sharp skerries," but the place is unidentified. The antiquary James Johnstone thinks it refers to Scarpey in Norway. Another theory is that it refers to Scarborough Castle in England (Rafn 106f).

Rafn konungr	Rafno rex	king Rafno	Rafno the king	the royal Rafno

Nothing is known about this king.

Inndyris-eyju	Indiorum insulas	isles of Indir	Indirian islands	Indirian islands

Unknown; may be fictitious. Rafn presents several interpretations, e.g., that it could refer to Inderø in the Trondheim bay in Norway, or possibly the Orkney Islands (Rafn 111).

Ullarakri	Laneo campo	the field	plains of Lano	Lano's plain

Here is an interesting mistranslation in the Latin text, which is then further mistranslated by Blair and then retained by Lovecraft. Consider the following passage from the Latin translation of *Krákumál* as quoted by Blair (his stanza 8):

> Altum mugierunt enses
> Antequam in Laneo campo
> Eislinus rex cecidit (78)

Blair renders this as

> Loud roared the swords in the plains of Lano. (86)

which of course is an abridgement—as you can see there is no "Eislinus [sic] rex" mentioned in the English text—and thus we get Lovecraft's

> (Weapons roared on Lano's plain.) (*AT* 92)

However, when we look at the Percy text, and at the Old Norse original, another image emerges. The passage is rendered thus by Percy who was working from the same Latin text (the Ólafsson/Wormius translation) as Blair:

Loud was the din of arms; before king Eistin fell in the field. (Percy 30f)

But the original text actually refers to a specific place:

> Hátt grenjuðu rottar,
> áðr á Ullarakri
> Eysteinn konungr felli. (*Krákumál*, stanza 7)

The place can thus be identified as Ulleråker in the vicinity of Uppsala in Sweden; the name means "Ull's field" or "Ull's place of worship" (Ull being a Norse god of hunting). But "ull" can also mean "wool," and this explains why the Latin text translates the original "Ullarakri" as "Laneo campo"—"field of wool"—an understandable but regrettable mistake.

But how did Blair translate "Laneo campo" as "the plains of Lano"? To get an answer I think we have to go to Macpherson—the very man whom Blair was defending against charges of literary hoaxing. In "The War of Inis-thona" the following passage can be found:

> "Cormalo," replied the king, "is a chief of ten thousand spears. He dwells at the waters of Lano, which sends forth the vapour of death. . . ." (Macpherson 35)

And in a footnote we learn that "Lano was a lake of Scandinavia, remarkable, in the days of Ossian, for emitting a pestilential vapour in autumn" (Macpherson 35). Therefore, we need look no further for Lano. It would seem that Blair, wishing to prove that the works of Ossian were authentic, misinterpreted the Latin "Laneo" as a reference to the mythical lake he had seen mentioned in Macpherson's text, and of course the mention of such a name in a text of demonstrably ancient provenance would reinforce his thesis. But Lovecraft was fluent in Latin and should have spotted Blair's mistake; unfortunately, even if he had he would have been unable to make a correct translation, since he did not have access to the original.

"Regner Lodbrog's Epicedium" will never be counted a major Lovecraft poem, but it is interesting in that it is one of his few translations, and its purported translator Olaus Wormius gained fame as one of the translators of the *Necronomicon*, as described in

"Lovecraft, Regner Lodbrog, and Olaus Wormius." Thus, it is far from unimportant.

Works Cited

Anonymous. *Krákumál.* URL: http://www.heimskringla.no/wiki/Krákumál. Retrieved 5 January 2012.

Blair, Hugh. "A Critical Dissertation on the Poems of Ossian, the Son of Fingal." In James Macpherson. *The Poems of Ossian: Volume I.* London: Lackington, Allen, & Co., 1803. 65–206.

Joshi, S. T. "Lovecraft, Regner Lodbrog, and Olaus Wormius." *Crypt of Cthulhu* No. 89 (Eastertide 1995): 3–7. In Joshi's *Primal Sources: Essays on H. P. Lovecraft.* New York: Hippocampus Press, 2003. 145–53.

Joshi, S. T. *Lovecraft's Library: A Catalogue.* 3rd rev. ed. New York: Hippocampus Press, 2012.

Macpherson, James. "The War of Inis-thona: A Poem." In *The Poems of Ossian: Volume II.* London: Lackington, Allen, & Co., 1803. 31–38.

Nordby, Conrad Hjalmar. *The Influence of Old Norse Literature upon English Literature.* New York: Columbia University Press, 1901.

Percy, Thomas. *Five Pieces of Runic Poetry Translated from the Icelandic Language.* London: R. & J. Dodsley, 1763.

Rafn, C. C. ed. *Krakas maal eller kvad om kong Ragnar Lodbroks krigsbedrifter og heltedød.* Copenhagen: Jens Hostrup Schultz, 1826.

The Shadow over "The Lurking Fear"

Michael Cisco

"The Lurking Fear" (1922) is not one of Lovecraft's more well-regarded stories; his literary productivity slackened after its completion, suggesting that his energies may have been flagging even as he was working on it. He makes disparaging remarks about it in letters to Clark Ashton Smith written around the period of its publication (*SL* 201, 213). Several of Lovecraft's characteristic themes recur in the story, but they are only indistinctly realized; the discovery of a monstrous familial legacy is one of them. Did Lovecraft begin writing "The Lurking Fear" with a revelation of the same kind that closes "The Shadow over Innsmouth" in mind for this earlier narrator as well? As the story stands, the narrator is only a disinterested party whose obsession with a mystery is apparently rooted in causes unrelated to the case. However, there are hints—and hints are all they are—of another storyline that Lovecraft seems to have dismissed during, not before, the composition of the piece, in which the narrator discovers he is an unrecognized descendent of Jan Martense.

The first chapter is the most directly suggestive, which might mean that a connection between the narrator and the Martense family was at its liveliest in Lovecraft's thoughts as he began the story, assuming that he wrote it straight through from beginning to end. The narrator sleeps in Jan Martense's bed in the Martense mansion, and the fireplace in Jan Martense's bedroom is ornamented with tiles illustrating the story of the prodigal son's return. While this has obvious significance for Jan Martense, who left the mansion on Tempest Mountain, it could just as readily foreshadow the possibility that the narrator himself is another prodigal, returned home without realizing it. The narrator is linked with Jan Martense so consistently that it seems possible that, at one time, Lovecraft might have considered making him the narrator's ancestor, as he could have fathered a child during his sketchily recorded absence. Considering that the murder of Jan Martense is the only other salient feature of his life story, and that this event takes place at the Martense mansion, it is hard to imagine what other reason Lovecraft might have had for deciding to send him away to fight in the Revolutionary War. Certainly, this detail helps root the story plausibly in history, and that might have been sufficient for Lovecraft, but this rooting could have been accomplished without sending Jan Martense away. On the other hand, coming up with a pretext for Jan Martense to leave, getting him out from under the scrutiny of the rest of the family, and making him a soldier, when soldier's trysts and the often unacknowledged or even unknown progeny resulting from them are a common enough feature of war stories, would have afforded Lovecraft an easy way to explain how an separate line of descent might exist.

Lovecraft places a great deal of emphasis on the fact that the narrator alone of the three men who sleep in the Martense mansion was inexplicably spared by the horror, and this is the most suggestive detail of all. This is only the first of at least three occasions on which the narrator has a near miss with the horror and escapes unscathed, the other two being the episode in which Arthur Munro is murdered (chapter two; D 189) mere steps away from the narrator, and the episode of the burrow, when the narrator comes face to face with the horror and is released by a bolt of lightning (chapter three; D 193–94). The degenerate Martenses are evidently mindless, bestial cannibals, who pounce on and rip to shreds any vulnerable or solitary human being they come across. The attack on Arthur Munro does not seem to have been prompted so much by hunger as by malice. Why should the Martenses, who kill for malice as well as for food, repeatedly spare the narrator, and what cause could there be for the "hideous wait" (D 194) or hesitancy of the Martense-being in the tunnel, unless perhaps it had recognized the narrator, by some subtle token, as a member of the family?

At the end of the story, the narrator witnesses one degenerate Martense devouring another, in a way that makes it seem obvious the Martenses eat one another. This makes it more difficult to claim that recognition of the narrator as a fellow Martense saved him from attack, but this difficulty dissolves if we assume that, as this cannibal episode only takes place at the story's end, and since it isn't clear until this point, so late in the piece, whether or not the Martenses eat one another, Lovecraft had only decided to include this scene after the idea of linking the narrator to the family had already faded from of his mind.

There are two other potential weaknesses in my attribution of the narrator's seeming immunity to Martense attacks to his being a family member himself.

First, as the story stands—that is, without any Martense connection—the elimination of Bennett and Tobey can be accounted for as a device foreshadowing the discovery by the narrator that what he has assumed to be a single monster is actually many. That, and the scare it induces, are sufficient reasons to include this detail. But this detail doesn't require that one of the creatures climb in bed and fall asleep beside the narrator, with an arm flung over him. It's creepy, and perhaps that was reason enough to include it, but Lovecraft could have achieved the same sort of scare by other means: the monster could have been staring at him from the windowsill, hanging above him from the ceiling, scrabbling directly under the bed, looming up at the foot of the bed. There are many possibilities, but Lovecraft chose one that, in addition to being fearsome, also implies familial intimacy.

Second, the narrator lacks the mismatched eyes, which are the only indication of Martense heredity that would not entail an elaborate scenario of verification, such as a blood test, that would require not inconsiderable inflation of the story, including at least an explanation of how a sample of Martense blood is acquired and how the facilities necessary for such a test were procured, and probably the introduction of another character to run the tests. It would have been far less cumbersome for Lovecraft to give mismatched eyes to his narrator, mentioning this detail at a convenient moment early on, then suppress the association of mismatched eyes with the Martense family until the last chapter. However, the story does end with a revelation of the Martense eyes, just as it would have done if the narrator were a member of the family. Strange eyes are also the first indication that the narrator of "The Shadow over Innsmouth" is not what he seems. It would be an irony consistent with Lovecraft's way of thinking to make the organs of investigation, the eyes, themselves into the sign of what the narrator would want at all costs not to see, to illustrate the terrible dangers of seeing and discovering.

Furthermore, the narrator of the story is all but wholly indistinct. While the narrator of "The Shadow over Innsmouth" is never described, it is not hard to get some idea of his appearance, especially after finishing the story. Lovecraft is careful to inform the reader where he lives and why he is in New England, to give a rough idea of his age, and he dilates on the subject of the narrator's heredity toward the close. The entire life of the last of the de la Poers is described in "The Rats in the Walls." Even the narrator of "Herbert West—Reanimator" is better known to the reader than the narrator of "The Lurking Fear." While the lack of information is not particularly noticeable, nor does it do any harm to the story, such as it is, it might suggest that Lovecraft was uncertainly weighing different possibilities and so chose not to be too specific too early. By the time he had determined how the story would play out, he no longer found it necessary or expedient to provide any information about the narrator. If this is true, then the absence of early data could imply a hesitancy about the importance of background information about the narrator, and that information could only be of importance if it pointed to Martense ancestry.

There are a number of other, admittedly more tentative, reasons to suspect an abandoned Martense connection.

The narrator admits a predisposition to ghoulish horrors and becomes frankly obsessed with the Martense family and the monstrous presence around Tempest Mountain. He experiences bizarre and apocalyptic dreams during this period, which seem to begin the night he spends in Jan Martense's bed, and is drawn "idiotically" (D 189) to dig in Jan Martense's grave for no clear reason. These facts, taking the story as written, point only to a morbidly curious man who is highly sensitive to weird atmosphere and so preoccupied with a mystery that he perseveres in his investigation despite numerous violent deaths and abductions, several of which took place in his presence, even to the point of irrational or mindless attempts to discover the truth. Anyone with a similar temperament would likely do the same. However, in "The Rats in the Walls" and "The Shadow over Innsmouth," it is implied that the narrators are drawn to their ancestral domains by a subtle influence reaching out from the past to retrieve them. It is worth noting here that, while Lovecraft is usually quite careful to spell out the important implications of his stories, nowhere in either of these examples does he ever explicitly say that the last of the de la Poers or the narrator of "The Shadow over Innsmouth" are drawn back home by any mysterious impulse. That implication is entirely tacit, yet easily emerges from the writing alongside other, more openly affirmed implications. If we accept the idea that Lovecraft did not habitually spell out this particular implication of atavistic homing, then the absence of such an explanation in "The Lurking Fear" need not be evidence that the idea did not play some role in the story's composition.

There is a pattern in Lovecraft's fiction that recurs with great consistency: a narrator, investigating some anomalous circumstance at the prompting of a vague and impractical motive, discovers he is, or is part of, the anomaly himself—whereupon the true nature of his fascination with it becomes obvious. This outcome is always foreshadowed by clues, often including mysterious dreams and what he calls, in "The Shadow over Innsmouth," pseudo-memories, which turn out to be atavistic premonitions or expressions of the investigating character's original, tainting connection to the anomaly. The identification of a character with that other, alien self is always signalled by a delirious exhibition in the language of the story itself.

In "The Tomb," for example, Jervas begins to speak in the colloquial eighteenth-century idiom of his Hyde ancestor and recites a ribald drinking song of the time. The last of the de la Poers reverts through the genealogical phases of his own family's speech customs, back to prehuman times. The narrator of "The Shadow over Innsmouth" begins to use proper names and phrases in inhuman language. He might have remembered Zadok Allen's recitation of the Cthulhu chant, but "Y'ha-nthlei" and the name of "Pth'thya-l'yi," his great-grandmother, were at most revealed to him in dreams, and their appearance in the story mark a degeneration or alienage in his speech designed to correspond with the degeneration of his body. The victims of the vampiric presence in "The Shunned House" utter execrations in French, despite their ignorance of the language. Robert Blake, in "The Haunter of the Dark," begins to identify with the being he summoned, seeing darkness as light and lightness as dark, presumably as the Haunter sees, and his final raving, heavily marbled with weird names and phrases, is a by-now recognizable hallmark of the Lovecraftian climax. At the end of "The Outsider," the narrator describes his subsequent travels through a phantasmagorical world of untraceable names and fantastical locations.

After his encounter in chapter one, the narrator of "The Lurking Fear" says that "the shock at the mansion had done something to my brain" (D 190). This could refer to nothing more than the shocked discovery of nightmarish possibilities, but it could also indicate the awakening of pseudo-memory. During the episode in the tunnel toward the close of the third chapter, the sight of his own light reflected in a pair of Martense eyes is said to provoke "maddeningly nebulous memories" (D 193). After recovering from this encounter, he avers that "the discovery that two monsters had haunted the spot gave me ultimately a mad craving to plunge into the very earth of the accursed region, and with bare hands dig out the death that leered from every inch of the poisonous soil" (D 195). Burrowing with bare hands, exactly like the beings he is hunting. "Innsmouth people . . . were as furtive and seldom seen as animals that live in burrows" (DH 321), and elsewhere Lovecraft mentions the tunnels and basements of Innsmouth. This means that the "Deep Ones" are not purely an aquatic menace. They can be included in a greater collection of Lovecraftian mirror-side beings who live below the surface, whether of the ground or the water; this resemblance to the Martenses perhaps is not enough to justify a claim that the two stories mirror each other in more ways, but it is a little better than irrelevant. The narrator of "The Shadow over Innsmouth," elaborating on the idea of pseudo-memory, speaks of "deep cells and tissues whose retentive functions are wholly primal and awesomely ancestral" (DH 312). The moment the narrator of "The Lurking Fear" figures out the puzzle of the mounds, he speaks of his "newly-opened mind" (D 197), so that it is possible his abrupt realization of the truth might in some way be the recovery of memories physically embodied in his tissues, passed on by his ancestors.

As the story draws to a close, the narrator, having at last realized the true nature of the horror, bursts out in a rhapsody of bizarre images:

> Shrieking, slithering, torrential shadows of red viscous madness chasing one another through endless, ensanguined corridors of purple fulgurous sky . . . formless phantasms and kaleidoscopic mutations of a ghoulish, remembered scene; forests of monstrous overnourished oaks with serpent roots twisting and sucking unnamable juices from an earth verminous with millions of cannibal devils; mound-like tentacles groping from underground nuclei of polypous perversion . . . insane lightning over malignant ivied walls and daemon arcades choked with fungous vegetation . . . (*D* 198–99)

The narrator here plainly speaks of remembering a scene. This could mean he is conjuring in his mind a flurry of variations on the scenes of mayhem he has encountered in the story, in order to populate the far larger scope of the horror he has now uncovered. However, it might also refer to something he himself has never experienced directly, the stirring of atavistic memories in his tissues. While he has wandered the monstrous forest, has he actually seen the underground nuclei, or know what kind of things there are in them? He may be referring to the shapelessness of the monsters themselves; Lovecraft often uses the adjective "shapeless" to mean, not amorphous or plastic, but lacking any familiar or known shape. However, "shapeless" here could also imply the existence below ground of some other evil or byblow of the Martense degeneration, perhaps even more radically deformed creatures, that are literally like polyps. He hasn't seen such things with his own eyes. Has he seen "daemon arcades" in the Martense mansion? Arcades are not included in Dutch colonial architecture.

Minus any familial link, this farrago must be considered a wildly vivid presentiment of the implications of his discovery, and a frantic, inchoate attempt to put into words an inexpressible monstrousness—which may be all there is to it. If there were a familial link, however, then this lexical rampage, which is often pointedly specific, would represent a cavalcade of unlocked "ra-cial" memories coinciding exactly with the moment at which the narrator discovers the true nature of the lurking fear.

The narrator also complains of restlessness and fear associated with thunderstorms. He speaks of the need to "calm [his] brain when it thunders" (*D* 199). This could be nothing more than a pho-bic association brought about solely by his discoveries, but of course it could mean he has the familial sensitivity to electrical storms. This was never mentioned in the story's earlier section, and, if the story were written in sequence, then the narrator's sensitivity would be entering it at a point when it would no longer serve to build up by touches an implied familial connection, which would be the only reason to mention it earlier. While this would suggest that Lovecraft was no longer thinking of such a connection, it is possible that it is a residue of thinking along those lines. One would expect Lovecraft to add this detail so near to the end if he were planning to close the story with a climactic revelation of kinship.

"The Lurking Fear" as a whole may not be one of Lovecraft's impor-tant stories, but it does contain a moment of great significance for anyone who wishes to look more closely at an essential element of Lovecraft's art: the carefully sustained ambivalence with which he handles the emotion of horror. In his essay, "What Is Poetry?," Ro-man Jakobson speaks of "the age-old psychological principle of the ambivalence of feelings—no feeling is so pure as to be free from contamination by its opposite feeling" (371). Lovecraft is often criti-cized for a lack of psychological complexity, largely because his corpus isn't populated by complex, Dostoyevskyian or Shakespear-ean characters. While Lovecraft's characters are often simple—and this is less a failure than it is a requirement of the kind of fiction he wanted to write—there is a psychologically complex attitude to-ward horror and wonder permeating his work, which is one of its most valuable aspects. The repulsion of horror in Lovecraft is often associated with a desire that coexists alongside it.

Turning, for example, to "The Outsider," the narrative runs most of its course in a slender channel, tightly centered on the solitary actor and what he does from one moment to the next. The ending of the story opens the channel out considerably, onto vistas of wild phantasmagoria analogous to those other climaxes I've mentioned. Crocodile tears notwithstanding, ultimately the Outsider is relieved to discover at last what he truly is; while the revelation is horrible, now that he knows he can never be accepted into the ordinary world under any circumstances he is liberated from any hope or desire to do so. He is, in fact, free to admit that the ordinary world of prosaic bourgeois modernity was never particularly appealing to him anyway, and, since the break with this world comes as a result of its rejection of him, he cannot be held responsible for rejecting it. This makes it possible for him to find the place and even the fellowship where he truly belongs; certain positive attributes are attached to this new place, and there is even a sense in which this destiny is superior to that of an ordinary mortal, a mark of distinction, a little like Caesar's rumored epilepsy or the hemophilia of the Romanovs. A few ride the night winds, but most ride the bus.

The bus-riding narrator of "The Shadow over Innsmouth" is not that different. The sea dwellers are not mindless monsters; they have a civilization of their own, with a magnificent city and refined artistic tradition, of which the tiara is an example. Their culture is ancient, sophisticated, unvarying, a Lovecraftian utopia in certain ways. Lovecraft doesn't do more than hint about it and most likely did not have any developed idea of that culture; the point is sufficiently achieved for his purposes by those hints. That point is: belonging to this fantastic lineage is, however initially horrifying to contemplate, actually a kind of promotion from the level of the merely human. This abrupt inversion in point of view is clearly meant to be an aspect of the fearful transformation of the narrator, but why then should every such transformation involve the realization of Lovecraft's values? Here, the horror transforms into an all-too-understandable ambition right before our eyes.

While the end of the last of the de la Poers is ignominious and wretched, he does get to live out Lovecraft's fantasy of settling in an archaic corner of England. In his final ravings there is a note of pride and defiance: "Shall a Norrys hold the lands of a de la Poer? . . . Curse you, Thornton, I'll teach you to faint at what my family do!" (*DH* 45). Is there perhaps too an implication that even a tradition of horror is nobler, or at least no worse, than modern rootlessness?

In "The Lurking Fear," the narrator says that at times it is a relief to scream in a nightmare, and more, to surrender to the nightmare and to allow oneself to be swept away by it. This passage is one of the most illuminating in Lovecraft's corpus:

> That fright was so mixed with wonder and alluring grotesqueness, that it was almost a pleasant sensation. Sometimes, in the throes of a nightmare when unseen powers whirl one over the roofs of strange dead cities toward the grinning chasm of Nis, it is a relief and even a delight to shriek wildly and throw oneself voluntarily along with the hideous vortex of dream-doom into whatever bottomless gulf may yawn . . . (D 195)

This is one of the least ambiguous indications that there is something like wish fulfillment in Lovecraft's horror stories. Considering his aversion to contemporary life, his avidity for the past, his immovable fixation on degeneracy and decline, just how bad does he seem likely to feel about the destruction of the contemporary world? Wouldn't the annihilation of present conditions by a force out of the past be something he would be more likely to cheer than to lament? Were Cthulhu to return, or had Wilbur Whateley been successful, the results would have been wholly terrible, even worse. However, the existence of Cthulhu or of Yog-Sothoth, minus any immediate threat, reverses the modern demystification of the world and is to be desired precisely to the extent that the grander scale of being they in part represent, just like the grander astronomical scale of space and the grander geological scale of time in Lovecraft's materialism, reduces modernity to a merely trivial episode in the history of ephemera. Wasn't this Lovecraft's revenge on life for bringing him into the world too late?

Reflecting on this passage, the reader must also reflect on the appeal of the horror story. The reader, in a small way, seeks out horror, while the narrator goes to great lengths to discover horror. Why? Lovecraft's narrators want to find and confront horrors so as to have reason to alter their idea of the world, enlarging and endarkening it at the same time, to set themselves apart from and very likely above people they label "ordinary" or prosaic. Of course, there are some who, very loosely sketched in by Lovecraft, enlarge and enlighten the world with conventional religious ideas that are usually represented, when discussed at all, as obviously confabulated notions intended to console. Then again, there are those who have a narrow view of the world, who are a kind of materialist, but among them Lovecraft is no more at home, because they lack the sense of wonder and yearning for broader horizons that was such an essential value for him. Lovecraft's narrators consider themselves to be steely-eyed investigators who gaze unflinchingly on cosmic insignificance, and who yet live in a mystically exalted, broader world of sublime depths and heights. It is a distinction to be doomed; most, according to Lovecraft, are unworthy of it. He saw, both in conventional religious and philosophical attitudes, and in business-minded, acquisitive materialism, a laughable anthropocentrism; his own idea was supranthropocentric, but a remnant of human vanity lurks in that idea, no less than there is a lurking desire within much Lovecraftian horror, namely those individuals who are able to adopt this idea see the world from a godlike vantage point. His narrators, to the extent they join in the cosmic mockery of human vanity, or to the extent they are susceptible to a supernal, unreal beauty, like Randolph Carter in "The Silver Key," seem to escape, in part, the galling limitations of the strictly human.

Was it the utter mindlessness of the Martenses that accounts finally for the absence of a connection to the narrator? The Martenses have no eerily beautiful otherworldly civilization, nor do they have the mocking sardonicism of Pickman's ghouls, nor the august tradition of the de la Poers, nor even the jungle city of Arthur Jermyn's inhuman forebears. There is nothing about them to lure a Lovecraftian narrator, apart from the fact that they are hidden. They are all but purely beasts and bear a far stronger resemblance to the merely degenerate throngs of modern city dwellers Lovecraft described in "The Horror at Red Hook," and in his racist diatribes, than to the always subtly majestic ancient or attractive beings of his other stories. Perhaps Lovecraft's own aversion to the mob guided him in deciding the fate of his proxy narrator as well.

Works Cited

Jakobson, Roman. *Language in Literature*. Cambridge, MA: Harvard University Press, 1987.

The Aboriginal in the Works of H. P. Lovecraft

James Goho

More than 400 hundred years ago, Francisco Vásquez de Coronado and his band of conquistadores ravaged the southwest in their quest for gold. The Superstition Mountain just east of Phoenix, Arizona, was one their targets. The Apache believe the Superstition Mountains are the home of the Thunder God; it is a sacred place, treated with reverence and honor, akin to a cathedral and not a place to plunder. Jill Pascoe writes that over hundreds of years countless people have vanished and died in this mysterious area, which continues to be fabled for lost gold. The Spaniards were unable to coerce the Apache to help them scour for gold in the Superstition Mountains, where many found only terror and death. The Spaniards viewed the Apache, along with all Amerindians, with distain, as primitives, perhaps with a touch of fear, but with a rapacious loathing.

Bartolomé de las Casas documented the savagery of the Spaniards as they subjugated the Americas, where they tortured and murdered millions. The extent of the "genocide" (33) is virtually unimaginable, according to Tzvetan Todorov.[1] The estimate of the population of the overall Americas pre-colonization is challenging and there are huge variations, as William Denevan ("Carl Sauer") and Russell Thornton[2] explore. Charles Mann writes that the bulk

---

1. Todorov asserts that in Mexico on the eve of Columbus's arrival there were 25 million Amerindians but in 1600 only one million.
2. Thornton provides 1492 population estimates in the Western hemisphere as ranging from 8.4 million to 112.5 million. Thornton himself suggests 72+ million for the Western hemisphere and 7+ million north of the Rio Grande, with 5+

of the evidence points to a loss of many millions of American Indians across North and South America after the European arrival. Thornton shows the decline of the American Indian population was a holocaust—precipitous, devastating and dreadful.

This devastation was founded on the notion of the inferiority of the indigenous people. Celia Brickman notes that the colonizing Europeans saw the American Indian as "the quintessential emblem of the first, primitive stage of human development" (17). Reneé L. Bergland suggests that the American "land is haunted because it is stolen" (9). Bergland argues that the source of the American uncanny lies in the history of "murders, looted graves, illegal land transfer and disruptions of sovereignty" (8) of the Native peoples and the landscape is now one of ghosts.

D. H. Lawrence writes: "The Aztec is gone, and the Incas. The Red Indian, the Sequim, the Patagonian are reduced to negligible numbers. . . . Not that the Red Indian will ever possess the broad lands of America. At least I presume not. But his ghost will" (39). Of course, American Indians were never completely gone and continue yet to protect and nurture their unique cultures and are not swallowed up by Lawrence's "great white swamp" (40). But Lawrence does hit on the hauntedness of America and the impact of the American Indian on American literature. To paraphrase a line from Toni Morrison's *Beloved*, there is no forest, prairie, valley, mountain, or town in the country not packed with some dead American Indian's grief, and that is why the American landscape is haunted.

The Ghosts of America

This haunting of the landscape, or geographic terror, is a key theme in the horror fiction of H. P. Lovecraft. That is because for Lovecraft the world in itself is sinister. Dread and horror are the

---

million in the US and 2+ million in Canada. Using information from the U.S. Census and the U.S. Commissioner of Indian Affairs, the American Indian population of the U.S. for the decade 1890–1900 was 250,000. David Stannard estimates the overall population of the Americas pre-Columbus at 100 million. In the United States and Canada, Ronald Wright says population approximations range from 7 to 18 million. Daniel Richter suggests that the population of eastern North America was over 2 million.

nature of existence, and his textual topography makes this alive. In Lovecraft's ontology the fundamental elements are indifferently malevolent. His haunted landscape was primarily in New England but also in other locales, such as the American Southwest. And the haunting in his stories, in many cases, has a particularly American shape to it. The argument of this article is that the haunting in many stories finds its origin in the American Indian. In the fictional woods[3] of Lovecraft the aboriginal is defined as essentially inferior to white Europeans, as demonic or unclean, as savage, as primitive. American Indians are also removed, effaced, overwritten by a legion of monsters, who are portrayed as previously occupying the land. These even more aboriginal beings, however, are really the reanimated indigenous peoples, for in the fiction of Lovecraft the millions of dead American Indians are the "soul of the forest" (D 5), who keep rising from the graves.

Of course, the fiction of Lovecraft is firmly in the mainstream of American literature on this. Joshua Bellin argues that the presence and dispossession of American Indians in America have shaped American literature and that this must be understood in the reading of all the literature. Charles L. Crow argues that to know American literature one must understand the Gothic, which he says is "the imaginative expression of the hidden fears and forbidden desires of Americans" (1). The American Gothic is pervasive in the mainstream and in genre form. It is a counter-argument to American exceptionalism and American triumphalism and American perpetual progress toward the promise land. Crow argues that the Gothic "patrols the line between . . . living and dead" (2). It is a literature at the frontier, which is especially relevant in the United States with a long fable of striking out into the wild frontier. In distorted and threatening form, the Gothic liberates what is hidden, buried away, taboo, and unspoken within a society. In American Gothic litera-

---

3. The terror of the forest pervades the works of HPL. In "The Lurking Fear," the unnamed narrator wonders what has "rotted and festered in the antediluvian forest darkness" and will come out of the "accursed midnight forests and strew fear madness, and death" (D 190). This is within the continuing flow of American literature. It is as if we are all aliens in nature. As Dickinson wrote: "Nature is a stranger yet / The ones that cite her most / have never passed her haunted house / nor simplified her ghost" (#1400).

ture the dreadful encounters with "monsters" reify fears and nightmares about the original inhabitants.

American Indians haunt the Gothic fiction of Lovecraft. But his mastery of the horror idiom opens new ground in understanding the foundation of the fear of the aboriginal. In the end, it is the loss of utopia, the realization that we cannot get ourselves back to the pristine garden (a garden we have destroyed), that there is no safe home; we will never really be homeward bound. Marianna Torgovnick argues that the desire of going home is akin to going primitive. It is a wish to return to origins and the familiar, in a way, that perhaps comforts, that helps us overcome our alienation from our culture and our world and perhaps from ourselves. Lovecraft turns this on its head; there is only a hostile strangeness everywhere. Joyce Carol Oates notes a pervasive and profound existential loneliness in Lovecraft's work, an "elegiac poetry of loss" (7). Some things are gone forever.

The ancient alien realms in Lovecraft's fictions are dystopias; there are no sacred places, just nightmare haunts. And over the mountains there is always something even more hideous as the Old Ones in *At the Mountains of Madness* knew and feared, and Danforth glimpses as he flies away from the Old Ones' abandoned city, and thus is reduced to gibbering. In a universe of dread, there is no salvation. Enmeshed in these themes is the problematical nature of storytelling itself. For Lovecraft is really a modern in Gothic literature. In many of his stories the narrator is not sure of what he has experienced; often the voice is confused, leaving the reader unsure. The narrative is sometimes constructed from fragments, as if all is artifice. He deploys varying styles and narrative voices. Moreover, as readers, should we trust the narrators of the stories? Lovecraft's fiction raises questions about how narratives are constructed and the reliability of those narrations. With a Gothic twist he explores the randomness of life, the disruption of conventional beliefs. His stories often express the loneliness of being and evoke an awful sense of existential despair. There are no absolute truths, and what truths we may find are likely to be terrifying. Although his stories deploy realism as a way of establishing the suspension of disbelief, the stories disrupt reality and question what is real. His library of imaginary texts establishes an alternate reality with alternative authorities. In addition, Lovecraft also deforms and reshapes American Indian models and beliefs into modern Gothic narratives in a manner akin to James Joyce's reshaping of Greek myths in *Ulysses*. The past is recast to a modern Gothic form.

The Aboriginal

What, then, is the aboriginal? Used as an adjective, "aboriginal" means being the first or earliest known of its kind present somewhere, having existed from the beginning, something in an earliest or original stage or state. The word is also indicative of or relating to aborigines and of or relating to the indigenous peoples of Australia. In Canada, the term is embedded in The Constitution Act 1982, which says the "Aboriginal peoples of Canada" include "Indian, Inuit, and Métis peoples of Canada." The synonyms of "aboriginal" include native, indigenous, autochthonous, original, first, earliest, primordial, and primitive. Torgovnick explores the complex and shifting meanings of "primitive" across a variety of fields: art, psychology, anthropology, and literature. In early usage it referred to the original state of something, that is, the aboriginal. This usage has changed and now, in the usage of a controlling society, it seems to refer to "the other," who is defined in distinction from accepted behavior or thoughts in that society. The primitive here is the uncivilized, the irrational, the uncultured, the unintelligent, the untamed, and the unrepressed. These words resonate with the sense of primary but also less advanced.

In Lovecraft's fiction there is often a loathing of the aboriginal or primitive and a pathological aversion to and fear of regression to a primitive state, sometimes expressed through a fear of miscegenation and sometimes in a fear of the regression of isolated populations or in the fear of finding out one's own origins. This is expressed in many stories. A sampling of these is provided here. In "Beyond the Wall of Sleep," Joe Slater is described as "one of those strange, repellent scions of a primitive peasant stock whose isolation . . . has caused them to sink to a kind of barbaric degeneracy" (*D* 26). The local population in "The Dunwich Horror" is "now repellently decadent, having gone far along that path of retrogression so common in many New England backwaters" (*DH* 157).

In the remote Catskills, the location of "The Lurking Fear," there is "a degenerate squatter population inhabiting pitiful hamlets on isolated slopes" (D 180). These inhabitants of the Catskills "having descended the evolutionary scale" (D 186) are "poor mongrels who sometimes leave their valleys to trade handwoven baskets for such primitive necessities as they cannot shoot, raise, or make" (D 180). Later in this story the unnamed narrator shoots one of the multitude of underground monsters, which are "the ultimate product of mammalian degeneration; the frightful outcome of isolated spawning, multiplication, and cannibal nutrition . . . the embodiment of all the snarling and chaos and grinning fear that lurk behind life" (D 199). It is a "dwarfed, deformed" (D 198), "filthy whitish gorilla thing" (D 199) that has descended from the Martenses, a once wealthy family.

This degeneracy can happen rapidly as expressed in "The Horror at Red Hook," where Detective Malone ruminates that "modern people under lawless conditions tend uncannily to repeat the darkest instinctive patterns of primitive half-ape savagery in their daily life and ritual observances" (D 248). Moreover, the story's language expresses much anguish and dread, as the primitive is "the root of a contagion destined to sicken and swallow cities, and engulf nations in the foetor of hybrid pestilence" (D 260).

"Facts concerning the Late Arthur Jermyn and his Family" evidences why Sir Arthur Jermyn soaked himself in oil to hasten his suicide. The story starts, "Life is a hideous thing" (D 73), and then asks the question whether humans are a separate species, that is, are we really civilized, are we really distinct from animals (in this story's case, apes), and not from an eon-long evolutionary perspective? Here it is a white ape, spawn of the great apes and a "prehistoric white Congolese civilisation" (D 74), that had fallen into the primal—the awful terror that many stories evoke. Arthur Jermyn "went out on the moor and burned himself" (D 73) after seeing the gift of the mummy of his great-great-great-grandmother—a white ape princess. Origins are not salutary in Lovecraft but awful.

For Lovecraft, "The past is *real*—it is *all there is*" (SL 3.31). But in the end that past is dangerous, as is found in many of his stories. And finding your ancestors is often full of horror. A fondness for the past is, in a sense, akin to trying to get back home. But Lovecraft's fiction tells us it is a fool's mission.

Illumination and Distortion

In "Supernatural Horror in Literature," Lovecraft identifies one of the sources of the weird fiction of American writers as "the strange and forbidding nature of the scene into which they were plunged. The vast and gloomy virgin forests in whose perpetual twilight all terrors might well lurk;[4] the hordes of coppery[5] Indians whose strange, saturnine visages and violent customs hinted strongly at traces of infernal origin" (D 401). He is on the mark with this assessment as a particular feature of the American Gothic. This demonization of American Indians started right away. Cotton Mather writes that witches call the devil the Black Man and that he resembles an Indian and that the Indians "used all their sorceries to molest the first planters" (74). In his *Map of Virginia, with a Description of the Countrey, the Commodities, People, Government and Religion*, John Smith states of Indian religion, "their chiefe God they worship is the Divell" (Smith 1.65–84).

Charles Brockden Brown in the preface to *Edgar Huntly* argues that "The incidents of Indian hostility, and the perils of the west-

---

4. But HPL, as well as nearly all others, is wrong about the first impressions of the landscape itself at the time of the first colonial incursions. Denevan ("Pristine Myth") provides evidence that "By 1492 Indian activity throughout the Americas had modified forest extent and composition, created and expanded grasslands, and rearranged microrelief via countless artificial earthworks. Agricultural fields were common, as were houses and towns and roads and trails" (370). Brandon and Mandell describe the New England landscape as first found by Europeans and described by them as nearly akin to an English garden with sweeping meadows and deep woods cleared of much underbrush and with clear sightlines, all to support native agriculture and hunting. However, the European colonists did dramatically alter the New England ecology to suit their agriculture and industry as shown by William Cronon.

5. The non-white skin of American Indians has always been a focus of racist words. In *In Cold Blood*, Truman Capote writes of Perry Edward Smith that "His mother had been a full-blooded Cherokee; it was from her that he had inherited his coloring—the iodine skin" (16). It is as if the flesh of Indians is infected and must be treated to stop contagion.

ern wilderness" (29) are the appropriate material for American writers. Brown's Gothic is the haunted forest where American Indians are akin to animals and represent natural evil.

Nathaniel Hawthorne in "Young Goodman Brown" takes the hero deep into a gloomy forest, where he says to himself: "There may be a devilish Indian behind every tree" (53). As Goodman Brown goes deeper into the "haunted forest" he hears "the yell of Indians" (59). According to Teresa A. Goddu, Americans for long have been taught from birth to see the Indian as a Gothic monster.[6] In Melville's *The Confidence Man*, there is a chapter, "Containing the metaphysics of Indian Hating." The following chapter recounts the exploits of the Indian-Killer Colonel John Moredock, whose family was purportedly massacred by Indians. Moredock "seldom stirred without his rifle, and hated Indians like snakes" (140), equating American Indians with demons in the Garden of Eden. Lovecraft elaborates this theme in "The Curse of Yig." Dirk Peters in *The Narrative of Arthur Gordon Pym of Nantucket* is almost bestial in appearance and the other to Pym. This dark companion is "the son of an Indian squaw[7] woman of the tribe of the Upsarokas" (84). This perspective[8] was a means of justifying the genocide of indigenous peoples and the continued violent expansion of Europeans across the Americas.

Leslie Fiedler writes that in the American tradition "the aristocratic villains of the European tale of terror are replaced by skulking primitives and the natural rather than the sophisticated is felt as a primal threat" (*Vanishing* 377). In the European Gothic, it is

---

6. The Declaration of Independence refers to "merciless Indian savages."

7. This is an offensive, obscene, and demeaning racist word.

8. There is another perspective of American Indians as emblematic of the noble savage, a sentimental image but no longer alive or only on display on reservations similar to zoos for exotic animals. This other image is just another way of removing Indians from the real landscape, leaving graves to be looted. The confrontation in the wilderness, at the frontier, between the white settler and the indigenous people is a continuing story element. The story has variations. In many, the American Indians are eliminated, opening up the land for the use of colonists. In others, a white person goes native, so to speak and joins the aboriginal either by being captured or by identifying as native. In *Avatar*, the disabled Marine goes native and saves the people of blue color, as if they are incapable themselves.

the power of church and state that is confronted, but in America it is nature and the indigenous people. In a sense, as Fielder argues the American Gothic is conservative and thematically is about building new power structures over killed ones in the wilderness. This demonization infuses American literature and is the foundation of a unique American literature, which is as Fielder writes "almost essentially a Gothic one" (*Love and Death* 129).

Depictions of American Indians in the Fiction of Lovecraft

Lovecraft's fiction is dense with images and themes of the primitive. There are also explicit mentions of American Indians and in most they are negatively portrayed, often referred to in derogatory language. For example, in *The Case of Charles Dexter Ward*, Curwen's servants "were a sullen pair of aged Narragansett Indians; the husband dumb and curiously scarred, and the wife of a very repulsive cast of countenance, probably due to a mixture of negro blood" (*MM* 119). They are presented as in league with the evil Joseph Curwen.

The story "He" takes place in New York City, where the narrator is shown around the secret places of the city by a stranger dressed in eighteenth-century garb. This stranger tells of an ancestor, the Squire, who learned of magical rituals by observing "sartain half-breed[9] red Indians" as "at full moon" they "stole over the wall" of his property and "performed sartain acts" (*D* 271). The Squire "sarved them monstrous bad rum"[10] (*D* 272) to kill them off. They were "mongrel salvages" (*D* 272). But they have their revenge. The stranger has the power to present vistas of different times. Upon

---

9. The progeny of mixed races seems to have been a particular bugaboo in the fiction of HPL. Of course this is another perennial theme in American literature. The secret theme of the Leatherstocking tales of James Fenimore Cooper, as Fiedler argues, is miscegenation. Natty Bumppo is for racial purity; in *The Last of the Mohicans*, he says he is "a white man without cross;" and has "no taint of Indian blood" (162). In *The Deerslayer*, he has "a white heart and can't, in reason, love a red-skinned maiden" (82). HPL drags this theme into the open. In *Tom Sawyer*, evil is personified in Injun Joe, who is half American Indian.

10. Mail and Johnson argue that the spreading of alcohol to the indigenous people was for colonist advantage and was an early form of chemical warfare.

seeing the future vista, the unnamed narrator screams and his shrieks seem to rouse something from the grave. The stranger, the Squire, admonishes the narrator: "The full moon—damn ye—ye . . . ye yelping dog—ye called 'em, and they've come for me! Moccasined feet—dead men—Gad sink ye, ye red devils" (*D* 274). In this story Lovecraft uses the images of American Indians as vengeful ghosts returning for payback, a theme that is featured in much of his fiction. They seem to be nowhere in the modern New York City of the story, as if they exist only in nightmares.

In "The Call of Cthulhu," a stone bas-relief of Cthulhu is reportedly worshipped in Greenland by a "singular tribe or cult of degenerate Esquimaux whose religion [was] a curious form of devil-worship." Moreover, "It was a faith of which other Esquimaux knew little, and which they mentioned only with shudders, saying that it had come down from horribly ancient aeons before ever the world was made" (*DH* 135). In the new world, there are even more aboriginal beings.

In "The Transition of Juan Romero," Romero's facial features although "plainly of the Red Indian type, were yet remarkable for their light colour and refined conformation, being vastly unlike those of the average 'greaser' or Piute of the locality" (*D* 338). Interestingly, this light color was due to "the ancient and noble Aztec" (*D* 338). But only his face was noble. "Ignorant and dirty, he was at home amongst the other brown-skinned" (*D* 338). In the story a great abyss is revealed after a dynamite blast at Norton Mine. The bottom seems lost in the depths, "the void below was infinite" (*D* 339). During the night, a great throbbing or drumming and chanting sound from the shaft awakens the unnamed narrator and Romero. They are drawn "irresistibly . . . to the gaping blackness of the mine" (*D* 341). As they descend Romero quickens his pace and leaves the narrator behind, who hears a shift in Romero's language, as if he is returning to his ancestral roots. Romero cries: "Huitzilopotchli" (*D* 339), the Aztec god of the sun and war. Romero returns to his ancient home and finds terror. The narrator catches a glimpse of Romero deep down in the chasm, but he dares not tell what he saw. It is a place that cannot be described. In the morning, Romero is dead in his bunk and it said that neither of them left the bunkhouse at night—nightmares are real.

In "The Dunwich Horror," the megalithic monument on a hilltop is "attributed to the Indians . . . as once the burial-places of the Pocumtucks" (*DH* 159). The horror in the story seems to have its essential source in the "unhallowed rites and conclaves of the Indians, amidst which they called forbidden shapes of shadow out of the great rounded hills, and made wild orgiastic prayers that were answered by loud crackings and rumblings from the ground below" (*DH* 157–58). Later in the story the odor at the Whateleys' is akin to that "near the Indian circles on the hills and could not come from anything sane or of this earth" (*DH* 164).

"The Whisperer in Darkness" begins with the sightings of strange creatures floating in the Vermont rivers after a mighty flood. "The Indians had the most fantastic theories of all" (*DH* 212) about the nature of the strange beings in the so-called Penacook myth of the winged ones. Their belief that the beings were not native to earth and came to extract a certain ore turns to be the most accurate. Standing stones are a geographical element in the landscape of the story, as in others. Such stones are sometimes used as a motif for American Indians and are a signal from the past and often mark a geographical entrance point for "monsters."

In "The Curse of Yig," Walker and Audrey Davis move from Arkansas to Oklahoma to start a new life in the former Indian Territory. Audrey has a "slight Indian admixture" (*HM* 84). The story centers around Walker's fears of snakes, rising to a crescendo after he learns Audrey killed a den of newborn rattlesnakes. He tries to atone to the snake god, Yig, modeled on Quetzalcoatl, the Toltec and Aztec god portrayed as a feathered serpent. Walker visits the "Wichitas, and talked long with the old men and shamans about the snake-god and how to nullify his wrath. Charms were always ready in exchange for whiskey" (*HM* 88). This all fails and during one night of terror Audrey mistakenly axes Walker to death. She goes mad and dies in an asylum. But first she gives birth to a rhumba of things, only one of which survives and is housed in the asylum. The creature is a "crawling and wriggling" thing "emitting every now and then a weak and vacuous hiss." It bears "some remote resemblance to a human form laid flat on its belly" but is "subtly squamous in the dim, ghoulish light" (*HM* 82) of its cell. This is another Gothic incarnation of the primitive, arising from the indigenous peoples.

"The Mound" is centered on a mysterious low tumulus or mound near Binger, Oklahoma. This mound turns out to mark an entranceway to the underground world of *Xinaián* or *K'n-yan*, which has seemingly existed for eons. The first narrator is an "American Indian ethnologist" (*HM* 99) who recounts several tales of expeditions to the mound, most of which result in strange disappearances. He hazards a way into the mound and finds a curious cylinder containing a scroll written by Pánfilo de Zamacona y Nuñez, who was part of Coronado's band. Zamacona[11] descends to the *K'n-yan* world[12] and is welcomed, apparently because he is of a "higher-grade" (*HM* 132) than the indigenous people of the area, referred to as "ignorant tribes of the plains" (*HM* 137). After centuries, the underground society finds only the European to be welcomed into their cities, although Zamacona is not free to leave. The story refers to American Indians in derogatory terms and the speech of the character Grey Eagle is a caricature. The sentinels on the mound seem to be biologically distorted images of American Indians, an embodiment of the American Indian terror hallucination haunting the white imagination.

Often Lovecraft's works have nearly a cinematic quality, including a soundtrack. For aboriginals, it is the sound of drums. The New Orleans police in "The Call of Cthulhu" track deep into the "terrible cypress woods" (*DH* 136) getting closer to the "beat of tom-toms" (*DH* 137), the auditory signal of the primitive in Lovecraft. In "The Curse of Yig" the "tom-toms . . . [of] the Pawnee, Wichita and Caddo country pounded endlessly" (*HM* 83) to ward off the snake god. In "The Mound" the real danger of American Indian drumming is told: "There are old, old tribes with old, old memories there; and when the tom-toms beat ceaselessly over brooding plains in the autumn the spirits of men are brought dangerously close to primal, whispered things" (*HM* 97).

---

11. Zamacona is told about the underground world by Charging Buffalo, who is nearly parental in his concern and caring for the Spaniard and gives him a talisman for protection. But Zamacona disrespects him by paying him off with "trinkets" (*HM* 120).

12. This world turns out to be the cities of gold searched for by Coronado, a nice twist by HPL.

These drums are the emblem of the wild primitive[13] and are a source of fear in a number of Lovecraft's works, as Leigh Blackmore illustrates. It is found also in "Herbert West—Reanimator," where Buck Robinson's face "conjured up thoughts of unspeakable Congo secrets and tom-tom poundings under an eerie moon" (*D* 146). Other examples include *The Dream-Quest of Unknown Kadath*, where "the muffled, maddening beating of vile drums" (*MM* 308) accompany Azathoth, and "The Elder Pharos," where "the last Elder One lives on alone / Talking to Chaos with the beat of drums (*AT* 75).

This deep aversion to drumming is expressed not only by Lovecraft. For example, the historian Robert Edward Leach, on the first page of chapter 1 of *Flintlock and Tomahawk*, takes this fear back to "1697 [when] the ominous drumbeats of large-scale organized resistance were heard in Connecticut as the enraged Pequots rose up against the English Settlers" (1).

The Return of Aboriginal Beings

But Lovecraft is a master; many of his monsters and horrific entities can be seen as a transformation of the primitive, the aboriginal, of American Indians.

Fictionally, his fiction displaces American Indians and replaces them with older beings, twisted and deformed in the Gothic tradition. It is as if New England is cleansed fictionally of any remnant of the real original inhabitants. Joel Pace suggests that Lovecraft's invocations of pre-American Indian ruins are an attempt to snuff out the Indian presence in the landscape, to write the Indian away.[14]

---

13. Joseph Conrad evokes this when he has Marlow think of "the heavy, mute spell of the wilderness--that seemed to draw him [Kurtz] to its pitiless breast by the awakening of forgotten and brutal instincts, by the memory of gratified and monstrous passions. This alone, I was convinced, had driven him out to the edge of the forest, to the bush, towards the gleam of fires, the throb of drums, the drone of weird incantations" (144).

14. Jean O'Brien [2010] writes of the concerted work of New England local narratives from 1820 to 1880 to write away the indigenous population and instil the myth of the extinction of the American Indian. The New Englanders claimed former Indian places as Euro-American. This was in part to solidify the superiority of the white population and to justify the appropriation of Indian land, as

This is another common thread in America's fabric of dispossession of indigenous peoples. William Bradford writes that where the pilgrims settled was the vast and unpeopled countries of America. "The place they had thoughts on was some of those, which are fruitful and fit for habitation, being devoid of all civil inhabitants, where there are only savages and brutish men, which range up and down, little otherwise then the wild beasts of the same" (25). In 1788, Philip Freneau in "The Indian Burying-Ground" made the American Indian "a shade" (3) and tried to write them out of the real "to shadows" (4); mere "delusions" (4) haunting the land.

In "The Colour out of Space" Ammi Pierce says that the woods around the blasted heath were not generally feared before the meteorite fell except for a "small island in the Miskatonic where the devil held court beside a curious lone altar older than the Indians" (*DH* 57). The unknown thing in the swamp of cypress woods and lagoons in "The Call of Cthulhu" "had been there before d'Iberville, before La Salle, before the Indians" (*DH* 137). This is of a piece with the looting of Native American artifacts and grave-robbing that started with the first invasions. Bergland points out that in the first year of settlement at Plymouth in 1620, the English plundered a number of gravesites. This progressed as the frontier was pushed across the continent, abetted by the military and museums.

In "The Mound" the tumulus is patrolled by ghostly guardians, and early in the story they are reported as American Indians: a male during the day and a headless female who carries a "blue ghost-light" (*HM* 106) at night. The narrator doubts the male is an American Indian, as he "was certainly *not a savage*. He was the product of *a civilisation*" (*HM* 108). These beings turn out to be former denizens of the underground world, one a "discredited

---

well as to provide a foundation for the continuing Indian wars in the West. Even the graves of Indians were obliterated either by looting or by such actions as planting trees on the grounds. But the extinction is false in New England and elsewhere. Still surviving are the Mashpee, Gay Head Wampanog, and the Nipmuck in Massachusetts; the Mashantucket, Pequot, and Mohegan in Conneticut; the Narrangansett in Rhode Island; the Abenaki in Vermont and western Maine; and the Passamaquoddy and Penobscot in Maine and others, as documented by O'Brien [1997]. In New York, Wright suggests the history of Iroquoia is overwritten with an alien history with names like Syracuse, Ithaca, Homer, Rome, and Ovid.

freeman" and the second, "T'la-yub who had planned and aided" (*HM* 157) Zamacona's first try at escaping from the underground world and, after they had failed, was punished. Even the ghosts of American Indians are usurped.

But in this dispossession, what Lovecraft's fiction achieves is the return of American Indians in the form of original beings, in Gothic form. American Indians are never really absent in his fiction; but they are often transformed. In "The Thing on the Doorstep," after Upton rescues Derby from Chesuncook, Maine, Derby explains his strange behavior as arising in part from his exploration of "certain Indian relics in the north woods—standing stones" (*DH* 291). This is the locale of "Cyclopean ruins in the heart of the Maine woods beneath which vast staircases led down to abysses of nighted secrets, of complex angles that led through invisible walls to other regions of space" (*DH* 285). American Indians are the source of the hauntings and transformations that come from the depths, as if they are arising from their looted graves.

In "He" the monster is prefigured by the "gleam of a tomahawk as it cleft the rending wood," and it opens the way for "a colossal, shapeless influx of inky substance starred with shining, malevolent eyes" (*D* 275). This is the return of American Indians in a shape twisted by the Gothic vision of Lovecraft.

In "The Electric Executioner," Meso-American Indian gods are blurred with Lovecraftian monsters into a mixed pantheon of beings. In this story, as Beherec identifies, Lovecraft displays considerable knowledge of Meso-American myths and geography. The story character, Feldon, who identifies strongly with Meso-Americans, intones the mixing of beings in his many chants. One goes: "In the mountains—in the mountains—Anahuac—Tenochtitlan—the old ones" (*HM* 68). As Beherec notes, this melds the land, the city, and Lovecraft's Old Ones. Another chant, in part, is: "Mictlanteuctli, Great Lord, a sign! A sign from within thy black cave! Iä! Tonatiuh-Metztli! Cthulhutl! Command, and I serve!" (*HM* 74). The lord of the underworld and the sun and moon are united with Great Cthulhu.

Beherec also illuminates Lovecraft's use of Aztec mythology in the "The Curse of Yig." In the story Yig is said to be an "older and darker prototype" (*HM* 81) of Quetzalcoatl. This is Kukulcan, the

Mayan god, which Lovecraft knew. Yig appears also in "The Mound" as one of the gods in the K'n-yan pantheon. In this story the longevity of the possession of the Americas by indigenous peoples is acknowledged, although it is overwritten by the K'n-yan people, who are portrayed as a sort of pseudo-human alien population of long duration on earth. For long the mounds in the United States were believed to be the work of some other agency rather than American Indians, as elucidated by George Milner.[15] This story describes the mound as perhaps "a product of Nature" or "a burial-place or ceremonial dais constructed by prehistoric tribes" (*HM* 98). It is really an entrance way to the underground society and is another example of an indigenous people's formation being usurped as the work of older beings. The story continues the narrative that any major structures or alterations[16] in the landscape could not have been accomplished by American Indians but must be due really to others. This is part of the appropriation of the North American landscape by Euro-Americans. However, there is a link with the indigenous people; in Zamacona's narrative the K'n-yan people "seemed to be Indians . . . [but] their faces had many subtle differences" (*HM* 129). And their language has "an infinitely remote linkage with the Aztec" (*HM* 131).

At the close of "The Dunwich Horror" professors from Miskatonic University kill off the invisible monster. In this story the locals are not capable of destroying the horror, only the white intellectuals are able to do so; the locals are powerless to repossess the land. The Miskatonic mission pulls down all the rings of standing stones on the hills, as if these are the source of the horror, whence the horror really arose, that is, from American Indian

---

15. Milner documents how from 3000 BC to the sixteenth-century American Indians quarried tons of earth to form thousands of mounds in the Eastern Woodlands. Some were burial sites, some effigies in the form of snakes and sacred totems, others platforms for dwellings. Much was looted but much also remained in the form of copper engraved stone palletes, shells, masks, stone figures and elaborately designed pottery. Stephen Plog itemizes the impact of the Hohokam and Anasazi on the American Southwest landscape with roads, irrigation canals, and towns.

16. William Romain argues the Hopewell built their massive earthworks using a standard unit of measure and aligned many to cycles of the moon and sun, providing evidence of sophistication in geometry, mathematics and astronomy.

haunts. In this story it is as if the force of the original inhabitants comes back in invisible form. The Dunwich Horror, the twin of Wilbur Whateley, is the reification of the fear of the vengeful return of the American Indian. In the Lovecraftian forest, the dispossession of American Indians continues but their ghosts keep on coming back.

Dystopia

Lovecraft's fiction is replete with images of a fallen utopia. No utopia is to be found in the past, the present, or the future. It is a vain quest. In "He" the vision of the past of New York is an "unhealthy shimmer of a vast salt marsh" (D 272–73). "The Mound" is particularly insightful in its dissection of the vision of utopia. It paints a disturbing picture of the K'n-yan culture that is lost in acedia, which is overcome with ennui and moral collapse, where hedonism and torture are the only reasons for living. It is hedonism of sadomasochistic dimensions, but where there is a realization that all is pointless. The progress of development of the underground people has led to a society of decadence. They are seemingly immortal, control advanced technologies, and seem to have magical powers to dematerialize and to communicate their thoughts; all things seem within their reach. But the society is repellent to the ancient Spanish adventurer, Zamacona. The society is founded on a deformed "half-human slave class" (HM 118) and an especially disturbing slave class continuously engineered through biological deformations and tortured into grotesque forms, something the Nazis dreamed of. Some of the elements of cultural collapse are akin to the orgies of coliseum mutilation and depravity of the Romans. But much is a spinoff of a post-industrial society, where leisure means torture and disgust. As Leonard Cohen sings about "The Future," it is murder. It is a civilization of savagery and cannibalism. Interestingly, there are several levels of this dystopia, a sort of circles of hell, with the known bottom ring of N'kai ruled by sluglike beings surging darkly as if liquefied excretions in gutters. The story hints that there may be even more subterranean rings with even more horrific entities.

In "He" Lovecraft displays a hellish image of the future New

York, with drumming as the sound track. It's like a dark bestial beating heart:

> I saw the heavens verminous with strange flying things, and beneath them a hellish black city of giant stone terraces with impious pyramids flung savagely to the moon, and devil-lights burning from unnumbered windows. And swarming loathsomely on aerial galleries I saw the yellow, squint-eyed people of that city, robed horribly in orange and red, and dancing insanely to the pounding of fevered kettle-drums, the clatter of obscene crotala, and the maniacal moaning of muted horns whose ceaseless dirges rose and fell undulantly like the wave of an unhallowed ocean of bitumen. (*D* 273–74)

The more we know, the more horrific things are; the deeper underground or farther in space or distant in time we venture or the more homeward we go, the more we find dread.

The Original

Near the end of *At the Mountains of Madness*, Danforth raves "the original, the eternal, the undying" (*MM* 106).

Lovecraft's fiction recreates American Indians, gothically transformed but powerful and fearsome, reifying fear as they arise from the deep memory. In a real way, his fiction tells the truth about America and its foundation on violence and dispossession and the ongoing fear of the aboriginal. America is founded and spread on violence. This violence, as Richard Slotkin argues, is a continuing impulse in American society and embedded in national historical and fictional narratives. Historically, Americans have not confronted the death and destruction that the country was founded on. It is forbidden, or unspeakable, or written away, or engulfed in a mythology of manifest destiny and always moving and conquering new frontiers where the inhabitants are inferior and have to be removed, in reality, in imagination, and in history. Lovecraft was an outsider himself in many ways, his work published in the pulps and excoriated frequently and viewed as amateur at best until relatively recently. From this outsider post, yet also a defender of the flag, Lovecraft created a new American Gothic clearly founded on its tradition of fear of the vanquished or enslaved. In his fiction they have returned in even more horrific form to terrify society. This theme is found throughout the fiction—in early stories, mature fiction, and the primary revisions. The eon-old monsters that Lovecraft invents are yet aboriginal themselves. Origins cannot be escaped.

The American Gothic is all about the aboriginal. The European Gothic can be thought of as an expression of rebellion against the obscenities of perverse power. The American Gothic is all about the killing of the powers of the natural, of origins, of the very source of our being. Lovecraft captures that overwhelming sense of loss in the New England landscape, in the great expanse of the United States. He expresses a familiar place changing into an alien place of ancient horror that cannot be escaped. And the horror cannot really be escaped because in the end it is not just in the landscape, it is inside us. His stories give voice to the American soul in torment, full of torture and anguish. The genocide of the indigenous population gave Euro-Americans their land, their wealth, their being. In Lovecraft, the dead original peoples of America keep coming back in colossal form to repossess their land. Lawrence writes of Americans as necessarily killers. Lovecraft's fiction rewrites this as self-killers in the end as all homes are full of ghosts.

Works Cited

Beherec, Marc, A. "The Racist and La Raze: H. P. Lovecraft's Aztec Mythos." In *The Intersection of Fantasy and Native America from H. P. Lovecraft to Leslie Marmon Silko*, ed. Amy H. Sturgis and David D. Oberhelman. Altadena, CA: Mythopoeic Press, 2009. 25–37.

Bellin, Joshua David. *The Demon of the Continent*. Philadelphia: University of Pennsylvania Press, 2001.

Bergland, Renée L. *The National Uncanny: Indian Ghosts and American Subjects*. Hanover, NH: University Press of New England, 2000.

Blackmore, Leigh. "Some Notes on Lovecraft's 'The Transition of Juan Romero.'" *Lovecraft Annual* No. 3 (2009): 147–68.

Bradford, William. *Of Plymouth Plantation*. Piscataway, NJ: Rutgers University Press, 1952.

Brandon, Kathleen, J. *Native People of Southern New England, 1500–1650*. Norman: University of Oklahoma Press, 1996.

Brickman, Celia. *Aboriginal Populations in the Mind*. New York: Columbia University Press, 2003.

Brown, Charles Brockden. *Edgar Huntly*. New Haven: College & University Press, 1973.

Capote, Truman. *In Cold Blood*. 1966. New York: Vintage, 1994.

Conrad, Joseph. *Heart of Darkness*. London: Folio, 1997.

Cooper, James Fenimore. *The Last of the Mohicans*. Cambridge, MA: Harvard University Press, 2011.

———. *The Deerslayer*. Teddington, UK: Echo Library, 2006.

Cronon, William. *Changes in the Land: Indians, Colonists and the Ecology of New England*. New York: Hill & Wang, 1983.

Crow, Charles, L. *American Gothic*. Cardiff: University of Wales Press. 2009.

de las Casas, Bartolomé. *The Devastation of the Indies: A Brief Account*. Trans. Herma Briffault. 1952. Baltimore: Johns Hopkins University Press. 1992.

Denevan, William M. "The Pristine Myth: The Landscape of the Americas in 1492." *Annals of the Association of American Geographers* 82 (1992): 369–85.

———. "Carl Sauer and Native American Population Size." *Geographical Review* 86 (July 1996): 385–97.

Dickinson, Emily. *The Poems of Emily Dickinson: Reading Edition*. Cambridge, MA: Harvard University Press, 2005.

Fiedler, Leslie. *Love and Death in the American Novel*. New York: Dell, 1966.

———. *The Return of the Vanishing American*. New York: Stein & Day, 1968.

Freneau, Philip. "The Indian Burying-Ground." In *The Little Book of American Poets: 1787–1900*, ed. Jessie B. Rittenhouse. Boston: Houghton Mifflin, 1915. 3–4.

Goddu, Teresa A. *Gothic America: Narrative, History, and Nation*. New York: Columbia University Press, 1997.

Hawthorne, Nathaniel. "Young Goodman Brown." In *American Gothic Tales*, ed. Joyce Carol Oates. New York: Plume, 1996. 52–64.

Lawrence, D. H. *Studies in Classic American Literature*. London: Martin Secker, 1933.

Leach, Douglas Edward. *Flintlock and Tomahawk.* Woodstock, VT: Countryman Press, 1958.

Mail, P. D., and S. Johnson. "Boozing, Sniffing, and Toking: An Overview of the Past, Present, and Future of Substance Use by American Indian." *American Indian & Alaska Native Mental Health Research* 5(2) (1993): 1–33.

Mandell, Daniel, R. *Behind the Frontier: Indians in Eighteenth-Century Eastern Massachusetts.* Lincoln: University of Nebraska Press, 1996.

Mann, Charles C. *1491: New Revelations of the Americas Before Columbus,* New York: Knopf, 2005.

Mather, Cotton. *The Wonders of the Invisible World.* London: John Russell Smith, 1862.

Melville, Herman. *The Confidence Man: His Masquerade.* Evanston: Northwestern University Press/Newberry Library, 1984.

Milner, George R. *The Moundbuilders.* London: Thames & Hudson, 2004.

Morrison, Toni. *Beloved.* New York: Knopf, 1987.

O'Brien, Jean M. *Dispossession by Degrees: Indian Land and Identity in Natick, Massachusetts, 1650–1920.* Cambridge: Cambridge University Press, 1997.

———. *Firstings and Lastings: Writing Indians out of Existence in New England.* Minneapolis: University of Minnesota Press, 2010.

Oates, Joyce Carol. "Introduction." In *American Gothic Tales,* ed. Joyce Carol Oates. New York: Plume, 1996.

Pace, Joel. "Queer Tales? Sexuality, Race and Architecture in 'The Thing on the Doorstep.'" *Lovecraft Annual* No. 2 (2008): 104–37.

Pascoe, Jill. *Arizona's Haunted History.* Gilbert, AZ: Irongate Press, 2008.

Plog, Stephen. *Ancient Peoples of the American Southwest.* New York: Thames & Hudson, 1997.

Poe, Edgar Allan. *The Narrative of Arthur Gordon Pym of Nantucket.* 1838. New York: Penguin, 1980.

Richter, Daniel K. *Facing East from Indian Country.* Cambridge, MA: Harvard University Press, 2001.

Romain, William, F. *Mysteries of the Hopewell.* Akron: Akron Ohio University Press, 2000.

Slotkin, Richard. *Regeneration through Violence: The Mythology of the American Frontier, 1600–1860.* Middletown, CT: Wesleyan University Press, 1973.

Smith, John. *Travels and Works of Captain John Smith.* Ed. Edward Arber and A. C. Bradley. Edinburgh: John Grant, 1910.

Stannard, David. *American Holocaust: The Conquest of the New World.* New York: Oxford University Press, 1993.

The Constitution Act, 1982, Schedule B to the Canada Act 1982 (UK), 1982, c 11. Retrieved from <http://www.canlii.org/en/ca/const/const1982.html> Feb. 2011.

Thornton, Russell. *American Indian Holocaust and Survival: A Population History Since 1492.* Norman: University of Oklahoma Press, 1990.

Todorov, Tzvetan. *The Conquest of America.* New York: Harper & Row, 1992.

Torgovnick, Marianna. *Gone Primitive: Savage Intellects, Modern Lives.* Chicago: University of Chicago Press, 1990.

Wright, Ronald. *Stolen Continents: The Americas through Indian Eyes since 1492.* Boston: Houghton Mifflin, 1992.

Briefly Noted

S. T. Joshi has published the first illustrated biography of Lovecraft, entitled *H. P. Lovecraft: Nightmare Countries* (New York: Metro Books, 2012). Although the text of the book comprises less than 40,000 words, it is lavishly illustrated with photographs of Lovecraft, his friends and relatives, his residences in Providence, and such rare items as his marriage certificate, death certificate, and the first page of his will. Also included are reproductions of the first page of the autograph manuscripts of *At the Mountains of Madness,* "The Thing on the Doorstep," and "The Shadow out of Time." The book will be sold exclusively in Barnes & Noble bookstores and on the Barnes & Noble website, for the bargain price of $19.98.

Envisaging the Cosmos: A Note on "The Dreams in the Witch House"

Scott Connors

Like its sister story "The Dunwich Horror," H. P. Lovecraft's tale "The Dreams in the Witch House" (1932) is a favorite with his fans but has not generally found favor with Lovecraft scholars and critics. Fritz Leiber lauded it as "Lovecraft's most carefully worked out story of hyperspace travel" ("Hyperspace" 146). More recent critics, while conceding the validity of Leiber's statement, have focused on the story's flaws, real and perceived. Donald R. Burleson stated that it falls "somewhat short of his usual level for this later period" (177); Peter Cannon called "The Dreams in the Witch House" "the weakest of his later tales under his own name" (114). Despite the vividness of his description of hyperspace and the inclusion of Brown Jenkin, one of his most memorable teratological horrors, many have echoed Steven J. Mariconda's assessment: "This story is best thought of as Lovecraft's Magnificent Failure—its uneven execution is not equal to its breathtaking conceptions, which are some of the most original in imaginative literature" (200).

Lovecraft biographer S. T. Joshi identifies several problems with the execution of "The Dreams in the Witch House." This essay concentrates on perhaps the most glaring of these: "How can Lovecraft the atheist allow Keziah [Mason, the titular Witch] to be frightened off by the sight of a crucifix?" (823). During the climactic struggle in the enclosed attic of the Witch House, Walter Gilman in desperation wonders "how the sight of the [crucifix] itself would affect the evil creature. . . . At sight of the device the witch seemed struck with panic, and her grip relaxed long enough to break it entirely" (*MM* 292). Witnessing the writer that Leiber described as the "Copernicus of the horror story [who] shifted the focus of supernatural dread from man and his little world and his gods, to the stars and the black unplumbed gulfs of intergalactic space" ("Copernicus" 50) describe a scene that would not be out of place in a Hammer Dracula film does tend to raise the eyebrow of even the beginning Lovecraftian. So why would Lovecraft have Keziah react in this manner?

Some dismiss Lovecraft's stories as dealing with "hairy squids from outer space," but David E. Schultz properly points out that the contrary is true, that "Lovecraft's stories are about people, not exotic monsters from strange places. His stories explore how individuals might be affected by knowledge of such things" (54). This raises the question as to the type of person Lovecraft envisaged Keziah Mason to be.

Lovecraft introduces her to the reader with an account of her unexplained escape from Salem Gaol during the 1692 witch trials (*MM* 263). He discusses this dark episode of Massachusetts history in an exhaustive letter to his fellow *Weird Tales* writer, the Texan Robert E. Howard, dated 4 October 1930, in terms that made it clear that he believed cult members posed a real threat to their societies. He cites Margaret Murray's 1921 treatise *The Witch-Cult in Western Europe*, which asserts that "the witch-cult actually established a 'coven' (its only one in the New World) in the Salem region about 1690, and that it included a large number of neurotic and degenerate whites, together with Indians, negroes, and West-Indian slaves" (*SL* 3.182–83).[1] Earlier in the same letter Lovecraft had explained how the Puritan colonists had imported

a vile class of degenerate London scum as indentured servants. . . . They had not learned the lesson that more actually anti-social perversion occurs among the decadent scum of a high race, than among the mentally and physically sound types of an inferior race. We can picture the result of this warped, inhibition-stunted, free and easy degenerate element under the domination of the iron-

---

1. Robert Waugh points out that "The Dreams in the Witch House" represents HPL's "last extensive use" of Murray (122). He had been an enthusiastic supporter of her thesis, that the witch cult was a real phenomenon and represented a survival of a rural pre-Christian fertility religion that still existed furtively into the late Middle Ages.

clad Puritan theocracy and moral strait-jacket. Repression and explosion—just as intelligent old William Bradford of Plymouth saw. "Wickedness more stopt up by strict laws . . . breaks out wher it gettes vente." (*SL* 3.177)

In the absence of anything in the story to the contrary, Keziah may be presumed to come from this class. It is unlikely (but not impossible) that this impoverished, stunted background would bring forth a prodigy capable of unlocking the secret of transdimensional travel, and no such suggestion appears in the tale.[2] The closest that Lovecraft comes to describing the origin of her knowledge is that she was "guided by some influence past all conjecture" (*MM* 266). This suggests a mechanism similar to that described in "The Call of Cthulhu," where the sleeping Great Old Ones communicate with mankind through the dreams of the sensitive (*DH* 140). Gilman theorizes later in the story that there exists a "kinship of higher mathematics to certain phases of magical lore transmitted down the ages from an ineffable antiquity—human or pre-human—whose knowledge of the cosmos and its laws was greater than ours" (*MM* 270). This implies that Keziah Mason's ability to use angles and curves to enter hyperspace was the result of such a revelation.

By suggesting a possible relationship between mathematics and elder lore, Lovecraft anticipated Arthur C. Clarke's famous third law, "Any sufficiently advanced technology is indistinguishable from magic." While Gilman, whose years of study and knowledge of the intricacies of "Non-Euclidean calculus and quantum physics" prepared him to make this distinction, it is doubtful that Keziah comprehended this in any terms but that of a satanic miracle. In a 20 February 1929 letter to Frank Belknap Long discussing the origin and decline of religious belief, Lovecraft opined that "By historic times it was so embedded in tradition as to be a permanent part of the heritage of all mankind. . . . The very processes of thought had become so chained to the traditional myths and for-

---

2. The case of Keziah Mason may be distinguished from that of her contemporary Joseph Curwen. Curwen, we are told, was "well fitted by education" to enjoy the company of the cream of Providence society, and that "His birth was known to be good, since the Curwens or Corwins of Salem needed no introduction in New England" (MM 120).

mulae that only generations of a scientific knowledge never dreamed of then could ever hope too liberate man's mind" (*SL* 2.270–71). Gilman, the beneficiary of the Enlightenment, of "Darwin and *my* friend Huxley" (*SL* 2.270) and of Herschel, Schopenhauer, Nietzsche, and Ernst Haeckel, was intellectually prepared to view the phenomenon of hyperspace in non-religious terms.

The same could not be said about Keziah. "The crude human animal," Lovecraft wrote to Woodburn Harris in a long letter written between 25 February and 1 March 1929,

> is ineradicably superstitious. . . . Rationalistic conceptions of the universe involve a type of mental victory over hereditary emotion quite impossible to the undeveloped and uneducated intellect. Agnosticism and atheism mean nothing to a peasant or workman. Mystic and teleological personification of natural forces is in his bone and blood—he cannot envisage the cosmos (i.e., the earth, the only cosmos he grasps) apart from them. Take away his Christian god and saints, and he will worship something else. (*SL* 2.310)

Keziah may well have been predisposed toward a certain type of worship by her environment. In the same letter to Robert E. Howard wherein he discussed the witch-cult, Lovecraft expounded upon the Puritan world view and its proclivity to see the hand of Satan at work everywhere ("there gradually grew up the commonly-accepted doctrine that the devil was making a special war in Massachusetts because of the holy purpose to which that saintly colony was dedicated by the Lord's Brethren" [*SL* 3.176]).

In summary, Keziah's worldview predisposed her to view the entities and phenomena with which she had come into contact in terms of what she had learned about witches and the devil from childhood. The Black Man, the Sabbat, hybrid familiars such as Brown Jenkin, signing the book in one's own blood: all these would have been familiar to her from old wives' tales. It is doubtful that Nyarlathotep or the other entities with whom she came into contact would have bothered to disabuse her of her error; understanding was not required, only obedience. What did it matter to Keziah that she was dealing with Nyarlathotep or Azathoth? She undoubtedly knew many names for the Devil, so what were two more? She was incapable of distinguishing an advanced technology from magic.

Although Keziah had, in her own mind, thrown in her lot with the Devil, she may well have retained residual belief in his Creator and opponent. It is conceivable that she might well react with fear if she were suddenly confronted with His symbol, not because it had any actual power *but because she believed it did*. Although Lovecraft owned the ninth edition of the *Britannica*, it is probably that he consulted later editions during his explorations of various libraries. The article on witchcraft in the eleventh edition discusses how a shaman's curse or magical object can be effective in the absence of any supernatural agency: "Ignorance of the effects of suggestion leads both the witch and others to regard as supernormal effects which are really due to the victim's belief in the possibility of witchcraft" (Thomas). Lovecraft was undoubtedly familiar with the principle from his reading of weird fiction.

Later in the same year that he wrote "The Dreams in the Witch House," Lovecraft wrote to E. Hoffmann Price (26 November 1932) in praise of the ability of their colleague August Derleth to create realistic characters in what he called "the literature of real life." Because Derleth possessed a genuine interest in ordinary people and could "see a vast significance tantamount to cosmic symbolism in the daily acts and thoughts and struggles of these people," he could "imaginatively [step] into their personalities for a while and [see] life through *their* eyes," not theirs. "Look how Derleth does it—he, a husky young egotist of 23, can for a time *actually be* in a psychological sense, a wistful, faded old lady of 85" (*SL* 4.113–14). While Lovecraft's assertion in "Some Notes on Interplanetary Fiction" that "The true 'hero' of a marvel story is not any human being, but simply a *set of phenomena*," the words that immediately precede this are sometimes overlooked: "we cannot expect to create any sense of life or illusion of reality if we . . . have the characters moving about under ordinary circumstances. The characters, *though they must be natural*, should be subordinated to the central marvel" (*CE* 2.179; my emphasis). Stated another way, while the marvel is the focus of the story, the human characters must still behave in a natural and believable manner. Keziah's reaction to this Christian symbol was an attempt by Lovecraft to "imaginatively step" into her personality. Unfortunately, its subtlety was overpowered by both cultural and literary memes that limited its effectiveness.

Works Cited

Burleson, Donald R. *H. P. Lovecraft: A Critical Study*. Westport, CT: Greenwood Press, 1983.

Cannon, Peter. *H. P. Lovecraft*. Boston: Twayne, 1989.

Joshi, S. T. *I Am Providence: The Life and Times of H. P. Lovecraft*. 2 vols., New York: Hippocampus Press, 2010.

Leiber, Fritz. "A Literary Copernicus." 1949. In *H. P. Lovecraft: Four Decades of Criticism*, ed. S. T. Joshi. Athens: Ohio University Press, 1980.

Leiber, Fritz. "Through Hyperspace with Brown Jenkin: Lovecraft's Contribution to Speculative Fiction." 1966. In *H. P. Lovecraft: Four Decades of Criticism*, ed. S. T. Joshi. Athens: Ohio University Press, 1980.

Mariconda, Steven J. "Lovecraft's Cosmic Imagery." In *An Epicure in the Terrible: A Critical Anthology of Essays in Honor of H. P. Lovecraft*, ed. David E. Schultz and S. T. Joshi. 1991. New York: Hippocampus Press, 2011.

Schultz, David E. "Who Needs the Cthulhu Mythos?" 1986. In *A Century Less a Dream: Selected Criticism on H. P. Lovecraft*, ed. Scott Connors. Holicong, PA: Wildside Press, 2002.

Thomas, Northcote Whitridge. "Witchcraft." *Encyclopedia Britannica*. 11th ed. 1911.

Waugh, Robert H. "Dr. Margaret Murray and H. P. Lovecraft: The Witch-Cult in New England." 1994. In *A Century Less a Dream: Selected Criticism on H. P. Lovecraft*, ed. Scott Connors. Holicong, PA: Wildside Press, 2002.

Lovecraft, Absurdity, and the Modernist Grotesque

Sean Elliot Martin

[The following is a slightly revised chapter of Martin's "H. P. Lovecraft and the Modernist Grotesque" (Ph.D. diss.: Duquesne University, 2008.—Ed.]

Literary designations can be problematic, especially when applied to writers who demonstrate unusual depth and innovation. However, in spite of a popular reaction against the limitations that can come with labeling, scholars continue to develop and debate literary categories because these designations have the potential to provide contexts that foster new discussion and insights. Yet certain writers create works that are so diverse, complex, and far-reaching that they continue to defy traditional designations, even after decades of study. H. P. Lovecraft exemplifies this dilemma. His early publication in popular genre fiction venues such as *Weird Tales* has led to his fiction commonly being labeled as "horror," "science fiction," or "fantasy." However, when placed in the context of the literary movements of his time, the majority of his work could just as easily be described as the "literary grotesque," "modernism," or "absurdism," labels that better reflect the sophistication and vision of his writing. Indeed, when analyzed in a wider literary context, it becomes evident that Lovecraft has more in common with Eliot, Joyce, and Kafka than he has with Shelley, Stoker, or Orwell. He belongs to a group of revolutionary writers whose work combines the disturbing, atmospheric, and even otherworldly elements of the "literary grotesque" with the far-reaching philosophical and stylistic experimentation of "modernism" and "absurdism." Although various Lovecraft stories may reasonably be placed into a range of literary boxes, he is one of the writers who appears to fall most squarely into a new literary category: the "modernist grotesque."

In his revolutionary study *The Grotesque in Art and Literature*, Wolfgang Kayser asserts that art and literature of the grotesque reflect three major elements: "THE ESTRANGED WORLD," "A PLAY WITH THE ABSURD," and "AN ATTEMPT TO INVOKE AND SUBDUE THE DEMONIC ASPECTS OF THE WORLD" (187–88; Kayser's capitalization). When these elements are compared to the most prominent modernist impulses, the connections between the grotesque and modernism become clear. Both of these artistic modes focus on the concepts of alienation, subjectivity, and absurdity, overlapping significantly in their approach to the subject of human limitations of perception, comprehension, and communication. It is possible to find some examples of grotesque literature that do not feature the high level of stylistic innovation ascribed to modernism, and modernist works that do not include the disturbing imagery and concepts so central to the grotesque. However, Lovecraft, Conrad, Eliot, Pound, Joyce, Kafka, Beckett, Woolf, and others seem to occupy the territory in the middle, the dimension in which modernism and the grotesque blend in a complex weave of dark imagination, cultural diagnosis, scientific theory, and stylistic innovation that lead to unnerving but unavoidable conclusions about the absurdity of human existence. If this fascinating literary shadowland has an ambassador, it is most certainly H. P. Lovecraft. By analyzing Lovecraft's work within the context of the modernist grotesque, a reader can more easily identify the importance of the concept of absurdity as one of his most important themes, the theme that communicates his perspective on all aspects of human civilization.

Absurdity lies at the very center of Lovecraft's universe. "Absurdity" is consistently defined in terms of that which is counter to reason, a definition that takes on new significance when applied to modernist grotesque literature. Modernism and the grotesque both tend to feature subjective approaches to meaning and reality. In the world of the modernist grotesque, reality is undeniably subjective, relative to individual perception, which means that objective truth is an unrealistic, impossible notion. To recognize the

inherent alienation of humans from their peers and their own experiences, and the inescapable subjectivity of human perception,
knowledge, and representation, is to recognize the fundamental
fallibility and insignificance of all human constructs. In effect, all
human beliefs are based upon nothing more than shared delusions.
Therefore, blind adherence to these constructs (religious, academic, scientific) in light of the principle of subjectivity that undermines them is counter to logic. It is absurd.

Absurdity as a general idea has been addressed in a number of
ways throughout literature, visual art, theatre, and film, in terms
of individuals and isolated incidents in which a person is represented as buffoonish in his or her actions or statements. The ancient icon of the fool is prevalent throughout world cultures, but
those representations depict absurd thoughts and behaviors as being unusual, easily identifiable, and even correctable. However,
the early twentieth century brought the idea of a new level of absurdity, one of universal meaninglessness and endless questioning
of the very foundations of human thought and existence.

Absurdity and Baseless Assumptions

The theme of assumption is prominent among the various incarnations of absurdity in literature, for baseless assumptions defy
reason, which is absurd. In previous centuries, these assumptions
were most often portrayed as isolated, and even tragic, in nature.[1]
The portrayal of individual characters who make absurd assumptions continues through the nineteenth and twentieth centuries,
especially in grotesque and modernist literature: Maturin's Mel-
moth assumes that someone else will take the same infernal bargain that he unwisely took; Shelley's Victor Frankenstein assumes
that he can abandon his creation without repercussions; Beckett's
Vladmir and Estragon assume that Godot will come; Eliot's Pru-
frock assumes that his actions may "disturb the universe." The circumstances that these characters face represent common
absurdities in human thought. As modernism develops and the

---

1. Oedipus, Faustus, and Hamlet, for instance, are characters whose assumptions
about their fate, their spirituality, or their actions lead to tragic results, but they
are represented as highly unusual individuals.

grotesque expands, both modalities tend to depict absurdity in more universal terms; absurdity is everywhere, not just in the lives of fools and madmen.

Satire is one of the most useful vehicles for the communication of absurdity, for it involves the portrayal of ideas and behaviors that are illogical, often on a symbolic level that mirrors elements of the world at large, mocking ideas and behaviors through exaggeration that can be ironic, wryly humorous, or outright comical. Satire is one of the many literary strategies shared by modernism and the grotesque, as seen in the works of Swift, Poe, Kafka, Eliot, Joyce, and Beckett, to name only a few. Lovecraft fits in among the ranks of modernists and writers of the grotesque who use satire for communicating the concept of cosmic absurdity. Fear was indeed a major concept in Lovecraft's writing, but his more sophisticated works focus on the fear of the paradigm shift, not the fear of any specific external stimulus; the "monsters" are not the objects of fear, but rather, the paradigm shift that they symbolize. In his modernist grotesque pieces, the terror that narrators face is one of human limitations of perception, knowledge, and significance. The dread of cosmic disinterestism and the absurdity of human thought processes and paradigms present a fertile ground for the grotesque union of absurdity and fear, or even comedy, as seen in Lovecraft's use of satire to depict absurd beliefs and behaviors. To portray the insufficiency of human perception, processing, and representation of reality through the absurd (and even ridiculous) failures of characters who represent the very pinnacle of rational thought is to address the fear of powerlessness and incomprehensibility in a universe that may have been better left unexplored. By addressing universal absurdity through plot elements associated with "weird fiction" and a synthesis of grotesque and modernist concepts and techniques, Lovecraft challenges assumptions of the validity and stability of human institutions: religion, physical science, behavioral science, and humanities scholarship.

Lovecraft's modernist grotesque works address the absurdity of human existence on a number of levels, undermining traditional human institutions that often go unquestioned. His nonfiction writing indicates that his rebellion against traditional religious ideas began as a child, developing into an intellectual questioning of physical science, behavioral science, and humanities. The questioning of assumptions of human significance is fairly recent in the scope of human culture. Even in the presence of their mighty gods, humans have tended to retain a belief in their significant position in the cosmic scheme. As a result, the beings that ruled ancient pantheons were generally human in their appearance, behaviors, and motivations.[2] In effect, the gods of the world tend to be humans on a grand scale, even including human faults on an epic level.[3]

Generally speaking, cultural constructs developed around the world with humanity at the physical and conceptual center. Aside from certain Pacific Island tribes who believed the shark to be the highest from of reincarnation (probably due to its place at the top of the food chain), world cultures have typically constructed cosmic views that revolve around specifically human-based perspectives. Within the monotheistic religions, the importance of humans is accentuated through the assertion that faithful mortals ascend to positions far above even the most ancient and powerful of angels and djinn, for humans must overcome the temptations and distractions that come with free will. In all these various outlooks, humans carve out a place for themselves at the center of the action. The assumption of privileged humanity may be reasonable in a world culture with limited scientific information about basic astronomy, but Lovecraft indicates that adherence to the assumption of privileged humanity is absurd in light of modern knowledge about the world and the universe at large.

Absurdity and Religious Institutions

Lovecraft's fascination with history, folklore, and mythology, combined with his lifelong dedication to science, prompted him

---

2. For example, Norse, Celtic, Hellenic, Babylonian, Egyptian, Sumerian, Hindu, Chinese, Aztec, and Incan gods are largely human in their appearance, behaviors, and communications. The beast-headed members of the Egyptian mythos and even the Winged Serpent Quetzalcoatl and the Jaguar Sun God Tezcatlipoca of South America were non-human primarily in appearance while reflecting human mental characteristics.

3, The Hellenic gods (especially Zeus, Hera, and Ares) are particularly given to rage, lust, jealousy, and other human faults.

to create a new, satirical mythology to relate his views on the absurdity of assumptions of the validity of religious institutions. This mythology, which later devotees would come to call the "Cthulhu Mythos," includes satires of major world religions—a pantheon of deities and their servants, a cohesive worldview and history, groups of worshippers, priests, holy relics, temples, and sacred texts. The primary difference between Lovecraft's mythos and the pantheons that presided over the world's populations for thousands of years is that Azathoth, Yog-Sothoth, Shub-Niggurath, Cthulhu, Nyartholotep, and their ilk could not possibly care less about the happiness or spiritual salvation of the human race. To these beings of infinitely superior and infinitely alien nature and power, certain cooperative humans are a minor convenience at best, a minor inconvenience at worst. Lovecraft was known among his friends as having a wicked sense of humor, which is identifiable in satirical elements that are the key to understanding his representations of absurdity. The comedy of Lovecraft's satirical religions is subtle, combining grotesque, modernist, and parodic elements in his mythos to create a statement about the absurdity of religious institutions that reflects a complex and ironic wit. The "Cthulhu Mythos" stands as a distorted carnival mirror reflection of world religions, his way of saying that, if there were godlike beings in the universe, there is no reason to assume that they would be anything like humans in appearance, morality, or motivation. In Lovecraft's religions, temples are secret and disturbing places, priests are sinister and often non-human, congregations worship through orgies and blood sacrifice, holy artifacts are alien and monstrous, sacred texts drive their reader mad, and the gods themselves are barely aware of the existence of the cult members who kill and die in their names. These themes are both disturbing and ironically humorous on a certain (twisted?) level.

Lovecraft's satirical pantheon is unique, but the concept of religious satire is prominent in modernism. Monique Chefdor, Ricardo Quinones, and Albert Wachtel explain in *Modernism: Challenges and Perspectives* (1986) that mythological parodies are an important element in modernist writing:

The large-scale parodies of myth, Joyce's *Ulysses* and Eliot's *The*

Waste Land, expand the techniques of quotation and allusion. Joyce's Homeric infrastructure provides a point-for-point analogue and critique of the "real" happenings in *Ulysses;* Joyce's tightly systematic double ordering of his materials resembles an allegory or expanded metaphor. Eliot's use of the Grail legend and fertility rituals is less systematic and somewhat after the fact; he had been reading *Ulysses* during the composition of *The Waste Land* and realized that "the mythical method" would be an important stylistic means for ordering "the chaos that was modern history." (132)

Lovecraft's parodies work similarly. For instance, S. T. Joshi compares *The Dream-Quest of Unknown Kadath* to the *Odyssey,* the *Aeneid,* and Greek and Roman mythology. This observation about Lovecraft's classical influences represents yet another link between Lovecraft and the canonical modernists, but he deviates dramatically from classical mythology in ways that accentuate his message of human insignificance. He also provides a more thorough vision of his parodied pantheon than any other writer of his time.

Perhaps one of the most powerful statements of human absurdity in all literature can be found in *At the Mountains of Madness,* when the narrator examines the pictorial history of the Old Ones and finds a depiction of the creation and true purpose of humans: "Dyer and Pabodie have read *Necronomicon* and seen Clark Ashton Smith's nightmare paintings based on text, and will understand when I speak of Elder Things supposed to have created all earth life as jest or mistake" (*MM* 22). The narrator reports that certain scenes "make Lake whimsically recall the primal myths about Great Old Ones who filtered down from the stars and concocted earth life as a joke or mistake; and the wild tales of cosmic hill things from outside told by a folklorist colleague in Miskatonic's English department[4] . . . Lake fell back on mythology for a provisional name—jocosely dubbing his finds 'The Elder Ones'" (*MM* 25). However, the explorers find that Lake's name for the creatures of the mysterious Antarctic city is more appropriate than they would have imagined. The scientists find various art objects and hieroglyphic depictions indicating that "an infinity of

---

4. This is an obvious reference to Wilmarth of "The Whisperer in Darkness."

other life forms—animal and vegetable, marine, terrestrial, and ae-rial—were the products of unguided evolution acting on life cells made by the Old Ones." Furthermore, images appear "in some of the very last and most decadent sculptures as shambling, primitive mammals, used sometimes for food and sometimes as an amusing buffoon by the land dwellers, whose vaguely simian and human foreshadowings were unmistakable" (*MM* 65). Unlike the human-created gods of world mythologies, the Old Ones create humans as nothing more than minor pets or food sources, not fit for the most basic of practical tasks.[5] *Homo sapiens* are the hamsters of the Old Ones, not dear enough to qualify as lapdogs, created for buffoonery and culinary delicacies, and eventually abandoned as a mere fleeting novelty. Nevertheless, isolated groups of human cultists like those featured in "The Call of Cthulhu" use artifacts and psychic impressions to reconstruct bits of their ancient past, voluntarily returning to a state of unappreciated servitude to their semi-dormant masters. Thus, Lovecraft makes his point about the absurd and slavish devotion of humans to the notion of servitude to powerful but uncaring forces.

Perhaps the only elements in Lovecraft's tales to supercede the absurdity of his creation myth lie in the nature of the Lovecraftian gods themselves. Azathoth is represented as the best equivalent to a king of the gods, the ultimate force at the center of the universe who is omnipotent, paradoxical, and absurd.[6] *The Dream-Quest of Unknown Kadath* describes Azathoth as

> that last amorphous blight of nethermost confusion which blas-phemes and bubbles at the centre of all infinity—the boundless daemon sultan Azathoth, whose name no lips dare speak aloud, and who gnaws hungrily in inconceivable, unlighted chambers be-yond time amidst the muffled, maddening beating of vile drums and the thin, monotonous whine of accursed flutes; to which de-testable pounding and piping dance slowly, awkwardly, and ab-

---

5. The shoggoths are the giant amoeboid work horses of the Old Ones, incredibly strong and able to change shape to fit any task.

6. HPL's religion of meaninglessness may remind a reader of Thomas Hardy's po-ems "Hap" (1898) and "Going and Staying" (1919), which address the idea that all human experience is random, without a divine plan.

surdly the gigantic ultimate gods, the blind, voiceless, tenebrous, mindless Other Gods whose soul and messenger is the crawling chaos Nyarlathotep. (*MM* 308)

"The Haunter of the Dark" depicts Azathoth's role as a god of meaninglessness and absurdity even more clearly through the narrator's reference to texts describing "ancient legends of Ultimate Chaos, at whose center sprawls the blind idiot god Azathoth, Lord of All Things, encircled by his flopping horde of mindless and amorphous dancers, and lulled by the thin monotonous piping of a demoniac flute held in nameless paws" (*DH* 110), a description that invokes Bakhtin's discussion of absurd carnivalesque celebrations in the early grotesque. This "daemon sultan Azathoth" and his court of Other Gods provide a parody of traditional mythological and religious entities, including a kind of satirical Christ figure in Nyarlathotep, who descends to earth in human form in the story "Nyarlathotep" as an avatar of chaos, bringing annihilation rather than salvation. Nyarlathotep incarnates in the form of an Egyptian prophet, a mystic priest who prepares the population of the world for the return of the Old Ones and, in turn, the direct rule of the God Azathoth. Cthulhu, worshipped by humans and non-humans alike, is also described in various works as a "priest," implying a parody of religious institutional hierarchies as well as satirized deities. The non-human religious hierarchy extends downward to the level of Azathoth's congregation of most devoted followers, "mindless and amorphous dancers" and flute players, accentuating the absurd elements that help to distinguish Lovecraft's modernist grotesque satire from the standard horror tale. Images of flopping, dancing, flute playing creatures arise in most descriptions of Azathoth, as well as in various accounts of narrators who glimpse the unknown on Earth (as in "The Festival"), indicating the prevalence of Azathoth's chaos in all parts of the universe. Members of Azathoth's "mindless" congregation are ironically enlightened: they worship the True god of the universe, but to properly commune with Azathoth they must be mindless, devoid of all logic. Perhaps this apparent paradox indicates that acknowledging and accepting cosmic absurdity is the most logical approach to understanding the nature of reality.

Although Lovecraft was an atheist, the presence of beings who are treated as gods in his tales is a stronger statement of absurdity than an exclusion of god figures. Atheism has the potential to lead to an unconventional yet strong sense of meaning. In fact, stripped of the sense of divinely granted purpose and assistance, the atheist may develop an even greater sense of human importance, the supremacy of humans in the universe, or at least on planet Earth. In Lovecraft's universe, however, the human has no such liberation from the impositions of higher powers, for all people are at the mercy of forces that could not be more indifferent to the human plight. Humans only have the meanings that they create for themselves. Ultimately, Azathoth, the center and origin of it all, exists as the very embodiment of absurdity, for Azathoth is not vengeful but oblivious—omnipotent, but completely uninterested in the affairs of any other beings. Humankind is trapped in every aspect—meaninglessness within meaninglessness, absurdity within absurdity.

Absurdity and Institutions of Physical Science

The questioning of religious institutions was not new in Lovecraft's time, especially for those who put their faith in the physical sciences. Scientific developments of the nineteenth and twentieth centuries impacted the world of literature dramatically, from the more tangible inventions of the applied sciences, like the automobile or the radio, to the new concepts of the fundamental nature of physical reality, like Einstein's Theory of General Relativity or Heisenberg's Uncertainty Principle. Many writers of the early twentieth century attempted to keep abreast of major developments in scientific theory and methodology, incorporating scientific thinking into their work (they were not trained scientists like Lovecraft, but they attempted to keep up with some of the general ideas). In *The Antimodernism of Joyce's* Portrait of the Artist as a Young Man (1994), Weldon Thornton addresses the problematic nature of scientific empiricism, where it is assumed that "instrumentalism supersedes and disavows fallible human perceptions" (36). In his examination of the influence of scientific thinking on modernist literature, Thornton asserts that

[we] must, then, recognize that the term "scientific empiricism" hides the treacherous implication that what science deals in is the empirical, with the implication that only valid "empiricism" is that amenable to instrumental science. We are thus deprived of the term for human use—i.e., empiricism no longer really implies a human perspective. (36–37)

Thornton points out that traditional ideals of empiricism fail to take into account the fact that science is carried out by human scientists who are confined to the limitations and fallibility of the human senses. Lovecraft, as an enthusiastic student of science, an experimental writer of "weird fiction," and an unconventional modernist thinker, combined a number of elements to create a new level of critical examination of the institutions of physical sciences and the problems with dogmatic adherence to those institutions and their paradigms. Lovecraft's thorough knowledge of the physical sciences is one of the most important biographical differences between him and his literary contemporaries. However, as Airaksinen explains, Lovecraft's lifelong interest in science did not influence him to accept scientific concepts unquestioningly. In fact, the criticizing of dogmatic adherence to traditional scientific modalities makes up one of his primary foci in his representation of absurd assumptions. Lovecraft perceived science as an ongoing process that humans may use as a tool to deal with their limited perspective of a much larger reality:

Lovecraft agrees that we tend to reason by using natural laws. We form our expectations and we plan our actions according to them. We trust them as if they were real. However, natural laws appear to fail in many cases where cosmic forces enter the realm of human perception. We may think that natural laws are no more than subjective regularities of perception which apply only in a given realm. In this way, Lovecraft returns to David Hume who claims that causal laws are nothing but psychological expectations based on repeated observations which have produced uniform results in the past. This is how we tend to think. If we add something to this realm, something that comes from outside, then we cannot trust any of the scientific norms. Hence, Lovecraft extends his social nihilism to science. (Airaksinen 74)

Lovecraft saw true science as open-ended and ever-evolving, which led him to create tales that question the motivations of scientific institutions by introducing hypothetical situations in which scientists fail to make necessary adjustments to their paradigms: they seek to confirm old ideas rather than exploring new ones.

Much of Lovecraft's critique of the institutions of the physical sciences comes through the characterization of his narrators. The stories in question are most often narrated by characters who suffer mentally due to the violation of assumptions based upon the institutions to which they attempt to adhere. These reactions are merely a symptom of the absurdity of the assumption that established human intellectual structures are sufficient to contain and process any and all possible content. As Robert A. Rubinstein, Charles D. Laughlin, Jr., and John McManus explain in *Science as Cognitive Process: Toward an Empirical Philosophy of Science* (1984), paradigm structures limit cognition:

> Structure in human cognition is the organization of thought. It should be distinguished from content, or that which is thought about. Structure is the information-processing system and content is the information processed. . . The definition of and responses to "objective" reality are determined by the structure of the apperceiving cognitive system. (38–39)

In the case of Lovecraft's narrators, the new "content" is so incompatible with the "information-processing system" that the observing characters simply cannot force the two to function together logically. Therefore, their thoughts and behaviors become absurd in the absence of stable and logical paradigms within which to operate. Their reactions to the incompatibility of old paradigms and new information are a painful process of questioning, obsessing, and analyzing that leads to absurd behaviors, ranging from paranoid secrecy to suicide.

One of Lovecraft's most inventive and effective literary devices is the use of a narrator who is so conventionally reliable that his adherence to objective documentation forces the reader to reevaluate the very nature of reliability itself. These narrators are presented as mentally competent and publicly respected individuals who are deeply rooted in scientific observation, empirical thinking, and rigorous documentation. The majority of Lovecraft's narrators in his modernist grotesque works are professional academics. Those academics who do not specialize in physical sciences demonstrate training in science that could reasonably accompany higher education in any chosen field. Lovecraft's scholarly narrators include a geology professor (*At the Mountains of Madness*), a literature instructor and folklore expert ("The Whisperer in Darkness"), and a professor of political economy ("The Shadow out of Time") among others. Although the principal narrator of "The Call of Cthulhu," Thurston, has no specifically named occupation, his scholarly compilation and presentation of the relevant documentation (as well as his relation to a renowned academic) implies academic training. Secondary narrators include a noted professor of Semitic languages, a professor of anthropology, a professor of biology, a police inspector, an experienced sailor, and a surveyor. Lovecraft's use of highly trained observers is crucial in his discussion of absurdity in institutions of physical sciences, for these characters are conventionally reliable representations of traditional empirical thinkers.

Unlike the often deranged, unreliable narrators of Poe, Lovecraft's narrators tend to establish themselves as sane and almost obsessively scientific in their thinking: "It is also critical for Lovecraft's narrators to be, on the whole, intelligent and rational men. . . . If these people can be convinced that something bizarre has happened, then how can the reader refrain from being convinced?" (Joshi, "Fiction of Materialism" 154). When faced with the alienating, "ESTRANGED WORLD" of the grotesque (Kayser 187), these pillars of the scholarly community find that their logic and beliefs no longer serve them. They face cataclysmic paradigm crises and try to explain them away through conventional concepts that simply do not work. In the end, many narrators choose to doubt their own minds rather than doubt their faith in traditionally dictated reality constructs provided by their scientific institutions. Everything that they have come to understand is taken from them, leaving them to struggle to force an alien reality into a conventional paradigm. In the light of new, irrefutable, earth-shaking data, a paradox arises, in which case the most absurd course of action is to cling to traditional beliefs and methods that no longer apply. The true absurdity of this struggle emerges as the breakdown of traditional thought leads them to erratic, obsessive, and even self-destructive behavior driven by the very investigative spirit that led them to their chosen professions. The stories themselves are portrayed as first-person documents: journal entries, letters, and scholarly records that typically include the narrator's reasons for recording the supposedly true events. As Leiber explains, Lovecraft "set great store by the narrator having some vitally pressing motive for recounting his experiences, and was ingenious at devising such motives" (55). These reasons may include warnings to others, personal edification and understanding, or a desperate attempt to maintain scholarly methodology (and thus, a faith in their own mental competence) by recording the unnatural events with as much objectivity as possible:

> Lovecraft's matured method of telling a horror story was a natural consequence of the importance of the new universe of science in his writings, for it was the method of scientific realism, approaching in some of his last tales (*At the Mountains of Madness* and "The Shadow out of Time") the precision, objectivity, and attention to detail of a report in a scientific journal. Most of his stories are purported documents and necessarily written in the first person. This device is common in weird literature . . . but few writers have taken it as seriously as did Lovecraft. (Leiber 55)

However, the described "scientific realism . . . precision, objectivity, and attention to detail" are complicated in these works by the very nature of what the narrators are reporting. The end result always includes an eventual questioning not only of the narrator's own sanity, but of the very constructs of human knowledge upon which the criteria for that sanity are based. The breakdown comes not from the events themselves but from the violation of the expectations and assumptions that the narrator has amassed over a lifetime of traditional scientific indoctrination.

"From Beyond," Lovecraft's earliest modernist grotesque story, stands as one of the most important examples of the criticism of scientific closed-mindedness. Crawford Tillinghast succeeds in creating a device that expands his senses to perceive entire worlds beyond his normal sensory range. Yet he feels betrayed by members of the scientific community who do not acknowledge how limited their own scientific perspectives have become. Tillinghast serves as the voice of his creator's sentiments when he exclaims: "Our means of receiving impressions are absurdly few, and our notions of surrounding objects infinitely narrow. We see things only as we are constructed to see them, and can gain no idea of their absolute nature" (*D* 91). As with most Lovecraftian alienated scholars, he is more enlightened than his fellows. However, Lovecraft, like Tillinghast, should not be confused for one who is anti-scientific. Lovecraft knew the history of the struggles between scientific pioneers and those who would suppress true breakthroughs on the basis of tradition and dogma. He knew the troubles of Copernicus, Galileo, Darwin, and others who were persecuted for their theories and discoveries because of the inability of others to adjust their thinking. A truly scientific approach, Lovecraft would say, includes the mental flexibility necessary to change world views as new information presents itself, no matter how radical the information may be. Lovecraft would open minds to new possibilities, acknowledge the limitations of scientific observation, and address the absurdity of adhering to old scientific paradigms when evidence reveals them as being insufficient.

Experts in various fields have examined the process of scientific paradigm shifts. For instance, Rubinstein, Laughlin, and McManus state that science passes through cycles of three phases, which include the construction of a paradigm, the application of the paradigm, and the destabilization of the paradigm. According to these theorists, the second phase is the one in which "the productive work of a mature science is carried out" (64–65), for the scientists can apply what is perceived as a stable paradigm. However, it is the third phase with which Lovecraft concerns himself. In the second phase, the phase representing the training of most of Lovecraft's scholarly characters, "Normal science is something of a closed loop, minimally, if ever, open to serious modification at the core. Scientific behavior serves to maintain and solidify a paradigm's dominance in addition to defining how problems are solved" (65). Rubinstein, Laughlin, and McManus go on to describe the trend in thinking when paradigms do not appear to fit a given situation:

> When paradigm-constrained behavior fails to produce solutions for research problems, anomalies result. Contrary to what might be supposed, these do not generally threaten the integrity of the paradigm unless (1) the anomaly is deemed critical or (2) these anomalies become too numerous. In both cases the paradigm is fiercely defended (and not always by methods that fall within the bounds of scientific decorum). (66)

The defense of threatened paradigms comes into play with Lovecraft's characters as they use any means possible to convince themselves that they and their institutions are correct.

While skepticism in the face of apparently anomalous information may be reasonable under most circumstances, major threats to paradigms often result in absurd behaviors:

> structural collapse inclines thought toward more categorical perceptions of the operational environment, increased affective response, and attendant bias on "objective" perception. Among the effects of such a collapse are increased egocentricity, . . . greater distortion of incoming information toward the internal model, and increased projection of internal content onto the operational environment. All this leads to less "objective" perception, dominated by the bias of earlier structures. (Rubinstein, Laughlin, and McManus 148–49)

The absurdity of this tendency of "scientifically minded" individuals to develop "less 'objective' perception, dominated by the bias of earlier structures" is a major factor in many Lovecraft stories where "rational" characters make attempts to rationalize anomalous criteria in ways that will maintain their intellectual status quo.

Lovecraft addresses absurd tendencies in scientific institutions through stories where narrators attempt in vain to understand the unexplained through traditional, entirely insufficient, scientific methodology. Some of Lovecraft's representations of the unexplained are noteworthy in their restraint, moving just far enough beyond traditional science to challenge the intellect and sanity of the narrator. He "starts from the given world of science and asks what happens if these laws are altered, and if we add as small a number of extraneous elements as possible to this new world"

(Airaksinen 74). These "extraneous elements" bring about threatening paradigm shifts, reflecting Ortega y Gasset's discussion in *Human Reality and the Social World* of the idea that "a priori principles are the conditions under which one conceives the ordered system of nature. The 'laws of nature' and all concepts of objects are specifications of the a priori forms: thus the 'objective reality' of phenomena consists in their conformity to the laws of the system as constituted" (27). Scientifically minded narrators and characters must rethink their training when it does not provide explanations, but Lovecraft does not create a world in which science must be thrown out entirely. In Lovecraft's tales, science must be developed and altered radically, not done away with: for instance, when the phenomena of electricity and animal magnetism (hypnosis) were first described, to claim, as some people did, that the laws of nature do not apply any more was too hasty. The laws still applied although their scope needed to be expanded (Airaksinen 77). As Airaksinen indicates, Lovecraft brings in only a "small number of extraneous elements," but he depicts those elements as causing bafflement and frustration among characters, the inflexibility of their perspective being a major source of their absurdity.

The paradigm shift resulting from the insufficiency of contemporary scientific paradigms is one of the most prominent themes in Lovecraft's work, aligning Lovecraft with both scientific theorists (like Rubinstein, Laughlin, McManus) and modernist cultural theorists (like Ortega y Gasset). In Lovecraft's stories, scientifically minded characters are confused by elements of nature beyond those they have come to understand: the strange meteorite in "The Colour out of Space," the non-terrestrial stone of the statue in "The Call of Cthulhu," alien corpses in "The Whisperer in Darkness," strange fossils and corpses in *At the Mountains of Madness*, and the extra-dimensional creatures of "From Beyond." The exposure of scientists to unusual items of study is alienating but is not, in and of itself, absurd. It is theoretically possible for scientists to approach new specimens with open-minded curiosity, but Lovecraft's characters tend to be more interested in maintaining the status quo than with developing new knowledge. Lovecraft's criticism of scientific institutions comes through in his depictions of how characters handle, or fail to handle, data that threatens their institutionally developed paradigms.

"The Colour out of Space" may be Lovecraft's strongest statement about the absurdity of closed-minded scientists, for the researchers who examine the meteorite dismiss a rare opportunity to gain knowledge due to the fact that their new subject of study is too different from anything they have previously seen. Eventually, they grow frustrated and simply give up their attempts to understand the object: not a very scientific approach to a perplexing problem. As Airaksinen indicates, Lovecraft takes the absurd representation of the scientists so far as to mockingly refer to them as "wise men" from the east (80). However, these satirical wise men have nothing to offer to the newly arrived gift from the stars. Airaksinen goes on to explain that:

> Here the problem of the "colour" involves the incompetency of scientists and the barrenness of their craft. Whether any laws of nature are violated is unclear. The only thing that becomes clear is that the scientists try to explain what they observed, but, after failing to do so, they give up. Their extraterrestrial particle vanishes in the laboratory, self-consumed via the radiation of energy. They try to measure it, and analyze its strange color, but nothing is revealed. This thing seems to come from somewhere where the world is epistemically foreign. (Airaksinen 76)

Rather than excitement at their discovery, the "wise men" recoil from the prospect of admitting their inability to comprehend the "colour." This is absurd.

At the Mountains of Madness provides the most thorough scientific account to be found in Lovecraft's works, and perhaps one of the most detailed fictional scientific accounts to be found anywhere. As Cannon observes, "In his close attention to geological and paleontological background, Lovecraft creates a sense of verisimilitude that certainly far surpasses that of Poe in the polar part of Pym" (103). In this novella, the narrator is open-minded enough to eventually consider that his discoveries that range far outside of his scientific training. The absurdity lies within the scientific community at large, leaving the narrator to struggle to make his experiences known and acted upon in the face of scrutiny, skepticism, and opposition: "I am forced into speech because men of science have refused to follow my advice without knowing why" (*MM* 3). The text of *At the Mountains of Madness* operates as a kind of scientific journal for the purpose of convincing the scientific community, that the narrator's findings are real, and that the expedition was too dangerous to repeat. However, the narrator indicates that his reports have been ignored or mocked, dismissed as implausible despite his reputation and his evidence. Even the rare Lovecraft narrator who is able to maintain a balanced psychology while examining the unexplained must still face the absurdity of the closed-minded scientific community at large.

Absurdity and Institutions of the Behavioral Sciences

The institutions of religion and the physical sciences are not the only institutions whose authority and validity Lovecraft questions. The behavioral sciences are also brought under scrutiny, especially psychology and anthropology. The idea of the absurdity of assumptions of the validity of the institutions of behavioral sciences calls into question the constructs through which scholars and mental health professionals evaluate human behavior. Like Lovecraft's physical scientists, his behavioral scientists face anomalies that range far outside of their institutional training. Yet they adhere to their learned perspectives, expectations, and practices, in spite of overwhelming evidence of the insufficiency of such strategies. Certain Lovecraft stories, including "The Shadow out of Time," *The Case of Charles Dexter Ward*, and "The Shadow over Innsmouth," address the insufficiency of the behavioral sciences directly in a clinical capacity by depicting mental health professionals who mis-diagnose and even commit to asylums patients who experience anomalous symptoms that they interpret as delusions. Many other stories provide more subtle portrayals of adherence to the institutions of behavioral sciences as characters evaluate the mental health and cognitive processes of themselves and others on the basis of standard conceptions of sanity and reality. The absurdity of these stories is particularly apparent when examined with relation to the critique of the natural sciences, for characters who adhere dogmatically to both types of institutions are guarded from paradigm crises by a double layer of rationalization: their institutions of physical science tell them to believe only what they see, while their institutions of behavioral science tell them that seeing anything outside of the norm means that they are mistaken or insane.

The complication of the concepts of intelligence versus ignorance, conscious versus unconscious mind, and sanity versus insanity addressed in various modernist and grotesque works undermine the validity of traditional, monolithic institutions of behavioral science that would attempt to preserve a clear distinctions in these dichotomies. Among the various scholarly narrators who make grievous errors, the narrator of "The Whisperer in Darkness," Albert N. Wilmarth, stands as one of the most absurd in his assumptions about facts that he has no evidence to confirm. Lovecraft reveals the absurdity of his assumptions through a satirical portrayal of the narrator's arrogance and closed-mindedness when he responds to reports of strange remains found in Vermont:

> They were pinkish things about five feet long; with crustaceous bodies bearing vast pairs of dorsal fins or membranous wings and several sets of articulated limbs, and with a sort of convoluted ellipsoid, covered with multitudes of very short antennae, where a head would ordinarily be. . . . It was my conclusion that such witnesses—in every case naive and simple backwoods folk—had glimpsed the battered and bloated bodies of human beings or farm animals in the whirling currents; and had allowed the half-remembered folklore to invest these pitiful objects with fantastic attributes. (*DH* 210)

Wilmarth is an English instructor and folklore expert who has not seen any of the remains in question. More importantly, he does not take into account that "naive and simple backwoods folk" may know more about the local animals than most university professors, or that they are more likely to handle and prepare their own dead. The rural folk have a better chance than a city-dwelling academic of knowing a "battered and bloated body" or a farm animal from something truly unusual. Wilmarth's errors reflect his traditional training in folklore study as it relates to anthropology and psychology, which leads him to be

correspondingly amused when several contentious souls continued to insist on a possible element of truth in the reports. Such
persons tried to point out that the early legends had a significant
persistence and uniformity, and that the virtually unexplored nature of the Vermont hills made it unwise to be dogmatic about
what might or might not dwell among them; nor could they be si-
lenced by my assurance that all the myths were of a well-known
pattern common to most of mankind and determined by early
phases of imaginative experience which always produced the
same type of delusion. (*DH* 213–14)

His faith in his own understanding of human psychology and culture creates an illusion of an elite and privileged position from
which he may judge even his colleagues, although he has no evidence upon which to base his assumptions: "The more I laughed
at such theories, the more these stubborn friends asseverated
them; adding that even without the heritage of legend the recent
reports were too clear, consistent, detailed, and sanely prosaic in
manner of telling, to be completely ignored" (*DH* 214). The narrator emerges as a satirical character whose adherence to conventional approaches to reality lead him to doubt on psychological
grounds the cognitive or intellectual abilities of anyone who might
propose the possibility of an event outside of the norm.

Wilmarth's reasoning borders on the comical when he is eventually contacted by an eye witness, Henry Akeley, who "had been
a notable student of mathematics, astronomy, biology, anthropology, and folklore at the University of Vermont . . . a man of character, education, and intelligence, albeit a recluse with very little
worldly sophistication" (*DH* 215). Even this expert witness is
doubted by Wilmarth, who simultaneously commends Akeley for
his scientific mentality and then himself violates that very type of
open-mindedness: "he was amazingly willing to leave his conclusions in a tentative state like a true man of science. He had no personal preferences to advance, and was always guided by what he
took to be solid evidence. Of course I began by considering him
mistaken, but gave him credit for being intelligently mistaken"
(*DH* 215). Akeley holds an important place in Lovecraft's works,
for he represents what Lovecraft seemed to have considered to be

a proper scholarly mentality. He is "willing to leave his conclusions in a tentative state like a true man of science," and there is no particular reason to believe him to be mistaken, "intelligently" or otherwise. Yet Wilmarth makes assumptions about Akeley's psychology that allow him to continue to maintain his belief that those whose opinions deviate from the status quo are naive, misguided, insane, or, at best, "intelligently mistaken." The characterization of Akeley makes him sound far more credible than Wilmarth himself, for Akeley has a wider base of learning, including biology. However, the narrator's desperation to avoid a paradigm crisis leads him to assume that the scholarly Akeley must be wrong. At one point, Wilmarth turns his scrutiny even upon himself: "Was it too presumptuous to suppose that both the old legends and the recent reports had this much of reality behind them? But even as I harboured these doubts I felt ashamed that so fantastic a piece of bizarrerie as Henry Akeley's wild letter had brought them up" (*DH* 220). Wilmarth's application of observational paradigms based upon traditional psychology appears to be one of his greatest sources of stress, for his anxiety related to his temptation to believe something outside the norm is greater than the anxiety related to any potential threat from the Mi-Go. "The Whisperer in Darkness" may depict the absurdity of assumptions of the validity of the behavioral sciences more acutely and more comically than any other Lovecraft story, but it is one of many Lovecraft works in which traditional concepts of behavioral sciences, like those of the physical sciences, prove to be insufficient for understanding new circumstances.

Absurdity and Institutions of the Humanities

Of all the institutions that Lovecraft challenges or undermines through his modernist grotesque writings, the institution of humanities scholarship is the one that provokes his most subtle and most experimental treatment of absurdity. Lovecraft addresses religion, physical sciences, and social behavioral through depictions of creatures, characters, objects, and actions that are absurd in a number of ways. However, he also explores absurd aspects of humanities scholarship through a unique approach to the modernist notion of literary difficulty. The topic of difficulty is nearly un-avoidable when discussing modernism; Leonard Diepeveen's *The Difficulties of Modernism* (2003) is a particularly useful guide when analyzing the role that difficulty plays in modernist literary stud-ies. As Diepeveen notes, difficulty "was the most noted character-istic of what became the canonical texts of high modernism; it dramatically shaped the reception of Faulkner, Joyce, Stein, Moore, Eliot, Pound, and Woolf, just to name those who early were considered to be central modernist writers" (xi). Difficulty was created in slightly different ways by various modernist writ-ers, revolving around the idea that difficulty encourages (or even forces) the reader to actively engage the text:

> For modern readers, difficulty was the experience of having one's desires for comprehension blocked, an experience provoked by a wide variety of works of art ('comprehension' is here defined broadly). Without dealing with this barrier in some way—and such dealings were not restricted to *understanding* or decoding the syntax of the difficult moment—it was impossible to interact sig-nificantly with the text. Difficulty thus drove its readers forward, for they realized that their bafflement was an inadequate re-sponse. (x–xi)

As Diepeveen explains, modernist literary difficulty involves the complication of a text for the purpose of forcing a reader to par-ticipate more directly with the text, an engagement that has the potential to enhance the intellectual experience of reading. Fur-thermore, literary difficulty serves to distinguish levels of reader-ship by providing material that less educated readers cannot fully comprehend. This aspect of the modernist motivation to create difficult texts has received a variety of responses, from admiration to accusations of exclusionary elitism.

Difficulty's incarnations are many and various in modernist lit-erature, resulting from a number of experimental literary tech-niques: fragmented narratives, countless historical/literary/cultural allusions, vernacular and dialect, multiple languages, liter-ary impressionism, collage, and stream-of-consciousness to name only a few. In the case of Lovecraft, modernist difficulty is pushed to new levels through the use of weird and grotesque elements.

Lovecraft's depiction of the absurdity of assumptions of the validity of humanities scholarship is particularly noteworthy because of the subtle elements of difficulty he uses for this purpose. By using practically every modernist technique for creating textual difficulty (including all those listed above), Lovecraft raises implicit questions about the nature of literary and historical authority and validity. However, in addition to the conventional modernist devices of difficulty, Lovecraft contributes his own strategies for engaging the reader and leading the reader to question the validity of literary and scholarly sources. One of Lovecraft's most unique contributions to literature may be found in his elements of hoax and verisimilitude with relation to absurdity and the modernist notion of difficulty. The difficulty represented by the canonical modernists through various types of allusions, language play, and cultural references tend to be traceable and somewhat linear. Diligent scholars have been able to unravel the difficulties of Eliot's *The Waste Land*, Joyce's *Ulysses*, and even Joyce's *Finnegans Wake* to a large extent. Lovecraft's literary difficulties are less accessible.

The concepts of history and literary scholarship are undermined in many of Lovecraft's works. In fact, the very notion of reliable documentation is attacked from several different angles through the use of alternate histories, suppressed histories, indecipherable communications, and the mixing of fact and fiction, one of Lovecraft's most noteworthy trademarks. This tendency toward verisimilitude is not a matter of a malicious hoax or pointless intellectual posturing. Lovecraft's realistic details involving documentation, geography, scientific practices, and historical events create a level of difficulty that truly challenges the reader. He brings a new aspect of difficulty to the dialogue by seamlessly blending his own fictional details with allusions, citations, and accounts from traditionally accepted sources. Fabricated details are added to established histories. Fictional locations are described in their proximity to actual places. Hoax texts are named along with real ones, and the whole of the "weird tale" is most often related from the point of view of scientific objectivity through a narrating character or characters who possess titles and occupations that imply intellect, integrity, and authority. The overall effect brings the concept of literary difficulty to a new level at which the active reader who attempts to research and decipher the "truth" behind the mingled facts and fictions is likely to uncover the deeper intrinsic absurdity underlying the verisimilitude of Lovecraft's fiction: the idea that the criteria by which most contemporary humans evaluate what is real and what is fictional are subjective, fallible, and very easy to imitate. Therefore, the active reader may experience first-hand the absurdity of his or her own assumptions about what representations of reality are valid and what ones are faulty, or even deliberately fabricated. By going beyond the depiction of a narrating character's catastrophic paradigm crisis, and encouraging the reader to face the absurdity of contemporary assumptions of what constitutes textual validity of secondary sources, Lovecraft pushes the dialogue of universal absurdity from the world of fictional depiction into the personal intellectual life of the reader.

In Lovecraft's modernist grotesque works, the readers cannot even enjoy the solace of approaching the modernist reality crisis from a distanced perspective, for the disorienting elements of the text invade the reader's world through the mixing of fact and fiction, leading to confusion as to which elements are facts and which ones are fabrications. There is no solid intellectual ground upon which to stand when reading Lovecraft, as addressed by Dziemianowicz with reference to Thurston's opening line in "The Call of Cthulhu," which states that the "most merciful thing in the world . . . is the inability of the mind to correlate its contents" (*DH* 125):

> [Lovecraft] says, in effect, that one does not need to investigate the dark corners of the universe to uncover mind-shattering cosmic truths; they may be evident in the events of the day if one knows the perspective from which to view the right events. The narrator's despair comes about simply through the realization of the pattern these events fit. In a sense, Lovecraft is expressing his belief that each one of us teeters on the brink of alienation along with Thurston. (Dziemianowicz 176)

This observation has the disquieting effect of indicating that, if any given person were to actually try to piece together all of the various and subtle clues available, he or she may have a chance at revealing patterns that lead to entirely new ways to perceive the fabric of reality. However, it is more than likely that this new paradigm would create panic, terror, and chaos. To this way of thinking, ignorance, indeed, is bliss (or at least a comfortable illusion of safety). Lovecraft's brand of difficulty brings the reader into Thurston's discussion by illustrating through textual hoax the ease with which the border between fact and fiction may be obfuscated. Just as Thurston faces the idea that his conception of reality is based on an illusion, Lovecraft's readers may face the uncomfortable realization that discerning "truth" is not so simple as they might have believed. Readers may even wonder what kinds of "dissociated knowledge" lies before them in their own lives, overlooked and waiting to be pieced together.

Lovecraft's mixing of fact and fiction goes beyond simple play, for it can be interpreted as a unique way to inspire scholarly inquiry on the part of his readers. Just as scholars have labored over the allusions, translations, and references of Joyce, Eliot, and Pound, Lovecraft's constant mixing of real and fictional texts, historical events, places, and scientific facts has led countless readers to expand their own knowledge. The works of Lovecraft provide puzzles that are just as convoluted and obscure as those of the members of the accepted modernist canon, challenging readers to research and differentiate established history, geography, and scientific thought from Lovecraft's own inventions:

> The reader's problem is that Lovecraft is such a demanding author. . . . His writings create a new kind of world, based on science, myth, and magic, so that he can be classified among the most difficult authors to understand. Without knowledge of this background philosophy, to discover what he is writing about is difficult. (Airaksinen 2–3)

Lovecraft's philosophical observations are often missed by readers, especially those who mistakenly expect nothing more than a mere pulp horror story. However, when combined with the difficulties of his innumerable factual and fictional histories, texts, scientific details, and geographical locations, the level of difficulty represented in his tales rivals that of any "high modernist."

Alienating documentation plays an important role in Lovecraft's works, especially when the topic of private libraries of real and non-existent books is applied to the responses of actual readers rather than the fictional characters. By placing actual texts on the same shelves as his "remarkable series of imaginary but deceptively realistic 'secret books,' chief among them the *Necronomicon*" (Leiber 55), Lovecraft confuses the issue of authorship, authority, documentation, and the veracity of human knowledge itself. As Edward S. Lauterbach explains in "Some Notes on Cthulhuian Pseudobiblia" (1980),

> the purpose of Lovecraft and his collaborators in creating this library of imaginary titles was to give a feeling of verisimilitude to their stories. Most of these titles have a proper, classical, even pedantic flavour and sound as if they originated in the ancient Orient or the Mediaeval and Renaissance worlds of learning. The pseudo-Latin, French, and German of many of the titles can easily be translated to hint at the forbidden contents. Such titles seem to echo lists of actual alchemical and occult treatises from the days of early printing, and the ability to quote passages of magical lore from such books, sometimes intermixed with actual occult titles, allowed a writer to add great authenticity to fictional supernatural narratives. (97)

The fact that Lovecraft incorporates not only his own invented titles but those of other writers with whom he associated further complicates the reader's sense of veracity, for the same titles come up in multiple works by multiple authors, creating a consistency that adds to the illusion of believability. The libraries of Lovecraftian scholars usually include the *Book of Eibon* (Clark Ashton Smith), *Unausprechlichen Kulten* and *People of the Monolith* (Robert E. Howard), *De Vermiis Mysteriis* and the *Cultes des Goules* (Robert Bloch), the *R'lyeh Text* (August Derleth), the Pnakotic Manuscripts, and the *Necronomicon* (Lovecraft). These are frequently placed, in relatively random order, with such titles as Frazer's *The Golden Bough*, Murray's *Witch-Cult in Western Europe*, W. Scott-Elliott's *Atlantis and the Lost Lemuria*, and Poe's *The Narrative of Arthur Gordon Pym*, leading many readers to confuse the fictional texts with the real ones, and challenging readers to decipher what sources are believable.

When examining the notion of "difficulty" in Lovecraft's writing, the *Necronomicon* deserves its own discussion. The *Necronomicon* is probably the most famous book that never existed. It is a useful recurring plot device in many of Lovecraft's stories, an ancient book penned by the "Mad Arab Abdul Alhazred" (the pseudo-Arabic name that Lovecraft created for himself in his childhood). This fictional text has become so believable to readers that even individuals who have never heard of Lovecraft have heard of the *Necronomicon*, and believe that it is an actual text of great historical significance. There seems to be no real evidence to substantiate the claim of many occult scholars that Lovecraft based this illusory tome on a real text. As Lauterbach explains, belief in the existence of the fictional text grew beyond the ranks of "weird fiction" fans: "Among collectors of supernatural fiction the *Necronomicon* had taken on near-corporality. Many bibliophiles have attempted to find actual copies of the *Necronomicon* in any edition and have plagued numerous book dealers to be on the lookout for this tome" (97). The fact that so many people believe in the authenticity of this fictional book is not entirely unreasonable, for Lovecraft composed a convincing peudo-scholarly paper entitled "History of the *Necronomicon*" (1927). This paper details the creation and distribution of the various copies, versions, and translations of the book, including the past and present locations of copies (many of them allegedly destroyed or lost). The *Necronomicon* has appeared in countless works of Lovecraftian spin-off fiction, films, and games, and in many films that have no direct relationship to Lovecraft at all. It stands as Lovecraft's most enduring hoax, and a testament to his ability to write fiction that is simultaneously "weird" and convincing. The mix of titles and authors is so believable, and so convoluted, that most readers would probably have a difficult time distinguishing the "real" from the invented ones, an effect that goes beyond a mere accentuation of the reader's reaction to a "weird tale." This mixture of fictional titles like the *Necronomicon* with actual texts like *The Golden Bough* calls into question the very nature of the written word and the amorphous sense of reality and authority given to any secondary textual source.

In addition to his mixed lists of titles, Lovecraft complicates the validity of humanities scholarship by providing allusions to supporting documentation in other publications, such as newspapers and scholarly journals. In this way, he brings an even deeper level of difficulty to the concept of authorship, scholarship, and literary validity by suggesting that the places, objects, and events portrayed in his works have some documented validity not only in old books but in current scholarly or journalistic sources. The tone of these references often bears a casual confidence in the reader's recognition, fortified by the Lovecraftian narrators' claim that various types of corroborating documentation appear in periodicals like the *Providence Telegram*, the *Journal*, the *Sydney Bulletin*, and his fictional *Arkham Advertiser*, bringing an additional element of complexity to the question of what types of literary sources are valid or trustworthy.

Lovecraft's unique approach to difficulty through the mingling of fictional and factual material brings into question the criteria by which factuality is assessed in secondary sources, thus providing the reader with a more direct experience and understanding of the absurdity of contemporary assumptions about the process commonly used to sort fact from fiction in humanities scholarship. The effect of Lovecraft's brand of difficulty upon the reader is complex. On one hand, the mixture of fictional and fact-based allusion develops a kind of distrust of information sources, for readers who realize that they have been tricked (to any degree) by Lovecraft's playful hoaxes face the question of whether or not other seemingly supportable information from other sources has been altered or entirely faked. Even the minor details of the stories are often hoaxes, leading the reader to wonder how much of his or her daily exposure to historical or literary documentation may be just as easily faked or altered.

By combining elements of the modern grotesque and modernism in much of his weird fiction, Lovecraft intensifies his absurdist statement of human insignificance. Modernism brings subtlety, intellectualism, and technical experimentation to the concept of absurdity, while the grotesque provides a greater textual tangibility, emotional force, and cosmic scope to the tales in question. With the modern grotesque and modernism combined as complimentary forces into the modernist grotesque, Lovecraft's works deliver a much more powerful representation of cosmic absurdity than would have been possible with either one modality or the other. In light of the apparent nihilism behind Lovecraft's statements of cosmic absurdity in his fiction, it is useful to bring his letters into the discussion to clarify his thoughts on the position of humanity within a chaotic and mechanistic universe, for his underlying statement about the value of humanity is elusive in his fiction: "It is . . . our task to save existence from a sense of chaos & futility by rebuilding the purely aesthetic & philosophical concept of character & cosmic pseudo-purpose—reëstablishing a realisation of the necessity of pattern in any order of being complex enough to satisfy the mind and emotions of highly evolved human personalities" (*SL* 4.280). Thus, the modernist grotesque exists as an important coping mechanism in developing "a slow, gradual approach, or faint approximation of an approach, to the mystic substance of absolute reality itself–the stark, cosmic reality which lurks behind our varying subjective perceptions" (*SL* 2.301). The "cosmic reality" to which he refers is that of his "fundamental principle" of cosmic disinterestism, the only higher truth to which he seems to give validity. Yet the approach to be taken by modernist grotesque art, to acknowledge and then cope with the ultimate alienation, subjectivity, and absurdity of human existence, is crucial because "although meaning nothing in the cosmos as a whole, mankind obviously means a good deal to itself" (*SL* 5.241). Thus, it appears as though Lovecraft attempts to find a kind of balance between intellectual realism and artistic optimism, acknowledging the problematic nature of human perceptions, representations, and institutional paradigms, while simultaneously suggesting that art can create a kind of mental life raft to which humans may cling in order to survive the surrounding cosmic maelstrom.

Works Cited

Airaksinen, Timo. *The Philosophy of H. P. Lovecraft*. New York: Peter Lang, 1999.

Cannon, Peter. *H. P. Lovecraft*. Boston: Twayne, 1989.

Chefdor, Monique; Quinones, Ricardo; and Wachtel, Albert. *Modernism: Challenges and Perspectives*. Urbana: University of Illinois Press, 1986.

Diepeveen, Leonard. *The Difficulties of Modernism*. New York: Routledge, 2003.

Dziemianowicz, Stefan. "Outsiders and Aliens: The Use of Isolation in Lovecraft's Fiction." In *An Epicure in the Terrible: A Centennial Anthology of Essays in Honor of H. P. Lovecraft*, ed. David E. Schultz and S. T. Joshi. Rutherford, NJ: Fairleigh Dickinson University Press, 1991. 159–87.

Joshi, S. T. "H. P. Lovecraft: The Fiction of Materialism." In *American Supernatural Fiction: From Edith Wharton to the* Weird Tales *Writers*, ed. Douglas Robillard. New York: Garland, 1996. 141–66.

Kayser, Wolfgang. *The Grotesque in Art and Literature*. Trans. Ulrich Weisstein. New York: Columbia University Press, 1957.

Lauterbach, Edward S. "Some Notes on Cthulhuian Pseudobiblia." In *H. P. Lovecraft: Four Decades of Criticism*, ed. S. T. Joshi. Athens: Ohio University Press, 1980.

Leiber, Fritz, Jr. "A Literary Copernicus." In *H. P. Lovecraft: Four Decades of Criticism*, ed. S. T. Joshi, editor. Athens: Ohio University Press, 1980.

Ortega y Gasset, José. *What Is Knowledge?* Trans. Jorge Garcia-Gomez. Albany: State University of New York Press, 2002.

Rubenstein, Robert A.; Laughlin, Charles D., Jr.; and McManus, John. *Science as Cognitive Process: Toward an Empirical Philosophy of Science*. Philadelphia: University of Pennsylvania Press, 1984.

Thornton, Weldon. *The Antimodernism of Joyce's* Portrait of an Artist as a Young Man. Syracuse: Syracuse University Press, 1994.

Sources of Anxiety in Lovecraft's "Polaris"

J. D. Worthington

"Polaris," the fourth tale Lovecraft wrote after taking up his fictional pen after an hiatus of nine years (if one includes the delightfully impish "A Reminiscence of Dr. Samuel Johnson" but excludes the round-robin tale to which he contributed, "The Mystery of Murdon Grange"), shows a further advance on his technique and range, being an example of a quasi-Biblical, almost prose-poetic style as well as exhibiting considerable subtlety in theme and structure. It has been pointed out—as Lovecraft himself did (*SL* 2.95)—that the tale bears a striking similarity to many early tales by Lord Dunsany, despite the fact that Lovecraft had not yet read Dunsany, nor would do for over a year. Yet when he did, this common chord would resonate so strongly that for some time the Irish fantaisiste would almost dominate Lovecraft's own work. It has also been noted by S. T. Joshi that much of the inspiration for the tale came from an ongoing discussion on religion between Lovecraft and Maurice Winter Moe, in particular a letter on the distinction between reality and unreality and the need to know which is which. Much of this letter is included in the first volume of *Selected Letters* (*SL* 1.60–68; see esp. 62–63). But little note has been taken of other writings and biographical facts that may have also played a role in, if not the genesis, then at least the development of the tale. These possible influences will constitute the subject of this paper.

"Polaris" (*D* 20–24) is the tale of an unnamed narrator who, haunted in some obscure fashion by the Pole Star, which "leers down from [. . .] the black vault, winking hideously like an insane watching eye which strives to convey some strange message, yet recalls nothing save that it once had a message convey" (20). This star seemingly influences his dreams, until he finally dreams of an unknown city; first as an unembodied watcher and eventually as an inhabitant. This city is threatened with attack by the warlike "Inutos," and the protagonist, though a close friend of the city's commander of troops, Alos, is "denied a warrior's part" because he is "feeble and given to strange faintings when subjected to stress and hardships" (22); yet he is granted the position of sole watch at the strategic watchtower of Thapnen, to warn of the Inutos' approach up a narrow pass which would allow them to attack the garrison unnanounced. Despite his intense love for his country and his determination to fulfill his post with honor, he soon finds himself lulled to sleep by a "damnable rhythmical promise" coming, by all appearances, from the Pole Star. In the end, he sinks to sleep, only to awaken once more to find himself in his modern-day setting, which he now deems a dream (his true life being that he lived within the dreams of the city), guilt-ridden for his failure to warn the city and keep his promise to his friend, certain that his sleep has doomed his beloved Olathoë to be overwhelmed by the Inutos, even though assured by those around him that all these things are a dream, and that "in those realms where the Pole Star shines high [. . .] there has been naught save ice and snow for thousands of years, and never a man save squat, yellow creatures, blighted by the cold, called 'Esquimaux'" (23). Meanwhile, the Pole Star, having made its promised round and returned to "the spot where [once it] burn[ed]," "leers down from the black vault, winking hideously like an insane watching eye which strives to convey some message, yet recalls nothing save that it once had a message to convey" (24). This ending, as noted by Donald R. Burleson (26), perfectly captures the cyclical nature of the tale, encapsulating the idea of the past reaching forth and affecting the present; a common motif in much of Lovecraft's fiction.

In structure and form, though a quite brief tale, it is a surprisingly complex one, and the questions it poses are skillfully maintained at an uneasy equilibrium from the first to the last. But it is not only the narrator's anxieties we have to deal with here, but those of his creator, which indeed may have much to do with why this story, insubstantial and minor though it is, continues to haunt its readers nearly a century after it was first written.

It might be best to begin by revisiting the most obvious "source of anxiety." As has been long noted, the dream of the city was first set down in the letter to Maurice Winter Moe of 15 May 1918; but, as Joshi points out (*I Am Providence* 1.256–57), this letter also provides the major theme of the tale: the anxiety of needing to know what is real and what is unreal (or dream).

> If there be not some virtue in plain TRUTH; then our fair dreams, delusions, and follies are as much to be esteemed as our sober waking hours and the comforts they bring. If TRUTH amounts to nothing, then we must regard the phantasms of our slumbers just as seriously as the events of our daily lives.

Lovecraft goes on to describe a dream he had recently had featuring just such a city as we see in "Polaris," save that here he remains "only a consciousness, a perceptive presence." He also senses that he "had once known it well," and that if he could remember, he "should be carried back to a very remote period—many thousand years, when something vaguely horrible had happened"; another aspect of the dream that he wove into the finished fabric of the tale. He continues by adding:

> At this point you will ask me whence these stories. I answer— according to your pragmatism that dream was as real as my presence at this table, pen in hand! If the truth or falsity of our beliefs and impressions be immaterial, then I am, or was, actually and indisputably an unbodied spirit hovering over a very singular, very silent, and very ancient city somewhere between grey, dead hills. I thought I was at the time—so what else matters? Do you think that I was just as truly that spirit as I now am H. P. Lovecraft? I do not. [. . .] I recognize a distinction between dream life and real life, between appearances and actualities. I confess to an over-powering desire to know whether I am asleep or awake—whether the environment and laws which affect me are external and permanent, or the transitory products of my own brain. (*SL* 1.62–63)

When it came to the writing of the tale, however, Lovecraft found it much more fruitful to take a position directly opposed to (or at least strongly questioning of) that of his letter, by arguing for or making plausible the idea that that dream-state, both disembodied spirit and later inhabitant of the city, were as real as the modern man who had the dream; that in fact the dream is a genuine memory of something from an unknown prehistoric past in which the dreamer, in a previous incarnation, played a part. Even more, the dream-self actually becomes more real than the "real" self, finally supplanting the modern man altogether in his own mind:

> [. . .] when next I looked up it was in a dream; with the Pole Star grinning at me through a window from over the horrible swaying trees of a dream-swamp. And I am still dreaming.
>
> In my shame and despair I sometimes scream frantically, begging the dream-creatures around me to waken me ere the Inutos steal up the pass behind the peak Noton and take the citadel by surprise; but these creatures are daemons, for they laugh at me and tell me I am not dreaming. They mock me whilst I sleep, and whilst the squat yellow foe may be creeping silently upon us. I have failed in my duty and betrayed the marble city of Olathoë; I have proven false to Alos, my friend and commander. But still these shadows of my dream deride me. They say there is no land of Lomar, save in my nocturnal imaginings; that in those realms where the Pole Star shines high and red Aldebaran crawls low around the horizon, there has been naught save ice and snow for thousands of years, and never a man save squat yellow creatures, blighted by the cold, whom they call "Esquimaux". (*D* 23)

It is this nagging sense of pseudo-memory, and the tension between the poles of possibility of it being a true memory or an obsessive dream, that gives the tale much of its power. While Lovecraft may well have meant such an ending as "a final tweaking of Moe's nose on the need to maintain such distinctions [between reality and dream] in real life" (*I Am Providence* 1.257), it is also true that this particular theme of the uncertainties involving real life and dream was one of the major keys of Lovecraft's fiction (cf. "The Tomb," "The Shadow out of Time," "The Call of Cthulhu," "The Dreams in the Witch House," etc.).

There are several other notable threads brought up in the passage given above, but before addressing these it may be well to make mention of an interesting similar confusion of the two states brought up by Lovecraft himself some years later, in which his "anxiety" to know which state was which is particularly vividly described. The following account is taken from a letter to J. Vernon Shea of 4 February 1934:

I still have some tremendously odd dreams—some of which I know to be such. Only last week I had a very curious one about the decay and ruin of the city. I tried to wake, but when I had come out of the dream *I felt that I was not really awake even then.* Something was wrong, even though a bright morning sun was shining on the bed from an east window. Then I realised. *There ought not to be any east window.* . . . . . I was in my old room at 598 Angell St., which I haven't inhabited for ten years! But how could I wake up? After all, *was* I asleep? Was it not possible that everything since early in 1924 was a dream? That I had never left 598—never gone to Brooklyn & Barnes St. & College St. . . . . ? But no! Here was the sun *where it hadn't been since 1912 or 1913* . . . . for a house had been built against my windows. I *knew* that. I couldn't swear I had ever lived away from 598, but I knew that my eastern sunlight had been cut off by a new house. And yet, there it blazed! Clearly, I was asleep . . . . asleep, & on that unstable plane where anything might happen. Into what vortex of nightmare might I be pitched without warning at any moment? But how could I escape? Pinching seemed to do no good. And even if I did have another awakening, how could I know that this *second* one would be final? At last, by a strong mental effort, I made the sunlit room dissolve around me, & emerged into a restful twilight. I stretched in relief . . . . & *then saw that I was still at 598.* My windows were shadowed this time, but the conviction that I no longer lived at 598 was stronger. The chances were about 8 to 2, it seemed to me, that I was still asleep. I shook myself, lifted myself on my elbow, & tried in every way to push myself through another layer of dream. No use. At last a current of cold blackness swept down from somewhere, & I was caught up in a vortex which dissolved all the visible world. Everything melted to chaos, & I soared through endless night against my will. Then hazy outlines began to form—the small panes of an old-fashioned window—daylight—*I was at 66 College St.!* But was I awake? Here was the sun shining in from the south, & I was in the house I ought to be in . . . . *but I could not be sure yet.* There was

an odd aura of doubt which grew & grew—& at last everything
dissolved again. No vortex this time, but just a diffusive greyness.
And then the outlines of the small-paned window again—this
time with only the College St. arc light at the mouth of the court
behind it. I shook myself once more, & speculated as to my degree
of awakeness. It seemed very doubtful. Still, I might as well test
my condition. I rose & turned on the light. 4 a.m. I raised the curtain & looked at the world outside. I went into the library & to
the bathroom, & returned to bed. Still devilish sleepy. Soon I was
dreaming of my old home at 454 Angell St. I definitely awaked
around 8 a.m.—*but do not yet know whether I was really awake &*
up at 4 o'clock. . . . (SL 4.361–62)

Obviously, even with his keen observation and general clarity of
thought, Lovecraft knew that firmly drawing the boundaries between the real and dream is not always an easy desire to satisfy.

Another thread of anxiety that forms a major theme in this
tale is the failure of the narrator to take a part—or, more accurately, to fulfill such a role—in the defense of his country. This,
too, reflects vivid experiences and feelings on Lovecraft's part; in
this case, his rejection for service by the R.I.N.G. and subsequently
during the draft, and his feelings of bitterness from that; his own
strong support of "moderate, healthy militarism as contrasted with
dangerous and unpatriotic peace preaching"; and of "Pan-
Saxonism, or the domination by the English and kindred races
over the lesser divisions of mankind" (CE 1.51), with his attendant
anxiety over the failure of each. These are each closely related, as I
hope to show, and so must be dealt with in a rather more complex web of references.

That a part of Lovecraft is not only reflected in the narrator,
but also in his friend Alos, is clear when we recall the narrator's
description of him as "a true man and patriot" who, like Lovecraft
in numerous passages in letters, essays, and verse of the period,
"spoke of the perils to be faced, and exhorted [his fellows] to sustain the traditions of their ancestors, who when forced to move
southward [. . .] valiantly and victoriously swept aside [those] that
stood in their way" (D 22). That Lovecraft also felt a keen anxiety
concerning the discarding of that "Pan-Saxonism" in favor of alli-

ances with "alien races," with the threat this implied, can likewise be seen in his letter to Rheinhart Kleiner of 23 December 1917:

> The pan-Teutonic ideal, attainable only by a compleat and amiable coöperation between Anglo-Saxon and Germanic races, has been fallaciously subordinated to a petty pan-Germanic ideal which is bringing about the virtual suicide of the Teutonic race, and driving Anglo-Saxons and Germans into equally unnatural alliances with alien races. [. . .] Progress is at a standstill, and everything human is lost in a mad scramble for a mutual victory. Even a recurrence of the Dark Ages is not [im]possible—a recurrence which will leave the Teutonic race so depleted numerically that the world's future is seriously threatened. (*SL* 1.54; bracketed emendation required by sense; cf. *Letters to Rheinhart Kleiner* 124)

That the Inutos, on the other hand, represent a symbol of what was to him a very real menace posed by the Oriental, and especially Mongol, races, seems quite obvious when we compare his description of them in the story with other passages in his letters, as well as one rather unexpected source. Here is his characterization of the Inutos as given in the story: "squat, hellish, yellow fiends [. . .] For the squat creatures were mighty in the arts of war, and knew not the scruples of honour which held back our tall, grey-eyed men of Lomar from ruthless conquest" (*D* 22). Compare that with the following, from a letter to the Gallomo, dated 23 September 1919:

> Of Japan I have not so far spoken, because I think it a certain enemy of the future, which no plan can permanently make a friend. It demands free access to Anglo-Saxon soil for its citizens, and this can never be given. Orientals must be kept in their native East till the fall of the white race. Sooner or later a great Japanese war will take place, during which I think the virtual destruction of Japan will have to be effected in the interests of European safety. The more numerous Chinese are a menace of the still more distant future. They will probably be the exterminators of Caucasian civilization, for their numbers are amazing. (*Letters to Alfred Galpin* 57)

His tone had not changed six years later (save, perhaps, to grow even more pronounced) when he described the denizens of

New York's lower East Side in a letter to Frank Belknap Long of 21 March 1924:

> The organic things—Italo-Semitico-Mongoloid—inhabiting that awful cesspool could not by any stretch of the imagination be call'd human. They were monstrous and nebulous adumbrations of the pithecanthropoid and amoebal; vaguely molded from some stinking viscous slime of earth's corruption, and slithering in and on the filthy streets or in and out of windows and doorways in a fashion suggestive of nothing but infesting worms or deep-sea unnamabilities. [. . .] I could not carry away the memory of any living face. The individually grotesque was lost in the collectively devastating; which left on the eye only the broad, phantasmal lineaments of the morbid soul of disintegration and decay . . . a yellow leering mask with sour, sticky, acid ichors oozing at eyes, ears, nose, and mouth, and abnormally bubbling from monstrous and unbelievable sores at every point. . . . (SL 1.333–34)

While I would readily agree that, in the preceding passage, Lovecraft quite deliberately exaggerated the language into such hyperbole as to be an exercise in verbal overkill, the genuine repugnance being expressed is nonetheless plain, while the description of the "*yellow* mask" (emphasis added) makes the comment even more pointed.

Nor was his view on this any milder when he painted a similar picture to the bellicose one given earlier, in—of all places—a satire aimed at the Providence astronomer J. F. Hartmann, as early as 1914:

> A conjunctional eclipse of Mercury by Saturn indicates that the English Emperor Theodoric IX of the United States will retake California from the Japanese through the remarkable strategy of Field Marshall Patricio Caeno.

> Japan will take but little part in the war, and indeed will engage in no tremendous hostilities until the great Mongolian invasion of 2142.

> This invasion will give rise to a frightful struggle between the white and yellow races lasting two and a half centuries [. . .] (CE 3.265)

> This was not a particularly unusual anxiety at the time—

consider, for instance, the plethora of tales by writers high and low on the theme of this "Yellow Peril," of which Sax Rohmer's stories of Fu Manchu are merely the most famous (or infamous) examples. Yet this fear was real enough to Lovecraft not only to engender such statements in letters and essays, but also to result in his creation of the Inutos and "the cruel empire of Tsan-Chan" (*D* 34) in "Beyond the Wall of Sleep" and "The Shadow out of Time." The same sort of thing is at work in the vision of a future New York (and, by extension, America) shown to the narrator by the preternaturally aged figure in "He"; a figure that, as has been noted by others, is itself quite similar to the "mystery man" of the melodramas of the period. The narrator sees a nightmarish city where the skies were "verminous with strange flying things," with a skyline almost a prototype of the alien geometries of R'lyeh. This is how he describes the inhabitants of that city: "And swarming loathsomely on aërial galleries I saw the yellow, squint-eyed people of that city, robed horribly in orange and red, and dancing insanely to the pounding of fevered kettle-drums, the clatter of obscene crotala, and the maniacal moaning of muted horns whose ceaseless dirges rose and fell undulantly like the waves of an unhallowed ocean of bitumen" (*D* 273–74). For all his intelligence, Lovecraft was not immune to the ethnic prejudices of his times.

That Lovecraft, like his protagonist, was unable to take part in the "great struggle for civilization" was apparently a considerable blow to him, given his comments on this in his letters to Kleiner and others. Even though he was initially approved by the examining physician at his attempted enlistment, the interference of his mother, who called in the family doctor as support, caused Lovecraft finally to be rejected first by the R.I.N.G., and eventually classed as "Class V. Div. G—totally and permanently unfit" (*Letters to Rheinhart Kleiner* 123). The first rankled, but the second caused a seeming depression in Lovecraft's spirits reflected in his comments to Kleiner that it "is not flattering to be reminded of my utter uselessness twice within the space of six months" (ibid.), and this feeling (expressed in a letter of 23 December 1917) was shortly exacerbated by the appearance in the *National Enquirer* of 17 January 1918 of a verse titled "Only a Volunteer," by one Sgt. Hayes R. Miller, which bemoaned the fact that, though the draftees were "fêted and extolled to the skies" (*Letters to Rheinhart Kleiner* 125), those who had volunteered and paved the way were given short shrift. Though the verse is, frankly, little if any better than doggerel, it apparently stung Lovecraft in this sensitive spot almost as if he himself had been accused of shirking his duty, prompting him not only to respond with a gentle refutation praising the earlier forces, "The Volunteer" (also published in the *National Enquirer* for 7 February 1918; both verses were also published in the [Providence] *Evening News* for 1 February 1918, on the same page), but, when this verse was printed in the April 1918 number of the *Tryout*, for him to write the following notes on the tearsheets for that appearance:

> The original poem by Sgt. Miller—"Only a Volunteer"— complained of the fashion in which volunteers—real men—were neglected whilst the skulking drafted herds were coddled & petted. [. . .] It is not my fault that my "military service" was with pen rather than sword. I did my best to enlist in the R. I. Nat'l Guard in the spring of 1917, but could not pass the physical examination. Have been in execrable health—nervous trouble—since the age of two or three. (*Winter Wish* 171n76)

Whether one believes that it was his mother's meddling or his genuine physical ailments that prevented Lovecraft's enlistment, the fact is that the peculiar circumstances—which he himself notes were barely countenanced by the examining board (*Letters to Rheinhart Kleiner* 109)—are quite likely to have embarrassed and possibly even humiliated him, making such a reminder as Sgt. Miller's verse painful indeed. It is to be noted that the reason the protagonist is "denied a warrior's part" is because he is "feeble and given to strange faintings when subjected to stress and hardships" (*D* 22), which certainly echoes his calling himself a "weakling" and noting it was information about his "nervous condition" that halted the enlistment (*Letters to Rheinhart Kleiner* 109).

There is one other peculiar note regarding this aspect, and that is the statement by the protagonist that his "eyes were the keenest in the city, despite the long hours I gave each day to the study of the Pnakotic manuscripts and the wisdom of the Zobnarian Fathers" (*D* 22), which is an odd inversion of his comment to Kleiner that "Fortune had sided with [him] in causing no attack of blurred eyesight to come upon [him] during the physical examination" (*Letters to Rheinhart Kleiner* 109).

Other themes common to Lovecraft's work also make their appearance in the tale, such as his notion or feeling that the modern day was a mad dream and that the past (in his case, particularly the "rational" eighteenth century) was the reality—cf. the letter to J. Vernon Shea cited above:

> I've always had a subconscious feeling that everything since the 18th century is unreal & illusory—a sort of grotesque nightmare or caricature. People seem to me more or less like ironic shadows or phantoms—as if I could make them (together with all their modern houses & inventions & perspectives) dissolve into thin aether by merely pinching myself awake & shouting at them, "Why, damn ye, you're not even born, & won't be born for a century & a half! God Save the King, & his Colony of Rhode-Island & Providence-Plantations! (*SL* 4.361)

This idea here combines with that of the past reaching forth to engulf the unlucky individual chosen by the whims of chance, yet another thread that runs through much of Lovecraft's work, one discussed with considerable skill by Donald R. Burleson, S. T. Joshi, and others.

Another similarity often overlooked is that to the verse "Astrophobos" (1917), which also tells of a narrator drawn by mysteries hinted at by a star, only to find the message it seeks to convey lays upon him a terror of the starry voids (cf. "The Colour out of Space") which will trouble him to the end of his days:

> Now I knew the fiendish fable
> > That the golden glitter bore;
> Now I shun the spangled sable
> > That I watch'd and lov'd before;
> But the horror, set and stable,
> > Haunts my soul for evermore. (*AT* 30, ll. 37–42)

Yet it is Lovecraft's artistry, even in such an early and minor tale as this, that allows for that "willing suspension of disbelief" which enables it to work. It is not only in the use of such autobio-

graphical material as noted above, but in the selection and manner
of their use, that Lovecraft's skill is exhibited. His careful choice
of what details to include and the choice of words and rhythms
are immensely important to the weaving of an atmosphere of
convincing nightmare and disturbing possibility. He had not read
Poe (see his comments on this aspect of Poe's work; *Annotated
Supernatural Horror in Literature* 43), the Gothics, and Hawthorne
in vain (though he was only to learn his most important lesson—
his haunted regionalism—from Hawthorne somewhat later).

While use of such terms as "uncanny light" for the Pole Star, or
north winds that "curse and whine"; Coma Berenices shimmering
"weirdly"; and so on—all from the first few lines of the tale—may
indeed, as others have noted, be "meaningless" in an objective or
literal sense, as descriptions of an emotional state or response to a
thing, they add a texture and color that incrementally slip the
reader from everyday reality to a particularly nightmarish vision
giving, upon finishing the tale, a new layer of perception of reality
itself. They also are very much a part of creating the idea of a sen-
tience within the very setting of a tale, another common motif in
Lovecraft's writing, reaching into even such an insignificant piece
as "The Street" (1920?; the date of the composition of this tale is
somewhat uncertain, though the triggering event—a news story
on the police strike in Boston—has been identified; see *I Am
Providence* 1.341).

In addition, choice of such details as how "the red-leaved trees
of the swamp mutter things to one another in the small hours of
the morning under the horned waning moon" (*D* 20); or "the night
of the great Aurora, when over the swamp played the shocking
coruscations of the daemon-light" (*D* 20); or the creation of the
Pnakotic manuscripts; or even the "damnable rhythmical promise"
seemingly chanted by the Pole Star—altered in wording after considering the criticism of amateur poet John Ravenor Bullen (*CE*
5.67n29), indicating Lovecraft's painstaking selection even of word
placement for the proper effect—are indeed carefully made, and
often hint of things beyond the view of the reader, giving the tale
a depth not only emotionally and historically (see, e.g., the Pnakotic manuscripts), but also in allusion to mysteries never explained but rich in possibilities.

Why call the aurora a "daemon-light," for example? Is it a portent of what is to come, perhaps even an irruption of the past into the present, a rupture in those "fixed laws of Nature which are our only safeguard against the assaults of chaos and the daemons of unplumbed space" (*Annotated Supernatural Horror in Literature* 23)? Note that, in the sequence of events given in the tale, it is only after the night of the aurora that the city appears and the protagonist's dream/memory begins; we may also recall that Aurora was the goddess of the dawn, so perhaps, in a punning sense, we have here a dawning of a particularly terrible kind. . . .

And here we may see what could be called the final "source of anxiety" in "Polaris": the anxiety of Lovecraft the artist, even in such a brief and minor piece, to choose what would enhance the effect, blur the lines of reality and dream, and give an emotional plausibility that is the hallmark of a consummate craftsman; an anxiety resulting in a body of work that continues to delight, fascinate, and haunt us long after Lovecraft himself has become a part of that past he made something to both revere and fear.

Works Cited

Burleson, Donald R. *H. P. Lovecraft: A Critical Study.* Westport, CT: Greenwood Press, 1983.

Joshi, S. T. *I Am Providence: The Life and Times of H. P. Lovecraft.* New York: Hippocampus Press, 2010. 2 vols.

Lovecraft, H. P. *The Annotated Supernatural Horror in Literature.* Ed. S. T. Joshi. New York: Hippocampus Press, 2000.

———. *Letters to Alfred Galpin.* Ed. S. T. Joshi and David E. Schultz. New York: Hippocampus Press, 2003.

———. *Letters to Rheinhart Kleiner.* Ed. S. T. Joshi and David E. Schultz. New York: Hippocampus Press, 2005.

———. *A Winter Wish.* Ed. Tom Collins. Chapel Hill, NC: Whispers Press, 1977.

Tekeli-li!
Disturbing Language in Edgar Allan Poe and H. P. Lovecraft

Lynne Jamneck

Edgar Allan Poe's *The Narrative of Arthur Gordon Pym* (1838) and H. P. Lovecraft's *At the Mountains of Madness* (1931) are texts that reveal the inconsistency and unreliability of language as a tool for expressing meaning. Pseudo-accounts of the past, they are ambiguous and uncanny, qualities that thwart ideas about reliability and truth. While these fictional accounts contain thematic similarities, ultimately they play out differently. However, it is their differences as much as their connections that are able to provide new insights into what are complex and layered narratives.

The Narrative of Arthur Gordon Pym (hereafter referred to as *Pym*) and *At the Mountains of Madness* (hereafter referred to as *Mountains*) are metanarrative texts. Attempts at interpreting them will benefit from an awareness and observation of how ideas about knowledge and understanding are paralleled with one another. The themes of the texts extend themselves outward, where they are doubled within the reader's imagination and personal context. Analogies can be drawn between this meta-nature and the practice of reading and writing. Both acts prolong themselves beyond the boundaries of the page, where they inevitably split into several suggested meanings. This differentiation is a result of a complex semiotic machine—"the living text"—always changing and reshaping itself to adapt to its social and cultural environment.

Mountains and *Pym* combine several genres, effectively destabilising our perceptions of textual meaning. Motifs and themes gain the dimensions of others they are contextually associated with. Though *Pym* is ostensibly representative of the travel narrative, Poe's interweaving of genres creates a hybrid text that stimulates and frustrates understanding. Like Pym in the hold of the *Grampus*, we are as much in the dark about where the narrative may lead us. It may leave us "strangely confused in mind" (70), struggling with it the same way Pym struggles against his own suppressed cannibalism, encouraging us finally to yield with "a dreaminess of sensation" (204) that will in due course lead us to "the skin . . . of . . . perfect whiteness" (206): the blank page, the birth of all texts. Interpretation inevitably leads back to the beginning; by the time we reach the end of *Pym*, our expectations have been challenged and suspicions, either confirmed or denied, have changed the way we view the text. We must start again with this new knowledge, repeating the process as we strip away textual layers that obscure our efforts.

To read a blank page is to read the void. This is where Pym finds himself at the conclusion of Poe's text. A void is not *nothing*; its existence gives it content. It simply lies beyond the threshold of perception. *Pym* exposes the "void" that an empirical approach runs into when matter can no longer be clearly distinguished. Studied emptiness creates meaning because it is observed. Furthermore, it exists in a state of flux and can be inscribed with diverse meanings. We *can* come to at least a partial observation of the abyss. To do so we need to go back not only to the text, but to the beginning of the text. It is here that all possibilities lie in state, blank, yet still imbued with meaning. Until we are convinced *by the text* not to trust the text, our interpretation of it will remain unsatisfying, "nothing but a dreary and unsatisfactory blank" (78).

The degree of separation between representation and perception is heightened the further we move from tangible, textual space. To gain a deeper understanding of *Pym* and *Mountains*, we may consider the landscapes of the narratives as symbolic of textual space. The principles of the Romantic, Gothic, and Adventure traditions come together in Poe's and Lovecraft's texts to express literal and metaphysical space. Pym's relationship to the physical spaces he inhabits is analogous to the psychic spaces he occupies. At various stages he is shut in the dark of a ship's hold; occupies the body of a dead sailor; navigates the space between civilisation (America) and barbarism (Tsalal); and finally enters the unknown Antarctic, the "white curtain . . . beyond the veil" (205–6). These spaces are dualistic; they facilitate Pym's physical journey and continue the narrative; they also hamper Pym psychically, inhibiting his psychological growth. Pym leaves Nantucket and the limits of being bound by family in a bid to gain freedom, only to find himself in a space even more restricted than before he left the mainland.

Pym is anything but a predictable adventure story. The narrative adheres to a Romantic framework only to cast the genre in a mocking light. Thompson suggests that *Pym* "conforms to the European definition of the arabesque, using genre conventions and conventional narrative to go against the grain of narrative conventions" (200). As in Islamic arabesques, *Pym* repeats linear patterns to create representations that extend beyond the borders of the text. *The end of the narrative is not the end of Pym's story.* As long as the final chapters of Pym's adventures remain lost, the text remains unresolved. The conventional, patterned narrative ending is circumvented. This "unfinished" state of the text affects interpretation in an ongoing process of repeat interpretation. Nonetheless, we *can* consider *Pym* complete *because* the text repeatedly subverts traditional form and structure. It is complete because it does not aim to be complete.

The "appearance of truth" is a constant double bind that threatens to undermine or inform our interpretation. We are told from the perspectives of Pym and *Mountains'* Dyer that their experiences are true, but the texts reveal inconsistencies that make the veracity of their narrators questionable. We cannot trust Pym and Dyer to reveal to us absolute truth, and their unstable and contradictory narratives support this. What is more, even if we could trust the narrators, absolute truth escapes human perception.

Writing and reading extends the life of a text indefinitely as a result of the unfixed nature of narrative. *Mountains'* and *Pym's* inconclusive endings extends the texts into an environment where they exist in a borderless state. As readers we become the conduit for this expanded existence; we are inextricably tied to the text, and the text to us.

Poe wrote at a historical time when the reading public demanded adventurous fiction with the *appearance* of truth. "Adventure" as it appears in fiction is rarely an accurate representation of truth. On the whole, *Pym* offers precisely the exciting narrative associated with adventure fiction. Yet it is aware of itself as fiction exactly because it pretends to pass itself off as an account of real events. From the start, *Pym* pretends to be something it is not. In his preface to the narrative Pym writes:

> One consideration which deterred me was, that, having kept no journal during a greater portion of the time in which I was absent, I feared I should not be able to write, from mere memory, a statement so minute and connected as to have the appearance of that truth it would really possess, barring only the natural and unavoidable exaggeration to which all of us are prone when detailing events which have had powerful influence in exciting the imaginative faculties. (55)

This is a fairly succinct summary of *Pym's* textual hybridity. Had Pym recorded his entire narrative as it had happened, at the time it happened, his telling of events would likely still have been exaggerated, either to satisfy his own, later recollection of events, or to satisfy his readers. Writing down his experiences is a way for Pym to make sense of it; however, making sense through writing is a suspect act because of the subjective nature of recollection.

Pym goes beyond the restrictions of genre taxonomy, guaranteeing the text a wide audience and expanding the scope of interpretation. Gitelman suggests that those condemning *Pym* on the basis that it does not adhere to the formal properties of a specific genre fail to properly consider the form and nature of the exploration narrative (Harvey 123). *Pym's* lengthy scientific digressions, discontinuity between and among episodes, and its anticlimactic end are all traits of the genre; they are outcomes fated by the nature of exploration (123). That we do not get the full story by the end of *Pym* is a realistic reflection of what a true exploration narrative would offer us as well. Even if a journey at sea would have been considered a success, the voyage in question is simply a part of a larger exploration within a bigger social context that continues long after ships have returned to port.

Pym mirrors what would likely have been a reality in cases where journeys at sea met with conflict or even disaster. The loss of the *Jane Guy* and the resulting failure of fixing some sort of foothold in the Antarctic may have offered reason enough for a follow-up expedition, as according to the note section, "these regions may shortly be verified or contradicted by means of the governmental expedition now preparing for the Southern Ocean" (207). Not only does *Pym* extend itself as an unfinished text, it also binds future potential texts to it, making its scope of influence even wider.

Of particular relevance in *Mountains* and *Pym* is the paralleling of fantastic language with scientific language. The function of both is to invoke ideas and imagery at opposite ends of the imaginative spectrum. Poe and Dyer are narrators in the tradition of scientific exploration, retelling their experiences within a prose narrative framework. The presence of scientific language also heightens our awareness of the past. Poe's and Lovecraft's metanarratives present history and the present as parallel textual presences; one reinforces the presence of the other, a consequence of opposite doubling. Juxtaposing fictional and scientific language creates the same effect. Both reflect their own set of codes and systems that at various instances illuminate or confuse reading.

Language and words are mysterious. Their meanings, connotations, and denotations can change according to context. Sometimes these changes cannot be easily explained, leaving us feeling uncertain and unnerved at our failure to decipher them. The metanarrative nature of *Pym* and *Mountains* adds to the enigmatic nature of the texts. Reading them becomes an uncanny act. Despite the attempts at grounding the narratives within a scientific framework, language is not "scientifically sound." When science fails to explain the events in Poe's and Lovecraft's narratives the texts become, like Nicholas Roerich's paintings, "disturbing" and "strangely painted" (*MM* 29). This causes "our notions of cosmic harmony" (*MM* 87) to crumble, and we enter into a realm of "unusual phenomena . . . a region of novelty and wonder" (Poe 203).

Burleson, writing on Lovecraft, highlights a thought-provoking analogy between science and language that comments on the unstable nature of texts:

Linguistic signifiers are like sums of differences. Like elements of the quantum field such as the electron, they are defined not in terms of self-presence or self-identity, but in terms of the field in which they are embedded. . . . Each field is essentially a relational realm, and each has its undefinable, elusive terms—the linguistic trace . . . is just as slippery, but just as necessary, as the quark. (4)

Burleson further notes that, since texts reside in language, they must take part of the mystery and complexity that this residence in language implies (5). The intrinsic instability of language affects a continuous and ever-present strain on the texts. As Dyer's and Pym's scientific views break down, so does their language for framing their experiences. They eventually find themselves adrift in hallucinatory-like environments, where they too are in relational realms. The texts become conflicted, having thus far been carried forward by procedural structure, exploration, and scientific discovery. Pym and Dyer are ill equipped for what they find, partly because they have based their expectations around specific outcomes and are now confronted with the incongruence of those expectations. There is inconsistency between what Dyer and Pym expect—or have convinced themselves they would find at the South Pole—and what they eventually do find. What is more, what they do find, they are unable to make rational sense of. A displacement of reality has taken place, destabilising Dyer's and Pym's views of the world.

The meta-nature of *Pym* and *Mountains* affects the same unsettling effect on the reader, alerting us to our preconceived expectations of the narratives. The inability to make definitive conclusions about the intentions of language renders the text indistinct; concurrently, textual uncanniness is transferred to the reader. Like Pym and Dyer, our own frameworks of reference break down and we are unable to view the texts as stable. Language, our strongest and most "trustworthy" tool for communicating meaning, has been compromised.

Accordingly, language itself is the barrier that hinders interpretation. Not only is it a formal construct—as well as having to be formally constructed—it performs according to a set of rules that are dependent on perception, as well as the context in which they are perceived. Poetic language differs from ordinary language; therefore, it has the potential to unsettle text, because it obscures the distinction between the figurative and the literal, the fictive and the real.

Pym serves as an example of the occult properties of language. Poe writes in his essay "The Philosophy of Composition" about the "step by step" (*Essays and Reviews* 14) process of working up a text from beginning to completion.

> Most writers—poets in especial—prefer having it understood that they compose by a species of fine frenzy—an ecstatic intuition—and would positively shudder at letting the public take a peep behind the scenes, at the elaborate and vacillating crudities of thought—at the true purposes seized only at the last moment—at the innumerable glimpses of idea that arrived not at the maturity of full view—at the fully-matured fancies discarded in despair as unmanageable—at the cautious selections and rejections—at the painful erasures and interpolations—in a word, at the wheels and pinions—the tackle for scene-shifting—the step-ladders, and de-mon-traps—the cock's feathers, the red paint and the black patches, which, in ninety-nine cases out of a hundred, constitute the properties of the literary histrio. (14)

Here we are given two notions about writers and writing: inspiration, and painstaking, hard work. Poe writes that the author *projects* an aura of creative genius, of being sensitively attuned to "an ecstatic intuition." He further claims that inspiration is something fleeting which the author must always be ready for, a conduit willing at any moment to be gripped by "fine frenzy." He then rejects this notion, explaining that it is nothing but a clever ruse to encourage a constructed image of The Author.

The nature of writing, Poe explains, is painful, but not in any romantic sense. Rather, it is a calculated process of "cautious selections and rejections." "The Philosophy of Composition" covers Poe's account—his *"modus operandi"* (14) of how he allegedly wrote "The Raven." In doing so, Poe effectively strips the enigmatic poem of its elusive and mysterious aura, demonstrating that our approach to text contributes significantly to how we perceive that text. Access to the workings of the author's creative process, while insightful, remains subject to the author's point of view. That is to say, such a process is shaped by the author's particular use of language to describe it. As Poe describes it, such carefully structured writing suggests a mind both creatively inspired and technically astute. "The Philosophy of Composition" may be an insightful and revealing essay on the creative process of an author, or it may be one of Poe's carefully structured hoaxes. It may be both. That Poe refers to his essay as "philosophy" can be taken as equally serious and satiric; "philosophy" implies particular knowledge, but also an aesthetic vision. As a writer whose work finds itself embedded in textual deception, Poe's reasons for writing the essay ambiguously can itself be argued as part of the Poe aesthetic.

Language reveals its philosophical properties through its unstable nature. Its mutability guarantees it a quality that is widely adaptable, able to reflect itself in a number of culturally and historically diverse contexts. *Mountains* addresses this adaptability through the idea of a transcendent realm "beyond words." Lovecraft's trademark use of adjectives like "unspeakable," "indescribable," and "unnamable" presents in words his things-that-cannot-be (Nelson 121). Though language pretends in this instance to break down and fail at describing Lovecraft's otherworldly entities, it does not. Just as the void is not unreadable, the unnamable or indescribable is not representatively blank. This is demonstrative of the aesthetic principles of language. Rather than directly describing a fantastic or bizarre image (by doing so limiting a wide interpretation of said image), Lovecraft uses the language of allusion and association to add to the uncanny thrust of his narratives.

Unlike Poe's *Pym*, Lovecraft finds a world where language truly breaks down undesirable. For the Lovecraftian personality, the inability to verbally articulate itself commonly leads to madness. After Dyer and Danforth have fled from the shoggoth and are flying away from the ancient Antarctic city, Danforth spies something so utterly dreadful that he is unable to put it into words. He refuses to tell Dyer what he saw (or thinks he saw), instead confining himself to "the repetition of a single mad word of all too obvious source: '*Tekeli-li! Tekeli-li!*'" (*MM* 106). Danforth's vision mentally unhinges him and leaves him psychically scarred forever. Dyer describes his partner's breakdown: "Danforth . . .

keyed up to a dangerous nervous pitch, could not keep quiet . . . turning and wriggling . . . his mad shrieking [bringing us] close to disaster by shattering my tight hold on myself . . . I am afraid that [he] will never be the same again" (*MM* 104–5).

Danforth's madness is induced by glimpsing the ancient past. What he sees sets up an intertextual reference in the Lovecraftian canon, to Lovecraft's story *The Dream-Quest of Unknown Kadath*. Kadath is a dream space that exists between Earth's dimension and another interdimensional space—one that, knowing Lovecraft, functions according to non-Euclidean geometry. Even the Old Ones fear Kadath, and "had made strange prayers to those mountains; but none ever went near them or dared to guess what lay beyond" (*MM* 71). Presumably, it is Kadath that Danforth glimpses. Kadath's image and the implications of its existence transfer themselves to Danforth, leaving a conceptual, perceptual, and psychological imprint on his psyche that he is unable to articulate intellectually. His only way of expressing the disturbing image is by repetitively shouting "Tekeli-li," a word that holds no meaning for the reader but supports the psychic weight of Danforth's madness—or keeps it at bay. Like the shoggoths who have learned the weird word from the Old Ones by way of mimicry, Danforth extends its status as a copy, ultimately an expression of language's inability to express the unknown.

Unlike Poe's internal dialogue with the unfamiliar, Lovecraft's designs about magic and the supernatural are directed toward a predatory, external force. Given that Lovecraft was an atheist and a materialist, it is worth noting that Russian painter and philosopher Nicholas Roerich's gallery, which Lovecraft often visited, had been a meeting place for theosophists. Lovecraft mentions theosophy in his short story "The Call of Cthulhu," written two years after his temporary move to New York. In the story, Francis Wayland Thurston relates his discovery of several notes and papers left behind by his grand-uncle, a Professor of Semitic languages at Brown University. Thurston recounts how "accounts of the queer dreams of different persons . . . citations from theosophical books and magazines . . . comments on long-surviving secret societies and hidden cults . . . references to passages in such mythological and anthropological source-books as Frazer's *Golden*

Bough and Miss Murray's[1] *Witch-Cult in Western Europe"* (*DH* 128) were among his grand-uncle's papers.

Both invented and real books play an important part in the Lovecraftian universe. They are regularly used as objects that facilitate the distribution of knowledge; this is, however, not always to the advantage of those who read them. Though they reveal secret truths, books are often harbingers of doom. Lovecraft created several fictional texts that feature in, or are alluded to, in his original fictional narratives. The most celebrated of these is the *Necronomicon*. A dreaded grimoire feared by many and sought by some for the inconceivable truths it reveals, the *Necronomicon* possesses the power to drive those who dare read it mad, a side-effect of its cosmically harrowing content. The *Necronomicon* is less subtle than anything Poe may have written as contemplation on the power of text\a text to affect its reader. Nonetheless, as a metanarrative prop, the *Necronomicon* effectively demonstrates the ability of language to "infect" other approximated texts.

"History of the *Necronomicon*" (c. 1927) is a brief account (approximately 650 words) written by Lovecraft, likely to keep track of the historical details of his grimoire as they relate to the greater context of his stories. The piece states that the *Necronomicon* had not always been referred to by this particular name. Instead, it had once been known by its original title, "*Al Azif—azif* being the word used by Arabs to designate that nocturnal sound (made by insects) suppos'd to be the howling of daemons" (*MW* 52). The book was "Composed by Abdul Alhazred, a mad poet of Sanaá . . . who visited the ruins of Babylon and the subterranean secrets of Memphis and spent ten years alone in the great southern desert of Arabia" (*MW* 52). Of Alhazred's death, "many terrible and conflicting things are told"; "Of his madness many things are told" (*MW* 52). Of the grimoire itself, "History of the *Necronomicon*" tells us that it was "suppressed and burnt by the patriarch Mi-

---

1. Anthropologist and Egyptologist Margaret Murray (1863–1963). HPL's own interest in Egypt is revealed in the story "Under the Pyramids" (1924), which he ghostwrote for Harry Houdini. One of HPL's fictional deities, Nyarlathotep, "came out of Egypt" (*MW* 32) and bears the Egyptian suffix *-hotep* to denote his origins.

chael," that "The Arabic original was lost as early as Wormius'
time," and that "no sight of the Greek copy . . . which was printed
in Italy between 1500 and 1550 . . . has been reported since the
burning of a certain Salem man's library in 1692" (*MW* 52–53).
Lovecraft then proceeds to write up a detailed summary of the
book's supposed publication history:

> An English translation . . . by Dr. Dee was never printed, and ex-
> ists only in fragments . . . Of the Latin texts now existing one
> (15th cent.) is known to be in the British Museum under lock and
> key, while another (17th cent.) is in the Bibliothèque Nationale at
> Paris. A seventeenth-century edition is in the Widener Library at
> Harvard, and in the library of Miskatonic University at Arkham.
> Also in the library of the University of Buenos Ayres. Numerous
> other copies probably exist in secret . . . a fifteenth-century one is
> persistently rumoured to form part of the collection of a cele-
> brated American millionaire. A still vaguer rumour credits the
> preservation of a sixteenth-century Greek text in the Salem fam-
> ily of Pickman; but if it was so preserved, it vanished with the art-
> ist R. U. Pickman, who disappeared early in 1926. The book is
> rigidly suppressed by the authorities of most countries, and by all
> branches of organised ecclesiasticism. Reading leads to terrible
> consequences. It was from rumours of this . . . that R. W. Cham-
> bers is said to have derived the idea of his early novel *The King in
> Yellow*. (*MW* 53)

"History of the *Necronomicon*" blurs fact and fiction to question
consensus about textual stability. That the *Necronomicon* was
written by a "mad poet" seriously undermines its credibility; on
the other hand, the notion of madness as a state that gives access
to special knowledge enhances the cosmic stature of the book.
Madness becomes a language in its own right, a secret code of se-
mantics that obscures truth from some while revealing it to others. Lovecraft uses madness as a conduit to truth, making us
question whether we can so readily either dismiss or accept the
content of the *Necronomicon*.

    That the *Necronomicon* undermines the trust we put in lan-
guage to reveal truth to us is further highlighted by the fact that
the book had once been known by its "original title," *Al Azif*. The

name change (dis)places the *Necronomicon* into a different frame-work where it gains new contextual meaning. Furthermore, incon-sistent facts about the original author, Abdul Alhazred, exist; "many terrible and conflicting things are told" about his death. Al-hazred's sanity is questioned, casting him in an uneven light. Not to mention the numerous lost copies and translations of the *Ne-cronomicon* into foreign languages, causing further derivation from the root text. Who can say with certainty if the *Al Azif* text was in fact semantically anything like the *Necronomicon*?

Numerous concepts about writing, reading, and interpretation are bound together in Lovecraft's fictional grimoire. Dyer high-lights these connections when his reaction to an unnerving sound has him recall Danforth's ideas about another text, Poe's *Pym:*

> The new sound . . . upset much that we had decided . . . It was, Danforth later told me, precisely what he had caught in infinitely muffled form when at that spot beyond the alley-corner above the glacial level; and it certainly had a shocking resemblance to the wind-pipings we had both heard around the lofty mountain caves. . . . I will add another thing . . . if only because of the sur-prising way Danforth's impressions chimed with mine. Of course, common reading is what prepared us both to make the interpre-tation, though Danforth has hinted at queer notions about unsus-pected and forbidden sources to which Poe may have had access when writing his *Arthur Gordon Pym* a century ago. . . . In that fantastic tale there is a word of unknown but terrible and prodi-gious significance connected with the antarctic . . . screamed eter-nally by the gigantic, spectrally snowy birds of that malign region's core. *"Tekeli-li! Tekeli-li!"* That, I may admit, is exactly what we thought we heard conveyed by that sudden sound behind the ad-vancing white mist—that insidious musical piping over a singu-larly wide range. (*MM* 97)

Dyer's account of events is not entirely shaped by *his own* under-standing and experience. This is evident in phrases like "upset much that *we* had decided"; "it had a shocking *resemblance*"; "*common reading is what prepared us both* to make the interpretation"; "a word of *unknown* but terrible and prodigious significance *connected* with the antarctic"; "exactly what we *thought* we heard conveyed" [my emphasis]. Writing, reading, and interpretation of a text follow a similar course of suggestion and influence, of "textual infection," giving it room to shape itself separate from author and reader. Dyer speaks of a "sound behind the advancing white mist," recalling *Pym*'s human figure, whose "hue of skin . . . was . . . the perfect whiteness of snow" (206). If Lovecraft's "white mist" and Pym's mysterious, white, shrouded figure are indicative of the blank page, Dyer's relation of the "sound" advancing from behind it comes to represent the text in a state of becoming. Similarly, the phrase *Tekeli-li* is itself a word in a state of becoming. Its unfinished state can only allude. That Dyer attributes the sound as being "insidious over a singularly wide range" suggests the idea of the text concurrently independent of its author and readers. The *Necronomicon/Al Azif* is symbolic of this independence. There is a certain sense of danger inherent in a text once it has been fashioned and released to the world, where it can exert an influence separate from what its creator may have intended.[2] Language cannot be forced into a singular understanding. Misreading is as much a side effect of unstable language as it is uneven perception, and when our vision—what we rely on to reveal truth—is compromised, our ability to read our environments, like texts, are similarly altered.

Ideas about concealment and misreading appear early on in *Pym*. Having been stowed away on the *Grampus* along with his dog, Tiger, Pym becomes trapped in the claustrophobic hold of the whaling ship when mutiny breaks out on deck. Augustus (having snuck Pym aboard the ship), fearing for both their lives, cannot immediately reveal Pym to the rest of the crew. Instead, he smuggles Pym a written note, but which the latter is unable to read; Tiger has eaten all the wax, leaving Pym without a source of light.

Unable to discover Augustus's message, Pym finds himself literally, literarily, and figuratively in the dark. He reacts with both slow desperation and careful calculation: "The hold was so intensely dark that I could not see my hand, however close I would hold it to my face. The white slip of paper could barely be dis-

---

2. Uncannily, HPL's fictional *Necronomicon* has done just this, with fringe "religions" adopting the text (of which several commercial copies are available) as their bible of choice, using it to practice "Lovecraftian Magic."

cerned . . . not even . . . when I looked at it directly; by turning the exterior portions of the retina toward it—that is to say, by survey-ing it slightly askance, I found that it became in some measure perceptible" (78). Pym's initial reaction to the frustration he feels is a reflectively astute one; it is as if he is doing a scientific ex-periment, his approach to a solution a decidedly rational one. This rational approach alone, however, is not enough. The "gloom of [Pym's] prison" (78) reflects his dejected state of mind, induced by the failure of an analytical approach to yield results. This in turn leads him to doubt the origin of the note, "if indeed it were a note from [Augustus]" (78), and threatens to further disquiet his "al-ready enfeebled and agitated mind" (78). The note begins to dis-turb Pym; he knows *something* is written on the piece of paper but he cannot see *what*. The message on the "slip" of paper persis-tently slips away from Pym, who is unable to grasp its meaning. His predicament makes his "reasoning [and] imaginative faculties flicker" (78) until he finally comes up with a plan:

> At last an idea occurred to me which seemed rational, and which gave me cause to wonder, very justly, that I had not entertained it before. I placed the slip of paper on the back of a book, and, col-lecting the fragments of the phosphorus matches which I had brought from the barrel, laid them together upon the paper. I then, with the palm of my hand, rubbed the whole over quickly, yet steadily. A clear light diffused itself immediately throughout the whole surface; and had there been any writing upon it, I should not have experienced the least difficulty, I am sure, in reading it. Not a syllable was there, however—nothing but a dreary and unsatisfactory blank; the illumination died away in a few seconds, and my heart died away within me as it went. (78)

Because he is in possession of a piece of paper to which he has as-signed the meaning of "note" and "message," Pym is singularly con-cerned with how he will be able to read it in the ship's dark hold and what the note will reveal to him; that it in fact will *reveal* something to him. He does not consider that, once he has effected the needed light, the note may not grant him the revelation he expects to find. He assumes that all he needs is to see words for its meaning to become clear, but does not consider that this may not be enough for truth to become apparent.

Pym illustrates in this episode the same expectations readers have when reading a narrative set within the framework of a particular genre. Pym's expectation about being able to find meaning in Augustus's message demonstrates the changing implications inherent in language. The word "message," contained within the anxiety-ridden context of his situation, instils in Pym the expectation of revelation. "Message," a word, is transferred to a physical object, in this case, a piece of paper. Categorising it as such, Pym imbues the object within a fixed state, i.e. *the thing that Pym expects it to be*. When it gives Pym the opposite "answer" to the one he was expecting—a "dreary unsatisfactory blank"—all his expectations are destroyed, his hopes for revelation shattered. This outcome anticipates the inconclusive ending of the *Pym* narrative. However, Pym faces the blank of the cataract with welcome anticipation, willingly moving into its "embraces" (206). In the incident with the note, Pym fails to recognise that a blank—the other side of the page—has meaning, too; as his journey comes to an end, his growth as character is evidenced by his submission to uncertainty. A blank page is impossible to "read," but not impossible to interpret. Pym has no idea what meaning he will find inside the void, but this is what sets him free from creating an experience limited by expectations.

Back in the hold of the *Grampus*, when Pym eventually manages a brief light from a few remaining fragments of phosphorous, he sees no actual writing on Augustus's note. In a rage of frustration and anger he tears the note to pieces and flings it into the dark. Only afterwards does Pym realise he must have had the paper turned the wrong side up. What follows is his attempt to recover the note piece by piece and put it back together. He is able to retrieve the scattered bits of paper (only three in total, his emotional outburst having warped his perspective of the situation); however, because he cannot see, he has to guess at how the pieces fit together. He manages to ascertain which side of the paper has been written on by using his fingers, tracing the paper with "a delicate sense of feeling" (79) to distinguish any remaining particles of phosphorus on the uninscribed side. This "delicate sense of feeling" translates to an inner, emotional experience of a text/text. The process of reading, though influenced by external contexts, is a personal one. Pym's initial approach to reading the note suggests the idea that external contexts (the dark hold of the ship) are able to render a text "blank." This is when internal context becomes the focus, i.e. the context of the Self.

With the very last of the phosphorus, Pym is able partially to read the note's deconstructed message: *"blood—your life depends upon lying close"* (80). Because Pym is physically and mentally in the dark aboard the *Grampus*, the note disconcerts him. Its incomplete nature puts Pym in a physically and psychologically precarious position. Though he succeeds in reading *part* of it, this unsettles him even more than the prospect of not being able to read the note at all. Apparently, a half-truth is worse than no truth at all. Pym's recoil from the very thing he wanted to see is tangible in his reaction immediately following the illuminated message:

> Had I been able to ascertain the entire contents of the note—the full meaning . . . that admonition, even although it should have revealed a story of disaster the most unspeakable, could not, I am firmly convinced, have imbued my mind with one tithe of the harrowing and yet indefinable horror with which I was inspired by the fragmentary warning thus received. And "blood" . . . that word of all words . . . rife at all times with mystery, and suffering, and terror—how trebly full of import did it now appear, how chilly and heavily (disjointed, as it thus was, from any foregoing words to qualify or render it distinct) did its vague syllables fall, amid the deep gloom of my prison, into the innermost recesses of my soul! (80)

Pym is unnerved because some part of Augustus's message remains hidden. It is not a far stretch to imagine the above paragraph as written by Lovecraft, possibly about the contents of the *Necronomicon*. Just as the secret language of Lovecraft's grimoire both obscures and reveals, language out of context makes *some* sense; what remains unknown distresses our conventional paradigm for relaying information. Processing what remains unidentified is easier than coming to grips with what is unveiled but not understood. Pym cannot comprehend Augustus's note because he does not have all the information. Nonetheless, what is not verbally communicated is *still present*. In this context of obscured information, the word "blood" and all its connotative meanings gives Pym reason to experience an impending sense of doom.

Pym's recoil is from the "vague syllables" of language itself. The power he assigns to the word "blood" exists in Pym's mind, "amid the deep gloom of [his] prison," in reality being no different from others he refers to as vague. What makes *blood* significant is that it relates to physiology, and is intimately connected with keeping us alive.

Pym comes to mirror the text in which he exists. Both are inscribed, but not fixed. Personality is formed and *read* by a converging set of external and internal circumstances. Interpretation is a complex process because it exists within the space where these inscribed bodies come together. Pym's "dreary and unsatisfactory blank" is part of the initial response engendered by this process. The coming together of such disparate bodies of knowledge causes resistance. Reading densely layered texts like *Pym* and *Mountains* can make interpretation seem like a process where "illumination [dies] away"; this is mirrored in the "textual body" of the individual—in this case, Pym—his "heart [dying] away within [him] as [the illumination] went."

Pym's frustration and inability to read Augustus's message works as a metaphor for the reading process and the cognitive interface with language. For reading to occur, two concurrent processes exist side by side: the physical act of seeing words on paper and the intellectual understanding of said words. From language, we draw conclusions, imparted by the meanings and connotations ascribed to each individual word. These meanings are derived from complex associative processes that ultimately result in a representation of derived meaning and become visible as a word printed on the page. Simultaneously, meaning is present in the phenomenological processes of the mind—Pym's alternating flickers of reason and imagination. The convergence of these two routes to meaning destabilises the notion of fixed significance. We become conscious of *other* meanings, though they may not be revealed to us in full. This is one of the primary responses elicited by weird fiction. Reading and understanding becomes an uncanny experience due to the uncertain nature of *what* it is we understand, *how* we understand it, and whether we are ultimately *willing* to understand it.

Arthur Pym, unable to make out Augustus's message, is mirrored in our own reading experience of *Pym*. The text has "two sides"; as Pym and his companion Dirk Peters are reflections of one another, so too does the text inhabit alternate spaces of meaning. While we, unlike Pym in the hold of the *Grampus*, may not be physically trapped in darkness, our perceptions of what the text says can be limited by our approach to it, echoing Pym's approach to Augustus's message. Poe's subversion of genre traditions is an example of how the text may lead us astray. It is an adventure story in which the hero does not always act heroically; in which the hero commits heinous acts; in which the hero is saved by the type of person who we expect would normally want to harm him; in which the ending is open-ended and mysteriously vague.

David Punter makes reference to the literary itself as uncanny, "something that becomes haunted, that resists and twists away from a definition to produce 'other,' 'unauthorised' meanings; of never reaching a fixed point . . . history and trauma endlessly rewriting one another . . . without origin or closure . . . a distorted mirroring of the world in which it functions" (6). Augustus's structurally incoherent note destabilises the language paradigm, thwarting Pym's opportunity to access knowledge about his situation aboard the *Grampus*. He is effectively severed from the rest of his immediate world (everyone else aboard the *Grampus*) and forced to evaluate his every decision as something that exists in a vacuum, the note itself having no origin or closure due to its restructured and reinterpreted nature.

As already suggested, it is the apparently disjointed nature of *Pym* as a text that signals its complexity. Ink on paper is only one phase of textual transference. To make better sense of what we read we have to return to the telling of the story continually.[3] One reading simply cannot clarify the complexities of language as a tool for transferring meaning. This pattern of repetition is characteristic of Poe's work as well as Lovecraft's. Poe employs it on a

---

3. Like the cursed mariner in Coleridge's Romantic poem.

microcosmic level, applying repetitive textual patterns to the individual's search for integration. Lovecraft uses the returning motif on a broader, macrocosmic scale to habitually return his characters into the same, seemingly unsuccessful confrontation with the unknown. This return to text creates a constant doubling of the reading experience, always forcing us to reassess our perceptions of what is being said.

Like Poe's mirroring of Pym in Dirk Peters and *vice versa*, his overlay of fiction on top of historical accounts is one of many doubling instances in *Pym*. The past is not distinct. When it comingles with fiction, the result is an ambiguous text where the expression of the historical "real" from within a fictional framework threatens to destabilise our sense of reality. It shows the past in an unsettling light and undermines our perception of truth. This shared context results in a new reality that is as true as it is false. Pym accurately claims, "the facts of my narrative would prove of such a nature as to carry with them sufficient evidence of their own authenticity" (56). The claim is true exactly because *Pym*/Pym contradicts itself/himself. Words like "facts," "prove," "evidence," and "authenticity" are accurate only in the sense that they are used as words on the page. They may or may not reflect claims that would stand up when taken in context with the narrative as a whole; in some cases—and this is particularly true in the case of Lovecraft—intertextual signposts draw other texts into interpretation, further broadening the scope for meaning. "Sufficient evidence" is gained by the measures we follow in solidifying a particular avenue of interpretation. What needs to take place is a move away from genre expectations and implications, as they affect the narrative to the point where meaning is not necessarily derived, but *instilled*.

Danforth's psychosis, elicited when he and Dyer are being chased by a shoggoth, is expressed in phrases and names from other Lovecraftian stories. This intertextual appropriation reflects the liminal nature of fantastic narratives. Fantasy exploits the gap between information given to the reader and associations made by related, insinuated information. In doing so, the text makes accessible all narrative layers (including the ones that are hidden) and bonds the experience of the external reader to that of the diegetic reader, with each intertextual reference acting as a moment of forced sub-jective doubling (Dillon 111). *Mountains* becomes a conduit for transferring hidden knowledge; once it is read, it exists outside it-self. With access to all narrative levels, overlapping themes and characters, the reader is placed in a privileged position of being able to connect all intertextual references, in charge of a greater inter-pretative agency than the diegetic reader (111). We become agents of the uncanny through whom the text reveals itself extradiegeti-cally, furthermore exemplifying its indeterminate nature.

Returning briefly to Nicholas Roerich, Joshi suggests that Lovecraft's references to the painter may, besides being inspira-tional, serve the purpose of explaining a textual anomaly in *Moun-tains*. The vast superplateau that Dyer and Danforth discover in the Antarctic is equated in *Mountains* with Lovecraft's fictional Plateau of Leng, a location he first mentions in the short story "The Hound." "The Hound" places Leng in Asia, but Joshi suggests that Lovecraft's admiration for Roerich's images may have had him shift the plateau to the Antarctic (2.784). This intertextual correction mimics the destabilised perceptions of Pym and Dyer and adds to the notion of texts as changeable, conflicting, and un-stable, perhaps even *wrong*.

As touched upon earlier, parallels can be drawn between the changing nature of a fictional text and changing perspectives of history. Recalling Lovecraft's textual transposing of Leng, what in the past has been perceived as constant and true can always be subject to change. This change is subject to what we allow our-selves to believe as truth, and what we allow ourselves to ques-tion. Changing perspectives affect meaning in the way they represent the effect of textual content upon the external "body" of the text—the reader.

Near the end of *Mountains*, Dyer comments on his colleague Danforth's insanity, pointing out how the latter "has on rare occa-sions whispered disjointed and irresponsible things about 'the black pit', 'the carven rim', 'the proto-shoggoths', 'the windowless solids with five dimensions', 'the nameless cylinder', 'the elder pharos', 'Yog-Sothoth', 'the primal white jelly', 'the colour out of space' . . . 'the original, the eternal, the undying'" (*MM* 105–6). The Lovecraft reader will recognise Danforth's ravings as references to other Lovecraftian narratives; one is even the name of a Lovecraft story, "The Colour out of Space."

Through Danforth's psychosis, Lovecraft's narrative becomes self-referentially doubled in its audience. The intertextual allusions signify a layered dimension to *Mountains* that exists separate from the text. Danforth's glimpses of truth are akin to interpreting text, to see connections that are not textually represented but imply meaning nonetheless. Like his psychotic state of mind, our analysis hinges not only on taking evidence at face value, but on being able to see what is not there. Distinctions between author, implied author, and narrator are relevant in this instance, as are those between narratee, implied reader, and actual reader.

In his preface, Pym claims that "it will be understood that no fact is misrepresented in the first few pages which were written by Mr. Poe" (56); that it will be "unnecessary to point out where [Mr. Poe's] portion ends and my own commences" owing to "the difference in point of style" (56). The narrative, however, does not offer up any obvious stylistic differences, making it nearly impossible to separate the implied author from the narrator. Pym's statement is indicative of the reading process. His claim that the stylistic differences between himself and "Mr. Poe" will be obvious (when they are not) creates a disconnect between narratee, implied reader, and the real reader. This separation generates gaps that, while holding the narrative together, produce a significant amount of confusion about who is being addressed, and who is addressing them.

Pym's preface presents itself as an exercise in working through this textual uncertainty. Poe seems to suggest that any inclination to disbelief, however, is the failure of the reader to recognise truth from lies. Pym observes that "I could only hope for belief among my family, and those of my friends who have had reason . . . to put faith in my veracity" (55). The public, Pym fears, will "at large . . . regard what I should put forth as merely an impudent and ingenious fiction" (55). Without certainty as to the validity of the claims, *Pym* demands to be read *for what it is*, not as a text by Edgar Allan Poe. Poe even fictionalises himself within the text, creating yet another level of confusion between what "Mr. Poe" means and what the real Poe may have intended his narrative to be.

Pym's preface excludes and obscures as much as it claims to explain. This is an ever-present facet of the narrative—textual presence acting as a means of confusion. In his preface to *The Uncanny*, Nicholas Royle writes:

> A preface is conventionally signed, dated, placed in a fashion that distinguishes it from the text that follows. Written at the end, it comes at the beginning. It appears to gather everything together, to give an impression of order and mastery over what it prefaces. Uncanniness entails a sense of uncertainty and suspense . . . As such, it is often to be associated with an experience of the threshold, liminality, margins, borders, frontiers. Perceived as being the threshold of the work, the preface inhabits a peculiar limbo—part of *and* separate from, before *and* after, what follows it. (vii)

Pym's preface is uncanny. It is dated "New York, July, 1838"—ten years after the point at which the narrative breaks off with Pym and Peters, heading "with hideous velocity" in a canoe toward the rim of a chasm at the South Pole (Irwin 90). Irwin comments further on this oddity using a so-called "explanation" in the opening paragraph of *Pym*'s final note:

> The circumstances connected with the late sudden and distressing death of Mr. Pym are already well known to the public through the medium of the daily press. It is feared that the few remaining chapters which were to have completed his narrative, and which were retained by him, while the above were in type, for the purpose of revision, have been irrecoverably lost through the accident by which he perished himself. This, however, may prove not to be the case, and the papers, if ultimately found, will be given to the public. (207)

Irwin notes that, at the point where the narrative is interrupted, Pym and Peters are about to descend into the abyss; yet this appears never to have happened, as ten years later Pym is back and writing his book (90). Royle's observations about a preface dealing in thresholds are emphasized in this instance. Pym's "accident" serves the same function as Lovecraft's "clever aluminum alloy,"[4]

---

4. The metal from which most of the exploring equipment used in *At the Moun-*

withholding specifics when the narrative needs it most to engender stability. The ten years between Pym's encounter with the abyss, his death, and writing the preface, are a liminal space where textual and spatial boundaries have blurred. Adding to the uncanniness is the fact that the unspecified accident that takes Pym's life also takes the last chapters of his text. *Pym's* confusing structure highlights the complex relationship of author to text, as well as the consideration of a text as an object in its own right. *Pym* is about reading and writing:

> That Pym's voyage to the pole is a symbolic quest for the origin of writing, a quest embodied in the written narrative's own oblique questioning of its origin . . . is subtly evoked by Poe's displacement of the dangers of the abyss from the act of exploring to the act of writing. It is not that the writing stops with the interruption of the voyage but that the voyage stops with the interruption of the writing. Writing in search of its origins *is* the self-devolving voyage into the abyss. (Irwin 91)

This ambivalence between writer and written can be explored further in Pym's feelings toward his own narrative. Pym is uncertain about the notion of publication, claiming, "I had several reasons . . . for declining to do so, some of which were of a nature altogether private, and concern no person but myself; others not so much so" (55). That Pym does not disclose any of his motives makes the reader question the veracity of both the narrator and his story. His private reasons for not wanting to publish may well obscure aspects of the text that could shed light on many of its mysteries. Pym claims that, in a bid to give his version of events "the appearance of . . . truth," he cannot write "from mere memory" for fear of "unavoidable exaggeration . . . when detailing the events which have had powerful influence in exciting the imaginative faculties" (55). Like Roerich's paintings and their emotional effect on Lovecraft, Pym recognises that what he remembers is not altogether true, clouded as it is by "powerful influence" (55). Even before the narrative proper starts, Poe is telling us to take

---

tains of Madness is made, apparently making it light and easy to move around. See *MM* 4.

note of *what* Pym is saying, and *how* he is saying it. The contradictions of travel writing are on display here: On one hand, travel writing must necessarily be occupied with boring facts to retain a sense of authenticity; on the other hand, travel narratives are expected to be exciting and adventurous. By writing his experiences so that they fulfil both qualities, *Pym* becomes ever more incredible and fantastic, ever more removed from anything remotely resembling reality.

Pym is convinced by "Mr. Poe" to publish his experiences *"under the garb of fiction"* (56). At this point in the narrative, we are presented by a text that is supposedly true but passed off as fiction, potentially inflamed by the imagination and the conflicting nature of memory. With the stipulation that "Mr. Poe" keep Pym's real name in the narrative, Pym consents to tell his story. However, the "shrewdness and common sense of the public" (55)—despite Poe's name appearing as author of the first group of Pym's accounts—"were not at all disposed to receive [Pym's account] as a fable" (56). Establishing itself in words as travel literature is seemingly enough for the narrative to prove its authenticity. In this instance, genre overrides the authority of narrator.

Tekeli-li[5] is the most concretely textual connection between *Pym* and *Mountains*. The word signifies the gap between written representation and the meaning we extract from it. *Tekeli-li* signals *something;* it instils fear, but the repetitive use of the word without fixed meaning suspends it in an indistinct textual space. For the Tsalalians it is a verbal expression of the taboo associated with the colour white, eliciting in them "horror, rage and intense curiosity" (Poe 190). As Pym has never seen men as black as the Tsalalians, the Tsalalians have probably never seen men as white as Pym. In this instance, *Tekeli-li* becomes an expression that rec-

---

5. Various meanings have been attributed to the phrase, including likening it to the Biblical MENE MENE TEKEL UPHARSIN, the writing on the wall from the book of Daniel, foreshadowing the demise of the Babylonian empire. (See Irwin, *American Hieroglyphics* 231–32.) Translated, this roughly means "to be weighed and found wanting." In the Pacific context, according to Edward Tregear's *The Maori-Polynesian Comparative Dictionary* (Lyon & Blair, 1891), Ridgely splits the word into *tiki* (god) and *lili* (angry). (See J. V. Ridgely, "The Continuing Puzzle of *Arthur Gordon Pym*," in *Poe Newsletter* 3, no. 1 (June 197): 5–6).

ognises the unknown, but fails to reveal it.

The word is nonetheless an integral part of Tsalalian communication. The impenetrable nature of this foreign language is most likely the reason Pym and the crew of the *Jane Guy* are led into a false sense of security. All but Pym and Peters eventually pay for this with their lives. *Pym* highlights that language is not universal and can develop separate from us. Language has agency—an uncanny thought, considering its uniquely human origins.

In *Mountains*, the subterranean horrors that have survived in the ancient Antarctic city of the Old Ones, the shoggoths, repeatedly cry out one word: *Tekeli-li!* The shoggoths have learnt the word from the Old Ones, but have likely appropriated it to mean something different from its original meaning. For the Tsalalians and the shoggoths, *Tekeli-li* is perhaps rather a meaningful *sound* as opposed to a word. In both *Pym* and *Mountains*, it is a word that is ceaselessly being shouted rather than being written down. This separation from language allows the word to be assimilated by Nature. In the moments before Pym and Parker are pulled into the cataract, Pym notes that "Many gigantic and pallidly white birds flew continuously now from beyond the veil, and their scream was the eternal *Tekeli-li!* as they retreated from our vision" (Poe 205–6). The word becomes ever more inexplicable, made even more bizarre by the intertextual relationship it holds to *Pym* and *Mountains*. In the two texts the word is used by native islanders, giant, pallid birds, star-headed aliens from outer space, shoggoths, and a madman. Pym's description of the word as *eternal* supports the notion that *Tekeli-li!* does not mean anything *as such*.[6] Rather, it signifies the breakdown of language in the face of the unknown and a reversion back to ritualistic state where repetition overtakes logic to connect us with the divine. It is a symbol of the failure of language to produce meaning indefinitely. Irwin suggests that if the ultimate root of Tsalal is *sl* (shadow) and that of its polar opposite *Tekeli-li* is *tkl* (original, fixed spot), then the two words combined are a "hieroglyph of Pym's final scene—'the shadow at the pole'—a pictograph of that shadowing or doubling

---

6. "Tekeli-li" has become a hybrid word, reflecting several inferred but not identified meanings.

that is the origin of the bipolar oppositions of the linguistic world" (232–33). The end of Pym's journey marks the end of the text as well. Within the void, language does not exist; therefore, the text cannot continue. Text/the text itself is an unequivocal border and a limit to what can be represented.

Works Cited

Burleson, Donald R. *Lovecraft: Disturbing the Universe*. Lexington: University Press of Kentucky, 1990.

Dillon, Sarah. *David Mitchell: Critical Essays*. Canterbury: Gylphi, 2011.

Harvey, Ronald C. *The Critical History of Edgar Allan Poe's* The Narrative of Arthur Gordon Pym: *"A Dialogue with Unreason."* New York: Garland, 1998.

Irwin, John T. *American Hieroglyphics: The Symbol of the Egyptian Hieroglyphics in the American Renaissance*. Baltimore: Johns Hopkins University Press, 1983.

Joshi, S. T. *I Am Providence: The Life and Times of H. P. Lovecraft*. New York: Hippocampus Press, 2010. 2 vols.

Nelson, Victoria. *The Secret Life of Puppets*. Cambridge, MA: Harvard University Press, 2001.

Poe, Edgar Allan. *Essays and Reviews*. New York: Library of America, 1984.

Poe, Edgar Allan. *The Narrative of Arthur Gordon Pym*. In Poe's *The Imaginary Voyages*. Edited by Burton R. Pollin. Boston: Twayne, 1981.

Punter, David. *The Literature of Terror: A History of Gothic Fictions from 1765 to the Present Day*. 2nd rev. ed. London: Longman, 1996. 2 vols.

Royle, Nicholas. *The Uncanny*. New York: Routledge, 2003.

Thompson, G. R. "The Arabesque Design of Pym." in *Poe's Pym: Critical Explorations*, ed. Richard Kopley. Durham, NC: Duke University Press, 1992.

Briefly Noted

Lovecraftian fiction continues to be a booming industry, with the publication of such anthologies as Ross E. Lockhart's *The Book of Cthulhu* (Night Shade, 2011), Paula Guran's *New Cthulhu* (Prime, 2011), and S. T. Joshi's *Black Wings II: New Tales of Lovecraftian Horror* (PS Publishing, 2012). Forthcoming volumes include an anthology of historical Lovecraftian tales being assembled by Darrell Schweitzer (PS Publishing), a second *Book of Cthulhu* by Lockhart (Night Shade), and Joshi's *Black Wings III* (PS Publishing). Joshi is also working on a two-volume set, *The Madness of Cthulhu*, to be published by Titan Books, the first volume of which will feature tales loosely based on *At the Mountains of Madness*, the second to include stories of a more general Lovecraftian sort.

Lovecraft's 1937 Diary

Kenneth W. Faig, Jr.

Perhaps the most widely circulated news story relating to H. P. Lovecraft relates to the diary he had commenced to keep for 1937. S. T. Joshi tells the story succinctly in *I Am Providence* (2.1009):

> On the evening of March 15 the *Providence Evening Bulletin* ran an obituary, full of errors large and small; but it made mention of the "clinical notes" Lovecraft kept of his condition while in the hospital—notes that "ended only when he could no longer hold a pencil." This feature was picked up by the wire services, and an obituary entitled "Writer Charts Fatal Malady" appeared in the *New York Times* on March 16. Frank Long, Lovecraft's best friend, learnt of his death from reading this obituary.

The fate of Lovecraft's 1937 diary is not known. We do know that Robert H. Barlow apparently had it in his possession on 31 March 1937, when he wrote a lengthy letter to August Derleth from the YMCA's William Sloane House in New York City. This letter is currently among the Derleth Papers at the Wisconsin Historical Society (WHS) in Madison. Starting on the third page of his referenced letter, Barlow copied out for Derleth "items from Howard Lovecrafts' [*sic*] 1937 diary," including (i) a "remembrancer" section of personal data and birthdays, (ii) an alphabetical list of friends/correspondents ("addresses"), and (iii) "entries in HPs 1937 diary," the famous "death diary," with transcribed entries dated between January 1 and March 11. Barlow transcribed complete entries only for January 1 and 2 and March 9, 10, 11; for other dates, he provided "condensations." From the reference to "page covering [January] 17–23" among the condensed entries, we may surmise that the diary purchased by Lovecraft contained one page per week. Since 1937 commenced on Friday, January 1, Lovecraft probably had extra room for his entries for the first two days of the year before the regular weekly sequence commenced on Sunday, January 3. In addition, to the principal diary section, commercial diary books of this kind typically also contained sections for addresses, personal data and birthdays.

Lovecraft does not appear to have been a diary-keeper by custom. The most significant exception is the diary he kept for January 1925–January 1926, which was first published in *Collected Essays* 5.149–79. This diary corresponded to the first thirteen months of the period that he spent at 169 Clinton Street in Brooklyn, after his wife Sonia departed to take a job in the Midwest. Writers have speculated that Lovecraft maintained this diary in order to facilitate the day-by-day accounts of his life in New York City which he sent primarily to his aunt Lillian D. Clark during this period. Then in 1932–33 Lovecraft purchased another notebook that he used primarily for notes on weird fiction. "Weird Story Plots" and "Notes on Weird Fiction" from this notebook were published in *Collected Essays* 2.153–69 and 169–75 respectively. The "remembrancer" section of this diary was published in *Collected Essays* 5.264. Some time during the fall of 1936, sensing that his health was deteriorating, he penned his "Instructions in Case of Decease," which survives in the form of a transcription that Annie E. P. Gamwell made for Robert H. Barlow (published in *Collected Essays* 5.237–40). We may surmise that he also purchased a commercial diary for 1937 during this period, with the intention of better organizing his records. The "addresses" section of the 1937 diary, for example, contains significantly more names than are found in "Instructions in Case of Decease."[1]

---

1. The only names listed in "Instructions in Case of Decease" which do not appear in the "addresses" section of the 1937 diary are T. Kemp Boardley, Jr., James Ferdinand Morton, Charles W. "Tryout" Smith, and Elizabeth Toldridge. The 90 names included in the "addresses" section of the 1937 diary include 36 names included in "Instructions in Case of Decease" and 54 names excluded from that document. Excluding Annie E. Phillips Gamwell, just 40 names appear in "Instructions." Of course, the document concerned the actual disposition of HPL's effects and therefore likely contained only his closest and most important friends. In addition, HPL made one disposition of all his amateur journalism papers, to

We may speculate concerning the fate of the original 1937 diary. It seems likely—although it is not absolutely certain—that Barlow had it with him when he wrote to August Derleth from New York City on 31 March 1937.[2] (The alternative is that he made a transcription of the diary contents while he was still in Providence and relied upon that transcription when writing to Derleth from New York City.) Whether he retained the diary, or returned it to Annie Gamwell after extracting data from it, is not known. For either Barlow or Gamwell, the diary would certainly have been a treasured keepsake—although potentially a painful one. It is possible that one of them eventually elected to destroy the diary because of its personal, painful character. Barlow sent virtually all his Lovecraft material to Brown University, some of it passing first through August Derleth in Sauk City. The major exceptions were the manuscript of "The Shadow out of Time," which he gave to his student June Evelyn Ripley (1915–1994), and his own letters from Lovecraft, which his literary executor George T. Smisor sent to Brown University following his death in 1951. (The manuscript of "The Shadow out of Time" reached Brown University years later, the gift of the children of June Evelyn Ripley.) If retained by Annie Gamwell, it is possible that the 1937 di-

---

Edwin Hadley Smith for the Library of Amateur Journalism (then at the Franklin Institute in Philadelphia, PA), so he may not have seen any need to include any but his closest friends in the amateur journalism hobby. Note that while James Ferdinand Morton and Charles W. ("Tryout") Smith are not included in the "addresses" section of the 1937 diary, they are included in the very short listing of birthdays in the 1937 diary. To some extent, the "addresses" section of the 1937 diary, while considerably more extended than that of "Instructions in Case of Decease," appears to contain a significant number of names whose principal connection with HPL was either relatively minor or significantly removed in time. It is possible that HPL compiled the "addresses" section shortly after Christmas 1936 and included a number of relatively minor associates from whom he had received Christmas greetings. It is important to remember that we have only Barlow's transcriptions of the 1937 diary in his letter of 31 March 1937 to August W. Derleth; it is possible that he made errors in the transcriptions.

2. Christopher M. O'Brien related to the author accounts that some members of the Kalem Club in New York City resented Barlow's display of the 1937 diary during his stay there following HPL's death. If these accounts are to be credited, Barlow apparently had the 1937 diary with him in New York City following HPL's death.

ary was missed by bookseller H. Douglass Dana when he went through the contents of Lovecraft's library following the death of Mrs. Gamwell in 1941. If retained by Barlow, it is possible that Smisor missed the 1937 diary in going through Barlow's literary effects. Of course, it is also possible that either Mrs. Gamwell or Barlow may have given the 1937 diary to another person before their deaths. If the 1937 diary were to be recovered today, I speculate that a bookseller might ask $50,000 or more for it because of its poignant personal contents. Only major letter groups or major holograph fiction manuscripts would be likely to be priced higher.

Regardless of the fate of the original 1937 diary, we are fortunate to have the Barlow transcriptions that survive in his letter to August Derleth. R. Alain Everts first published the "death diary" transcriptions in *The Death of a Gentleman* (1987).[3] S. T. Joshi included Barlow's "death diary" transcriptions in *Collected Essays* 5 (2006). The "addresses" section of the 1937 diary is first published in the Appendix of this essay. The addresses in particular contain a number of individuals elsewhere unmentioned, or little noticed, in the vast secondary literature concerning Lovecraft. I have added a few annotations on some of the more obscure individuals in the notes for the appendix. For example, he was surprised to find not two, but four, Providence residents in the addresses:

[12] Harry Brobst, Hayward Apts., 61 Beacon Ave.
[23] C. M. Eddy, Jr., 1 Providence St.
[25] Thomas S. Evans, 145 Medway St.
[86] Frederick A. Wesley, 6 Hammond St.

Harry Brobst (1909–2010) was probably the last of Lovecraft's surviving close personal friends. Brobst knew Lovecraft while working as a nurse and attending school in Providence in the 1930s. Clifford Martin Eddy, Jr. (1896–1967) and his wife, Muriel (Gammons) Eddy, knew Lovecraft from an earlier period, and Clifford collaborated with Lovecraft on several projects, including work for the

---

3. The "death diary" transcriptions appear on pp. 25–28 of Everts's work. He reproduced the final entries from March 9, 10, 11 in facsimile from Barlow's letter of 31 March 1937 on p. 22 and also published the contents of the "remembrancer" (personal data) and the "birthdays" sections of the 1937 diary on p. 17.

magician Harry Houdini. The names of Thomas S. Evans and Frederick A. Wesley were, however, completely unknown to me when he first encountered them in the 1937 diary. David E. Schultz subsequently informed me (e-mail dated 14 September 2011) that Thomas S. Evans receives three mentions in the surviving Lovecraft correspondence, while Frederick A. Wesley receives none. Lovecraft wrote to Frank Belknap Long on "Sun's Day April 1931":

> This epistle is a two-day job, broken by one of my very rare excursions into the outside world. The amiable if not excessively profound Thomas S. Evans—he of the dramatick and playwriting predilections—called me up and urged me to accompany him to a concert of the newly organised Providence Concert Band in historick Infantry Hall (now remodell'd on the interior, tho' still possesst of that nauseous Victorian belfry), and having no striking objection, I acquiesced.

After he had departed for his southern journey of that year, Lovecraft wrote to Lillian D. Clark on 5 May 1931: "This outfit which I put on for the Infantry Hall concert with Evans is going to see St. Augustine yet—though it may not last till next Christmas" (ms., JHL). He wrote again to Mrs. Clark on 30 May 1931: "Interested to hear that Evans called up. I wasn't sure about how we left the telephoning business, and that accursed typing job erased nearly everything else from my memory. I have dropped Evans one or two cards from along my route" (ms., JHL). Evans was still on a 1934 "List of Correspondents to Whom Postcards Have Been Sent" (CE 5.267).

Thomas Stuart Evans was born in Providence on 1 February 1885, the son of (Ashton[4]) English-born engineer Thomas Evans (1841–1927) and his Pawtucket-born wife Martha Alice (Pollett) Evans (1844–1921). The elder Thomas Evans, the son of Ephraim Evans and Hannah (Jenkins) Evans, had emigrated in 1863 and become a naturalized citizen in 1875. His wife Martha Alice Pollett was the daughter of William Pollett (1820–1888) and Susan (Scott) Pollett (c. 1811–1888). The elder Thomas's and his wife Martha's daughter Anna Louise Evans (1868–1949), who like her brother Thomas never married, was born in Providence on 17 Feb-

---

4. Probably Ashton-under-Lyne in Greater Manchester.

ruary 1868. There is a 22 February 1881 Rhode Island death record
for Winslow J. Evans, age 18, with kin Thomas S. and Anna L. Evans. I do not know whether Winslow was a full-sibling, half-
sibling, or other relation of Thomas S. and Anna L. Evans. When
Thomas and Martha (Pollett) Evans and their children were enumerated at 94 Almy Street in the 1900 census, Thomas was working as a steam engineer and his daughter Anna as a bookkeeper,
while son Thomas S. was still in school. In 1910, Thomas S. Evans,
age 22, was living at 410–412 West 23rd Street in New York City,
pursuing his career as a theatrical actor. By 1920, however, son
Thomas S. was back in his father's home, then at 405 Lloyd Avenue in Providence. The elder Thomas Evans was continuing to
work as a mechanical engineer, while no occupations were listed
for either daughter Anna or son Thomas. Martha (Pollett) Evans
died in Providence on 22 May 1921, only two days before Lovecraft's mother died on 24 May 1921. By 1923, the widowed Thomas, still working as a consulting engineer at 75 Westminster St.
(room 15), was living at 145 Medway Street, which remained the
family home until the death of daughter Anna L. Evans on April
30, 1949. The senior Thomas Evans, age 86, died at home of a
cerebral hemorrhage on 17 June 1927. Son Thomas and daughter
Anna continued on in the family home at 145 Medway Street. In
the 1930 city directory, Thomas S. Evans still listed his occupation
as actor. When Evans died on 8 November 1940, five days after
suffering a heart attack, he was a self-employed cosmetician working from his home at 145 Medway Street. The death certificate
noted that he had been employed in this occupation for ten years.[5]
He and his sister Anna L. Evans were both buried by Horace B.
Knowles' Sons, in the family lot at Pocasset Cemetery.

Thomas S. Evans's interest in the theater would certainly have
provided the basis for a friendship with Lovecraft. How they originally became acquainted is not known to me. Evans was more than
five years older than Lovecraft, so it does not seem likely that they

---

5. A 1935 Rhode Island state census punch card uncovered by Chris Perridas on
FamilySearch recorded Evans's usual occupation as actor (independent) and his
present occupation as chemist (research). It also recorded that he was employed
for twelve months in 1935.

were schoolboy acquaintances. They lost their mothers within two days of each other, so one wonders if they might have become acquainted at the Horace B. Knowles' Sons funeral parlor, patronized by both families. Is it possible that Evans's knowledge of theatrical makeup qualified him for employment by one or more Providence undertakers as a cosmetician? Of course, we also know from Sonia Lovecraft's memoir that her husband suffered from ingrown facial hairs—whether this might have provided an occasion for Lovecraft to meet a cosmetician remains unknown. A detailed check of Providence directories 1885–1937 might reveal whether Lovecraft and Evans were at any time close neighbors. Otherwise, it does not seem particularly likely that we will gain more knowledge of the friendship of H. P. Lovecraft and Thomas S. Evans in the future.

I regret that the friendship of H. P. Lovecraft and Frederick Allen Wesley will likely remain an even tougher puzzle to resolve. Frederick Allen Wesley was born in Providence on 14 October 1885 and died in the same city of colon cancer on 20 April 1948. His death certificate shows his parents as Warren B. Wesley and Martha A. (——) Wesley, both born in Plymouth, Massachusetts. However, the 1900 census shows Fred A. Wesley, son, born October 1888 Rhode Island, living in the 42 Hudson Street household of his father Martin A. Wesley, born December 1853 in Connecticut, of Connecticut-born parents and his mother Martha A. Wesley, born March 1861 in Rhode Island of a Massachusetts-born father and a Rhode Island-born mother. Martin Wesley was then working as a shoe store manager. He and Martha had been married for fifteen years and Fred was their only child. Perhaps Martha's Massachusetts-born father represents the family link with Plymouth.

By 1910, Fred A. Wesley and his wife Corinne A. Wesley had their own home at 330 Plainfield Street. Fred was working as a streetcar conductor. Their son Frederick R. Wesley, born 6 January 1910, was also living in the household. The 1910 census confirms the Connecticut birth of Fred Wesley's father. Fred's wife Corinne was the daughter of a Philippines-born father and a New York–born mother. When he registered for the draft in 1917, Fred was working as a steamfitter's helper for Smith Gibbs Company at 11 South Main Street in Providence. He and his wife resided at 161 Newell Avenue in Pawtucket. A second son, Robert H.

Wesley, had been born to Fred and Corinne on 29 November 1913. The 1930 census recorded Frederick A. Wesley residing at 6 Hammond St. in Providence and working as a furnace steamfitter. He was then divorced from his former wife Corinne, who married John (Gorm) A. Giguere in Providence on 20 April 1926. In 1930, the Giguere family, including the two Wesley stepsons, were living at 27 Woodlawn Avenue in Pawtucket. John (Gorm) A. Giguere, of French-Canadian parentage, was working as a streetcar motorman, while his wife Corrine M. Giguere worked as a cook's helper at a golf club. On 26 August 1930, Frederick A. Wesley married Edna C. Allen in Providence. When he registered for the draft in 1942, Frederick Allen Wesley was working for Brown & Sharpe and residing with his second wife Edna at 243 Adelaide Avenue in Providence. In the 1944 city directory, Frederick continued to work as a helper at Brown & Sharpe and resided at 222 Thurbers Avenue. He worked as a machinist's helper at Brown & Sharpe for seven and a half years and only stopped working in January 1948, a few weeks before his death on 20 April 1948. He was still a resident of 222 Thurbers Avenue at the time of his death, although he spent the last five days of his life at Price Nursing Home. On 23 April 1948, he was buried at Grace Church Cemetery. His widow Edna was 52 years old at the time of her husband's death. His second son Robert H. Wesley died in August 1961 in Rhode Island, aged only 47. His first son Frederick R. Wesley died in February 1981 in Scituate, Massachusetts, aged 71.

Like Thomas S. Evans, Frederick Allen Wesley seems too much older than Lovecraft to have been a likely schoolboy acquaintance. We know that Lovecraft vastly appreciated the steam heat furnished by Brown's John Hay Library when he lived at the adjoining 66 College Street. Whether Wesley or his employer might have been under contract with Brown to provide maintenance for the heating system we do not know. Certainly, such a circumstance could have provided an opportunity for Lovecraft and Wesley to meet. What would have formed their common ground is more difficult to speculate. Lovecraft was willing to admit acquaintances from all walks of life and seems to have been friendly even with the Negress Delilah Townsend (c. 1870–1944), who provided housekeeping services for Lillian D. Clark. As far as we know, Lovecraft's butcher, baker, and candlestick-maker do not occupy places of honor in the "addresses" section of his 1937 diary.

One possibility that may merit consideration is that Lovecraft's acquaintance with Evans and Wesley may have been related. The senior Thomas Evans's occupation was recorded as steam engineer in the 1900 U.S. census and Frederick Allen Wesley was working as a steamfitter by the time he registered for the draft in 1917. From the recollections of Brown University professor Robert Kenny, confirmed by Harry Brobst, we know that Lovecraft held a job as a ticket seller at a downtown Providence movie theater in the late 1920s (Joshi, *I Am Providence* 2.821). It seems likely that Lovecraft was under some pressure from his uncle Edwin E. Phillips (1864–1918)—and from his mother and his aunts after Edwin's death—to secure gainful employment in order to supplement the family finances. I wonder if Lovecraft might have worked at some time in the downtown Providence office of Thomas Evans Senior, thereby making the acquaintances of his son Thomas Stuart Evans and of steamfitter Frederick Allen Wesley. Thomas Evans Senior was a contemporary of Lovecraft's uncle Dr. Franklin Chase Clark (1847–1915), who might possibly have helped his nephew secure a position. If Lovecraft's relationships with Thomas S. Evans and Frederick A. Wesley are linked, two lesser possibilities are that (1) they participated with him in the Men's Club of Providence's First Universalist Church in 1908–12 or (2) they participated with him in the Providence Amateur Press Club in 1914–16. Evans was living in New York City in 1910, and neither Evans nor Wesley is mentioned in the surviving issues of the *Providence Amateur*. While it seems unlikely that we will ever know more about the relationships of Evans and of Wesley with Lovecraft than the little we know today, their presence in his life, as documented in the 1937 diary, seems worth noting for what we can make of it.

I hope that the "addresses" section of Lovecraft's 1937 diary will continue to yield useful information concerning his friends and relationships. I have attempted to shed some light on some of the more obscure individuals in the notes, but even where individuals can be identified from the census or by other means, the connection with Lovecraft sometimes remains unknown. The opening of the 1940 U.S. census in 2012 may provide some additional clues. Perhaps it is not beyond hope that the 1937 diary it-self will one day be recovered. We can be grateful that the young Robert H. Barlow took the time to transcribe most of the 1937 diary contents for August Derleth from his New York City YMCA room on 31 March 1937. Barlow's intention in transcribing the "addresses" section of the diary was doubtless to provide Derleth with as many leads as possible for the already-projected collection of Lovecraft's letters, finally realized in five volumes from Arkham House in 1965–76. We can surmise that Barlow transcribed or summarized the diary entries from January 1 through March 11 because they so movingly recorded the final illness of his friend.

I wish to acknowledge the assistance of Marcos Legaria, Christopher M. O'Brien, Chris Perridas, David E. Schultz, and the Rhode Island State Archives. However, I remain solely responsible for all opinions and any errors contained in this paper. Readers should refer to S. T. Joshi and David E. Schultz's *An H.P. Lovecraft Encyclopedia* (2001) as a primary reference for most of the names included in Lovecraft's 1937 diary. My objective in the notes for this paper is to provide supplementary information about lesser-known associates of Lovecraft, such as his Providence friends Thomas S. Evans and Frederick A. Wesley discussed in the body of the paper. Evans [25] and Wesley [86] have in common with Curtis F. Myers [53], Horatio L. Smith [71], and C. L. Stuart [78] the fact that I can identify them with fair certainty, but have not been able to establish the basis of their relationships with Lovecraft. Establishing the connection of any of these five individuals with Lovecraft would constitute exciting progress. For Bell c/o Dixon [6] of Nebraska and Geo. FitzPatrick [29] of Sydney, Australia, I have not even identified a specific individual as Lovecraft's correspondent.

With ongoing conversion of vital records and other information to electronic form, it seems probable that future generations will know far more about Lovecraft and his associates than we know today. I hope that the readers of the future will forgive my errors; if I have succeeded in shining a little light into some obscure corners, I will rest content. The vital statistics appearing in this paper and its notes are not fully cited, but most (including all U.S. census, draft registration, and Social Security Administration Death Master File references) can be readily validated using Ancestry.com. The Rhode

Island State Archives provided me with death records establishing many of the facts about Thomas S. Evans [25], Frederick A. Wesley [86], and their families; the Archives also provided a death record for Evelyn M. Staples. The acronym SSDI stands for the Social Security Administration Death Master File. The acronym SSN stands for Social Security Number, cited only by state of issuance.

APPENDIX

ITEMS FROM LOVECRAFT'S 1937 DIARY
TRANSCRIPTION BY ROBERT H. BARLOW
(Robert H. Barlow to August W. Derleth, March 31, 1937, WHS)

Editorial Notes:
1. Annotations by Barlow appear in italics.
2. Correspondent numbers in brackets added by me.
3. Correspondent numbers followed by an asterisk indicate an individual not included in "Instructions in Case of Decease."

Height 5 foot 11[6]
Weight 145
Sleeve length 34
Gloves 7¼
Collar 14½
Hat 7
Shoes 8½

Birthdays

SL 1-14-1887[7]
MS 4-26-18[8]

---

6. These data can be compared with the data published as "Remembrancer" in CE 5.264, which derives from a separate notebook used mainly by HPL for "Weird Story Plots" and "Notes on Weird Fiction" as published in CE 2.153–69 and 169–75 respectively.

7. Samuel Loveman (1887–1976).

8. Margaret Sylvester (1918–2010). Christopher M. O'Brien discovered an SSDI record for Margaret (Sylvester) Ronan (SSN issued NY before 1951), born 25 April 1918 (only one day different from the date of birth shown in HPL's di-

FBL 4-27-02[9]
EAE 10-4-67[10]
JFM 10-18-70[11]
CWS 10-24-52[12]

Addresses

[1*] Fred Anger 2700 Webster St Berkeley Calif
[2*] Victor E. Bacon[13] 1965 A Bund Ave St Louis Mo (*amateur journalist prob. not in touch recently*)
[3*] J. O. Baily Box 414 Chapel Hill, N.C. (*might have good letters in conn. with science-fiction thesis*)
[4*] F. Lee Baldwin, Gen. Deliv. Grangeville, Idaho
[5] (Barlow)
[6*] Bell[14]—15 Pine Ave., Old Orchard, Ne. c/o E Dixon, Box 292 (sic)

---

ary), died 14 December 2010, Hudson, Summit County, OH.

9. Frank Belknap Long (1901–1994). Long's record in SSDI indicates that he was born 27 April 1901, not 1902.

10. Ernest Arthur Edkins (1867–1946).

11. James Ferdinand Morton (1870–1941).

12. Charles W. ("Tryout") Smith (1852–1948).

13. Victor E. Bacon (1905–1997) was HPL's recruit for the Hoffman-Daas branch of the United Amateur Press Association and served as its final Official Editor in 1925–26. Bacon was also President of the National Amateur Press Association in 1930–31. His own amateur journal was *Bacon's Essays*.

14. I did not find the surnames Bell and Dixon in membership lists of the National Amateur Press Association or the United Amateur Press Association in the 1930s. (HPL's "Hoffman-Daas" faction was extinct by this time, but the "Erford-Noel" faction based in Seattle continued and in fact experienced several subsequent splits.) No place named Old Orchard appears in NE gazetteers. Johnson County, NE, has a small community named Crab Orchard (population 49 in the 2000 census); it is possible that Barlow mistranscribed "Crab" as "Old," given the similar shapes of the initial and final letters. However, Internet maps show no Pine Street in Crab Orchard. The 1930 U.S. census recorded a Nancy (or Waney) C. Bell, a white female widow age 78, born NC of NC-born parents, in nearby Sterling, Johnson County, NE. There was a Millard D. Bell, a 29-year-old school superintendent born NE of NE-born parents, in Edgar, Clay County, NE, in the 1930 U.S. census. He and his wife Elisa M. Bell, age 28, born NE of German-born parents, had been married for four years. There was also Ira E. Bell, a 46-year-old farmer, born NE of WI-born

[7] Mrs. D. W. Bishop 5001 Sunset Dr. KC Mo
[8*] Jim Blish 69 Halsted St E. Orange NJ
[9] Robt. Bloch, 620 E. Knapp St, Milwaukee Wis
[10*] J E C Blossom,[15] 117 Church St., Rutland Vt
[11*] Hyman Bradofsky, 315 W Second St, Pomona Calif. (*amateur journalist, not likely to have remarkable material*)
[12] Harry Brobst,[16] Hayward Apts, 61 Beacon Ave, Prov RI
[13*] Paul J Campbell,[17] 5720 Westmoreland Pl, E St Louis Ill
[14*] E H Cole, 53 Freeman St, Wollaston Mass
[15] W. Paul Cook 1305 Missouri Ave, E St Louis Ill.

---

father and VA-born mother, in Logan township, Antelope County, NE. He had been married for ten years to his wife Ora A. Bell, age 41, born NE of NE-born parents. They had a son Nal C. Bell, age 4, born NE. No connection with HPL is known for any of these persons. HPL did have relatives bearing the Dixon surname, since Whipple V. Phillips's sister Abbie Emeline Phillips (1839–1873) had married Henry D. Dixon (1835–1905) in Sterling CT on October 26, 1859. The Dixons had four sons, three of whom, Wilfred H. (b. 1861), Walter S. (b. 1865), and Alva J. (b. 1867), were living with their families in CT when the 1920 U.S. census was taken. One son, Whipple Van Buren Phillips Dixon, born 31 July 1870, died 29 February 1872, as a result of a scalding accident.

15. Josephine E. Crane Blossom was born 17 July 1861, Mayatta KS, and died 4 January 1952, Rutland VT. In the 1900 U.S. census, she was recorded in Shrewsbury, Rutland County, VT in the household of her husband William R. Blossom, born April 1854 VT of VT-born parents, a physician. They had then been married twenty-one years and Josephine was the mother of seven children, of whom five were then living, all of them in the paternal household: Elsie C. (b. August 1885 VT), Ethel C. (b. March 1889 VT), Fay E. (b. August 1890 KS), Franklin O. (b. August 1890 KS), and Wilhelmina J. (b. August 1896 VT). Josephine Blossom was active as a poet in amateur journalism.

16. Harry Kern Brobst (1909–2010) was probably the last survivor of HPL's personal friends. A memoir of Brobst by Christopher M. O'Brien was published in the *Lovecraft Annual* 4 (2010).

17. Paul Jonas Campbell was born 8 November 1884 in Georgetown IL. He married fellow amateur journalist Eleanor J. Barnhart as his second wife in Chicago on 4 October 1918. A longtime stalwart of the United Amateur Press Association, he died 16 August 1945 in East Saint Louis, IL. His memoir of his career in the amateur journalism hobby, "Adventures in Amateur Journalism" (originally published in *Courage* for December 1941–January 1942), was republished in the *Fossil* for January 2006 (www.thefossils.org). Two of Campbell's best-known amateur magazines were the *Scotchman* and the *Liberal*.

[16*] William Crawford, 122 Water St, Everett Penn
[17*] Edw F. Daas, 1723 W Cherry St, Milwaukee Wis (*introduced HP to amateur journalism, 1914, Out of touch later*).
[18*] W. L. Davies,[18] Westville, N.H
[19] Adolphe de Castro, 1732 S. Catalina St, Los Angles Cal
[20] Willis Conover, Jr. 27 High Street, Cambridge, Md
[21] August W. Derleth.
[22] Bernard Austin Dwyer, Box 43, West Shokan NY or CCC Camp SP-8 Co. 26, Peekskill NY
[23*] C. M. Eddy, Jr. 1 Providence St., Prov. RI
[24] E A Edkins,[19] 925 Lincoln Ave, Highland Pk, Ill. (San Sebastian Hotel, Coral Gables Fla in winter)
[25*] Thomas S. Evans, 145 Medway St Providence
[26*] Harold S. Farnese, 4001 S. Harvard Blvd, Los Angles. (*This man, dean of a calif. music inst., wanted H P to co-operate in a*

---

18. Barlow has mistranscribed M. L. Davies (i.e., Myrta (Little) Davies) as W. L. Davies. Myrta Alice Little was born 15 January 1888 NH, the daughter of Albert Little (b. June 1852 NH) and Abbie J. Little (b. June 1860 NH). In the 1900 U.S. census, she was recorded in Hampstead, Rockingham County, NH, along with her younger sister Edith M. (b. January 1893 NH) and her parents in the home of her paternal grandfather Tristram H. Little (b. December 1816 NH), a widowed farmer. The household was the same in 1920 U.S. census except that grandfather Tristram was deceased and sister Edith was working as a stenographer. Myrta Alice Little was involved in the amateur journalism hobby and HPL visited her and her mother in their NH home in 1921 and 1922. On 5 May 1923, Myrta Little married Arthur R. Davies. In the 1930 U.S. census, Arthur R. Davies, age 60, born England of English-born parents, a teacher, was recorded with his wife Myrta L., age 42, writer, and their son Robert L. Davies, age 6, born NH, in their home on East Road in Hampstead, Rockingham County, NH. SSDI shows that Myrta Davies (SSN issued NH 1956–58), born 15 January 1888, died in West Ossipee, Carroll County, NH, in December 1967. I acknowledge the special assistance of Chris Perridas on Myrta Alice (Little) Davies.

19. Ernest Arthur Edkins was born 4 October 1867 in Aston, Warwickshire, England, and died 3 July 1946 in Coral Gables FL. He and his parents emigrated to Canada in 1867 and to the United States in 1869. He had a career in the amateur journalism hobby stretching from 1883 until his death. Late in life, he collaborated with HPL in publishing *Causerie* and with Timothy Burr Thrift in publishing the *Aonian*. The April 2006 issue of the *Fossil* (www.thefossils.org) was devoted to his life and work.

weird opera—never done—and set two of his sonnets to music, holding the only copies. I suggest transcriptions be obtained)
[27] Virgil Finlay 302 Rand St, Rochester NY
[28] Harry O. Fischer, 3515 W. Kentucky St, Apt 15, Lousville, Ky.
[29*] Geo. FitzPatrick,[20] Box 3413 R, G.P.O. Sydney, NSW, Australia
[30*] Nils H. Frome, Bx 3, Fraser Mills, B.C. Canada
[31*] Alfred Galpin, 723 E. College Ave, Appleton Wis. (*likely to have a long series of 1920–25 philosophical letters*)
[32*] Arthur Harris,[21] "Caynton," Llanrhas[?] Road, LLANDUD-NO Wales
[33] Woodburn Harris,[22] Route 1, Vergennes, Vt. *should have*

---

20. George Fitzpatrick, born c. 1885 Parrametta, Australia, arrived in San Francisco CA from Sydney, Australia on 10 September 1934. George Fitzpatrick, born c. 1887, arrived in Sydney, Australia from London, England on 22 November 1889. George D. Fitzpatrick was born in Sydney, Australia in 1891. George L. Fitzpatrick was born in 1899 in Sydney, Australia. George Fitzpatrick married Jessie J. Browne in Sydney, Australia in 1920. Whether any of these can be identified with HPL's George FitzPatrick remains unknown. It seems likely that George FitzPatrick is the unidentified "Fitz P" in the 1934 "List of Correspondents to Whom Postcards Have Been Sent" (*CE* 5.267).

21. Arthur Harris was a Welsh amateur journalist. He published *Interesting Items* as a monthly over many decades, beginning with a handwritten journal as early as 1904. He discovered organized amateur journalism in 1912. Harris died 15 March 1966, at age 73. His large amateur journalism collection, estimated at 15,000 items in 1962, passed to Eric Webb, then to Almon Horton, then to Roy Heaven (see Willametta Keffer, "After Many an Irish Moon," *Fossil*, January 1981). His letters from HPL were acquired by Gerry de la Ree in 1970s and are now held by the Lovecraft Collection at Brown University.

22. Woodburn Prescott Harris was born on 17 July 1888 in Mendon, VT, and died on 20 June 1988, in Bristol VT. In the 1900 U.S. census, he was living with his parents Sidney and Alice Harris and five siblings on a farm in Panton, Addison County, VT. In the 1910 U.S. census, Woodburn P. Harris was still living with his parents, now in Middlebury, Addison County, VT; the occupation of his father was now given as Methodist Episcopal clergyman. Woodburn Harris had no occupation in the 1910 U.S. census. However, he had found employment as a teacher in Epping, Rockingham County, NH, when he registered there for the draft on 5 June 1917. In the 1920 U.S. census, he and his 23-year-old English-born wife Pauline E. Harris were living in Littleton, Middlesex County, MA, where Harris was employed as high school principal. However, by the time of the 1930 U.S. census, Harris had returned to Panton, Addison County, VT,

many pink discussions

[34*] Hazel Heald, 249 School St. Somerville, Mass. or 15 Carter St Newtonville, Mass

[35*] Chas. D. Hornig 121 Jefferson Ave, Eliz. N.J.

[36*] Dr. I. M. Howard L.B. 313, Cross Plains Texas

[37*] George W. Kirk, Chelsea Bk. Shop, 58 W 8, NYC

[38] Rheinhart Kleiner, 116 Harman St Brooklyn

[39] H C Koenig 540 E 80th NYC

[40] Eugene B. Kuntz Bx 736 Clovis NM.

[41] Henry Kuttner 145 S. Canon Dr. #3, Beverly Hills Calif.

[42] Arthur Leeds Hotel Rutledge, 161 Lexington Ave. NYC

[43] Fritz Leiber Jr. 459 N. Oakhurst Dr. Beverly Hills

[44] FBL 230 W 97 NYC

[45] Samuel Loveman, Rm. 1705 105 5th Ave NYC

[46] Wm. Lumley.[23] 742 Wm. St, Buffalo, NY.

[47*] J. Bernard Lynch,[24] 17 Hemenway St, Boston

---

where he operated a farm. His 32-year-old English-born wife (now listed as Ethel) and his 44-year-old sister Jennie (who worked as a stenographer in an insurance office) were also in his household in 1930. Harris was a widower by the time he died at age 99 in 1988, less than one month from the century mark. Refer to *An H. P. Lovecraft Encyclopedia* for additional information regarding Woodburn Harris.

23. William Sylvester Lumley, then resident in Buffalo NY and working as a porter, claimed a date of birth of 20 March 1880 when he registered for the draft on 12 September 1918. In the 1900 U.S. census, he was enumerated in the home of his parents, Edward Lumley (b. August 1844 NY of English-born parents) and Belle M. Lumley (b. January 1857 PA of English-born father and NY-born mother) on West Farms Road in Bronx NY. William (b. March 1881 NY), a sister Marie (b. June 1898 NY) and a brother Benjamin (b. March 1896 NY) also lived in the Lumley household in that year. Edward Lumley was working as a roofer. The family of Edward and Belle M. Lumley was located in the same place when the 1910 U.S. census was enumerated; by then Edward was working in real estate and his son William S. Lumley's occupation was listed as writer and artist (magazine work). In the 1930 U.S. census, William Lumley, a 50-year-old single white male employed as a watchman, born NY of a NY-born father and a PA-born mother, was rooming in the Buffalo NY home of Lewis and Lena Groner. Today Lumley is best known for his 1935 story "The Diary of Alonzo Typer," which was revised by HPL. Refer to *An H. P. Lovecraft Encyclopedia* for additional information regarding William Lumley.

[48*] A. Merritt 235 E 45 NYC
[49] Moe,[25] 1810 W Wisconsin Ave, Milwaukee
[50*] Robert E Moe, 334 Ridgefield Ave, Bridgeport, Conn
[51] C. L. Moore, 2547 Brookside Ave., S. Dr. Indianapolis Ind
[52] Richard E. Morse 40 Princeton Ave Princeton NJ
[53*] Curtis F. Myers,[26] 70 Clifton Ave, Clifton NJ

---

24. Longtime Boston-area amateur journalist, organizer of the famous 4 July 1923 "roundup" that included a Boston Harbor cruise. Joseph Bernard Lynch was born 27 March 1879 in Boston MA, the son of Irish immigrants Thomas and Catherine Lynch. He lived in the parental home at 17 Peabody Street when the 1900, 1910, and 1920 U.S. censuses were taken, with occupations listed as author, advertising manager, and insurance agent, respectively. In the 1930 U.S. census, with occupation reverted to author, he was living with his MO-born wife Florence M. Lynch, a hairdresser in a beauty parlor, on Cortes Street in Boston. The Lynches had then been married six years. Lynch was the author of one published collection of stories, *Props: Tales of the Pawnshop and Other Stories* (Boston: Meador Publishing Co., 1932), collectible today because some of the stories have mystery elements. He was also involved with a trade journal for hairdressers. As a composer of music, he published "On a Starry Irish Night" (H N Publishing Co., 1936) and "Boston Is My Home Sweet Home" (Meredith Music Co., 1946).

25. Maurice Winter Moe (1882–1940). Robert E. Moe [50] was one of his sons.

26. Curtis F. Myers, born 15 August 1897, son of John Myers, registered for the draft in Brooklyn NY on 24 August 1918. In the 1910 U.S. census, John D. Myers, age 40, a widowed boatman, was recorded on Orrington Avenue in Brooklyn NY with his daughter Eva E., age 18, twin sons Harold A. and Herbert B., age 16, and son Curtis F., age 12; everyone in the household was born NY of NY-born parents. In the 1920 U.S. census of Brooklyn NY, John D. Myers, age 55, a marine broker, was recorded at 44 Waldorf Court with daughter Eva E., age 28, unemployed, and son Curtis, age 22, secretary for a chiropractor. (In this census, John Myers was recorded as married, with parents born in Germany.) In the 1930 census, Curtis F. Myers, age 32, born NY of NY-born parents, was living with his wife Leolia L., aged 36, born NJ of Alsace-Lorraine-born parents, at 32 Harrison Place in Clifton, Passaic County, NJ. Curtis was then working as a machinist in a woollen mill. The couple had been married for seven years in 1930, but there were no children in their household in that year. Christopher M. O'Brien found a 15 August 1897 Brooklyn NY birth certificate (#12898) for Curtis F. Myers as well as an SSDI listing for Curtis Myers (SSN issued NY before 1951), born 15 August 1897, died July 1985, St. Augustine FL. I have not been able to find any connection between Curtis F. Myers and HPL's second cousin George Francis Myers (b. 23 February 1865; d. 25 March 1937), the son of Andrew Gormley

[54*] Frederic J. Pabody,[27] 1367 E 6th St, Cleveland O
[55*] Chas A A Parker.[28] 114 Riverside Ave, Medford Mass.
[56*] Emil Petaja, Bx 85 Milltown Montana
[57*] Dean P. Phillips,[29] 1676 E 117, Cleveland O

Myers and Georgia Frances Lovecraft and grandson of Aaron and Althea (Veazie) Lovecraft. The 1930 U.S. census recorded George F. Myers, a NY-born patent attorney (airplanes), age 65, in Queens, Queens County, NY, with his wife Edith, secretary for a wholesale paper company, born in Scotland, age 50. George and Edith Myers had then been married for eight years. For additional information concerning the descendants of Aaron Lovecraft, refer to Richard D. Squires's *Stern Fathers 'Neath the Mould: The Lovecraft Family in Rochester* (West Warwick, RI: Necronomicon Press, 1995).

27. Fred J. Pabody (b. 23 March 1910, Hamilton, Butler County, OH; d. 18 December 1993, West Lake, Cuyahoga County, OH) wrote to HPL after noting the character Professor Frank H. Pabodie of the Miskatonic University Antarctic Expedition in *At the Mountains of Madness*. In the 1930 U.S. census, he was recorded at 1237 Ramona Avenue in Lakewood, Cuyahoga County, OH, in the home of his father Earl Pabody, a 47-year-old insurance company agent, born in PA of OH-born parents, and his wife Jessie (Daggett) Pabody, age 45, born NY of OH-born parents, along with a brother Charles, age 17, and a sister Mary, age 14, both born OH. The Pabody family had been at 412 14th Avenue in Columbus OH in 1920 and at 414 Park Avenue in Hamilton, Butler County, OH, in 1910.

28. Charles A. A. Parker (1878–1965) was a longtime Boston-area amateur journalist. His best-known journals were the *Literary Gem* (1900–11), *L'Alouette* (1921–34?), and *Bavardage* (1935–44). Parker printed the ultimate issue (July 1923) and probably the penultimate issue (March 1923) of HPL's amateur journal, the *Conservative* (see Joshi, *I Am Providence* 1.179). His private press did subsidy publishing in the 1920s and the 1930s. He published two subsidy poetry anthologies, *Threads in Tapestry 1934* and *Threads in Tapestry 1935* (both subtitled *An Anthology of Verse*), with Rachel Hall and Marcia A. Taylor as co-editors. He served as President of the National Amateur Press Association in 1942–43. The January 2011 issue of the *Fossil* (www.thefossils.org) contained material by and about Parker.

29. In the 1920 U.S. census, Dean Phillips, age 5, born OH, was living in the household of his parents Edwin and Flora A. Phillips at 10615 Eventon Avenue in Cleveland OH. Edwin Phillips, age 38, born OH, was a dentist with his own office. His wife, Flora A., age 40, was NE-born. Dean had a sister Margaret, age 11, born OH, and a brother Edwin, age 8, also born OH. It is possible that this Dean Phillips is the same Dean P. Phillips, born 15 December 1914 OH, whose 17 December 1998 death at Auburn, Placer County, CA, is recorded in SSDI. Dean Phillips is mentioned as a friend of Samuel Loveman in HPL's correspondence

[58*] Jennie K. Plaisier[30] 1321 Albion Ave. Chicago
[59] E. H. Price, R. 2 Bx 100 U5, Redwood City, Calif
[60*] Seabury Quinn, 34 Jefferson Ave, Brooklyn NY
[61*] Anne T. Renshaw, 1739 Conn Ave NW, Washington DC
[62] Duane W. Rimel 1009 Chestnut Clarkston Wash
[63*] J. M. Samples,[31] 742 Walnut, Macon Ga

---

files with Barlow, Bloch, and Rimel (information courtesy David E. Schultz).
Dean Phillips is probably the unidentified "Phillips" of the 1934 "List of Correspondents to Whom Postcards Have Been Sent" (CE 5.267).

30. Jennie Irene Plaisier was born Jennie Irene Maloney in IL in February 1884,
the daughter of Timothy Maloney (b. November 1840 Ireland) and Mary Maloney (b. December 1846 Ireland). The family was recorded at 84 East Clifton
Avenue in Chicago when the 1900 U.S. census was enumerated. Jennie and two
sisters and two brothers were then residing in the parental home; her mother
Mary had had eleven children, of whom eight were then living. Jennie was still in
the parental home at 2107 Clifton Avenue in Chicago when the 1910 U.S. census
was enumerated; she was then working was a stenographer in a law office. Jennie
became involved in the amateur journalism hobby during the first decade of the
twentieth century and met her husband Frank Austin Kendall in the hobby.
Kendall was elected president of the National Amateur Press Association for the
1913–14 term but died in November 1913 and was succeeded by his widow.
Jennie married John Plaisier in Cook County, IL, on 7 January 1920. In the 1930
U.S. census, they were recorded in Chicago at 7123 Merrill Avenue: John, age 53,
born Holland of Holland-born parents, was a public school teacher, and his wife
Jennie, age 47, was working as secretary to an attorney. Also in their home in that
year was Jennie's daughter Betty J. Kendall, age 17, born MO of a NE-born father
and an IL-born mother. Jennie Kendall Plaisier remained active in the amateur
journalism hobby for many more years. During the tumultuous 1935–36 official
year, Jennie served with HPL and Vincent B. Haggerty as executive judges of the
National Amateur Press Association. They had during the year to resolve several
contentious disputes raised by Edwin Hadley Smith. Jennie's daughter Betty J.
Kendall Heitz (1912–2011) became a successful copywriter and was a frequent
contributor of poems to the Chicago Tribune's "Line O'Type or Two" column.

31. John Milton Samples published the Silver Clarion for the UAPA in 1918–20.
It was one of the publications most frequently mentioned in HPL's reviews in
the United Amateur and also featured contributions by HPL. At the time he was
publishing the Silver Clarion, Samples was living in Macon GA (still his address
in 1937), and taking courses at Mercer University. (HPL's UAPA faction concen-
trated much of its recruitment efforts among high school and university stu-
dents.) John M. Samples was the eldest of seven sons of William M. Samples (b.

[64*] J. Schwartz 255 E 188 NYC
[65] R F Searight 19946 Derby Ave Detroit
[66] E F Sechrist, Bx 191 Papeete, Tahiti
[67] J. V. Shea, Jr. 4779 Liberty Ave, Pittsburgh
[68*] W. Shepherd, Oakman Ala
[69] C A Smith, #385 Auburn Calif
[70] E. H. Smith,[32] 235 Emerson st, NW, Wash D.C. (*amateur journalist, said once he did not keep letters*)
[71*] Horatio L. Smith,[33] 36 Dodd St, Montclair NJ

April 1865 GA) and Mollie A. Samples (b. April 1869 GA), and was living with his parents and his brothers in Fairplay District, Douglas County, GA, when the 1900 U.S. census was enumerated. His father William M. Samples was a farmer. When the 1910 U.S. census was enumerated, John M. Samples was boarding in the Fairplay District, Carroll County, GA, and working as a teacher in a literary school. He self-published a collection of his poetry, *Visions in Verse*, from Carrollton GA in 1912. (Today WorldCat records only one copy, at the University of Virginia.) When he registered for the draft on 5 June 1917, Samples was residing in Macon GA and working as a rural letter carrier and already married. He gave his date of birth as 9 January 1887 and his place of birth as Carroll County, GA. When the 1920 U.S. census was enumerated, Samples and his 30-year-old SC-born wife Mamie (Knight) Samples were recorded in Macon, Bibb County, GA, with their 2-year-old daughter Layce Ruth Samples. Samples was still working for the post office when the 1920 U.S. census was enumerated. His wife can probably be identified with Mamie F. Knight, born October 1889 SC, living with her parents Joseph C. Knight (b. June 1846 SC), her mother Nancy L. Knight (b. July 1848 SC), and her niece Ruth E. Knight (b. February 1898 GA) in Appling County, GA, when the 1900 U.S. census was enumerated. I have not succeeded in finding John Milton Samples in the 1930 U.S. census. Mamie Samples, age 55, born SC, normal school graduate, no occupation, was recorded at 1204 14th Street in Precinct 24 of Manatee County, FL, when the 1945 FL census was enumerated. Living with her was B. Samples, age 22, born GA, high school graduate, Salvation Army employee. I am indebted to Christopher M. O'Brien for assistance on John Milton Samples.

32. Edwin Hadley Smith (1869–1944) was a longtime amateur journalist. His bound collection of amateur journals was purchased by Charles C. Heuman for The Fossils in 1916 and formed the basis of the Library of Amateur Journalism Collection owned by the University of Wisconsin (Madison) Special Collections Department since 2004. HPL left his own amateur journalism collection to Smith for the Library of Amateur Journalism.

33. When he registered for the draft on 5 June 1917, Horatio Lawrence Smith (b. 2

[72*] Louis C Smith,[34] 1908 98th Ave, Oakland Calif
[73*] Truman J. Spencer,[35] 2525 Whitney Ave, Hamden, Conn.

September 1889, Binghamton NY) was living at 26 Arthur Street in Binghamton NY and working as an agent for Adams Express Company. In the 1900 U.S. census, he had been recorded in the home of his parents Charles R. and Jennie Smith at 87 Prospect Street in Binghamton NY, along with a brother Charles H. and sisters Georgiana and Clarissa. He was still residing in the paternal home in Binghamton NY when the 1910 U.S. census was taken. In the 1930 U.S. census, Horatio L. Smith, age 40, born NY of a NY-born father and a MA-born mother, was living with his wife Iola, age 39, born PA of Welsh-born parents, at 36 Dodd Street in Montclair, Essex County, NJ. Horatio was working as a clothing salesman. In their household in that year were son Lawrence W., age 9, and daughters Evelyn R., age 9, and Shirley A., age 4. When he registered for the draft in 1942, Smith repeated the date and place of birth which he provided in his 1917 registration. He was living at 66 Dodd Street in Montclair, Essex County, NJ, and was working at the offices of Boston-based A. S. Tower Company at 66 Worth Street in New York City. His wife Iola was listed as his closest relation. SSDI has a record for an Horatio Smith (SSN issued NY before 1951) who died August 1966 in Sarasota FL; the date of birth (2 September 1889) of this Horatio Smith matches the date of birth of Horatio Lawrence Smith from the 1917 and 1942 draft registrations. I wonder if Horatio Lawrence Smith might have been a relation of either Charles W. ("Tryout") Smith or Edwin Hadley Smith.

34. Louis C. Smith was an early collecting fan, mentioned in Sam Moskowitz's *The Immortal Storm*. He may be the Louis C. Smith, age 8, born CA, recorded in the 1920 U.S. census in the Bernicia, Solano County, CA, home of his parents Benjamin F. Smith, age 46, born CA of OH-born father and MO-born mother, a locomotive engineer, and Margaret (Cunningham) Smith, age 41, born Scotland of Scottish-born father and Irish-born mother. Also in the household that year were sisters Marie, age 11, and Lois, age 9, both born in CA, and grandfather Alex Cunningham, age 68, widower, born Scotland. This Louis C. Smith may be identified with SSDI's Louis O. C. Smith, born 15 June 1912, died 26 August 2000, Downey, Los Angeles County, CA. Louis C. Smith, age 55, married Stella G. Anderson or Harrington in Madera CA on 9 August 1967. Another SSDI Louis C. Smith was born 16 September 1918 and died 3 January 1999, Irvine, Orange County, CA.

35. Truman Joseph Spencer (1864–1944) was a longtime amateur journalist whose most famous journal was the *Investigator*. He published a 512-page collection of writing by various amateur journalists under the title *A Cyclopedia of the Literature of Amateur Journalism* in 1891 and was well-known for his own writings on the works of William Shakespeare. He served as President of The Fossils in 1934–35 and as Official Editor of the *Fossil* from 1934 until his death. His own

[74*] Helm C Spink,[36] 513 Belgravia Court, Louisville Ky
[75] Kenneth Sterling Room A-11, Lionel Hall, Harvard College
[76*] Corwin F Stickney[37] 21 Jefferson St, Belleville, NJ
[77*] Carl F. Strauch,[38] 812 Washington, Allentown Pa
[78*] C. L. Stuart[39] 17 Brockett St, E Milton, Mass

---

collection of amateur journals was bequeathed to the American Antiquarian Society in Worcester, MA. His work *The History of Amateur Journalism* was posthumously published by The Fossils in 1957; an index volume followed in 1959.

36. Helm C. Spink was born 22 March 1909, the son of Thomas F. and Juliet B. Spink. His father, a medical doctor, had been involved in amateur journalism in Indiana in 1880–83. While working as printing foreman for George G. Fetter in Louisville KY, Spink supervised the printing of HPL's *Further Criticism of Poetry* (1932). In the 1940s Spink moved to Cleveland OH to work as managing editor for William Feather, a magazine printer/publisher. In 1948 Spink married fellow amateur journalist Bernice McCarthy, the niece of Vincent and Felicitas Haggerty. Spink served the National Amateur Press Association as Official Editor for three terms: 1929–30, 1930–31, and 1935–36. He became President of The Fossils in 1963 but had to retire following a debilitating stroke. He died in Cleveland OH, in September 1970. His obituary appeared in the *Fossil* dated July 1970 (apparently released later). His letters from HPL, once the property of Sheldon and Helen Wesson, are now in the Lovecraft Collection at Brown University.

37. Corwin F. Stickney was born 10 October 1921 and died 15 November 1998 in Glen Ridge, Essex County, NJ. He knew HPL through science fiction fandom. August Derleth attacked his use of HPL material in the commemorative chapbook *HPL* (1937).

38. HPL's letters to Carl Ferdinand Strauch (1908–1989) were published in the *Lovecraft Annual* 4 (2010), with annotations and a biographical sketch of Strauch by S. T. Joshi.

39. Charles Stuart, a single white male age 42, born MA of Canadian-born parents, was recorded as a boarder at 227 Pleasant Street in Milton MA in the 1930 U.S. census. His occupation was fireman for the town fire department. He can probably be identified with the Charles Stuart of 57 Center Street, single male, born July 14, 1888, occupation chauffeur for the town of Milton MA, who registered for the draft on 5 June 1917. It seems likely that he can be identified with Charles Stuart, born July 1888 MA, son, in the Milton MA home of Alexander Stuart (b. August 1854 Canada of Canadian-born parents), park laborer, and his wife M. Ann (b. May 1865 MA of Canadian-born parents) in the 1900 U.S. census. M. Ann Stuart had eleven living children when the census was compiled, of whom nine were living in the family home. However, the Charles Stuart employed by Milton MA may not have been HPL's correspondent. In the 1910 U.S.

[79*] Edw. F. Suhre,[40] 3641 Juniata St, St Louis Mo
[80*] Sutton-Morgan,[41] 505 W 167 NYC

---

census, there was a Charles L. Stuart, while male age 23, born MA of Scottish-born parents, living at 194 East Street in Milton MA and working as a machinist in a machine shop. He had been married for two years to his wife Bella, a white female age 23, a weaver in the worsted mill. Also living in their home was their eight-month-old son James Stuart (born MA) and Charles's 73-year-old grand-mother Jane Stuart (born Scotland). I wonder if there is any significance that Charles Stuart's surname was also the second given name of Thomas Stuart Evans [25]. Perhaps there is some obscure family connection lurking here.

40. Edward Frederick Suhre was born 24 March 1879 in St. Louis MO, the son of Herman Suhre. A longtime amateur journalist, he was a founding member of the United Amateur Press Association in 1895 and served as Edith Miniter's succes-sor as President of the National Amateur Press Association in 1910–11. He died 18 August 1939

41. A surviving letter of HPL to Mayte Sutton addressed to her at 100 Spring Ave-nue, Troy NY, from 66 College Street in Providence RI, on 2 November 1933 is held in the Lovecraft Collection at Brown University. Another letter to Mrs. Sut-ton, dated 6 August 1936, was excerpted for the Arkham House Transcripts. Mrs. Sutton can probably be identified with SSDI's Mayte Sutton (SSN issued NY 1957–59), born 7 July 1879, died September 1968 Ithaca NY. Her first husband John L. Morgan was born in Scotland in March 1877, the son of William and Margaret (Duncan) Morgan. John and a younger brother James came to the United States with their mother in 1883, a year after their father arrived. Mayte (maiden name unknown to me) married John L. Morgan about 1905 and the 1910 U.S. census found the couple at 606 Bessmer Avenue in East Pittsburgh PA, with their daugh-ters Christine M., age 3 years, born NJ, and Terrace [Jerrace?] F., age 3 months, born PA. Mayte E. Morgan was recorded as born NJ of a NY-born father and a ME-born mother. Mayte became a widow and remarried between the 1910 and 1920 U.S. censuses. The 1920 U.S. census recorded Mayte and her new husband Frank M. Sutton at 5707 Warrington Street in Philadelphia PA (ward 40). Frank M. Sutton, age 53, born in PA of PA-born parents, was working as traffic manager for an elec-tric company. His wife Mayte E. Sutton, age 38, was recorded as born NJ of a VT-born father and a NY-born mother. With them in their household were Frank's stepdaughters Margaret Morgan, age 13, born NJ, and Terrace Morgan, age 9, born PA, both with Scottish-born father and NJ-born mother. In the 1930 U.S. census Mayte E. Sutton, age 48, once again widowed, was recorded in Dryden, Tompkins County, NY, as a dormitory house mother in a private school. The 1930 U.S. cen-sus recorded Mayte Sutton as NJ-born, with ME-born father and NY-born mother. There may be two records of her daughter Margaret in the 1930 U.S. census: one as a 20-year-old student nurse Margaret C. Morgan, born NY of NY-born parents, at

[81] Margaret Sylvester, 612 W115 NYC

[82] W B Talman, 135 E 42 NYC

[83] Donald Wandrei

[84*] Howard Wandrei

[85*] Henry Geo. Weiss Bx 190, Route 4 Tucson Ariz—*Weiss, a Red, had many vast political tussles with HPL, whose changing social views are probably embodied in letters if they've been preserved—*

[86*] Frederick A. Wesley, 6 Hammond St, Providence

[87*] Lee White, Jr.[42] 2834 Bush Blvd, Birmingham Ala.

[88*] Eola P. Willis[43] 72 Tradd St, Charleston SC

[89*] D A Wollheim 801 West End Ave NYC

[90*] N H Wooley[44] 18 S Mill St, Rosedale, Kansas

St. Mary's Hospital & Nurses' Home in Niagara NY and one as a 23-year-old trained nurse (nurse trainee?) Margaret Morgan, born PA of PA-born parents, at Bellevue Hospital in New York City (Manhattan Borough) NY. HPL's letters to his aunt Annie E. P. Gamwell written from the Long family home in NYC during the 1933–34 Christmas holiday recorded several meetings with Mayte E. Sutton and her daughter. Mayte E. Sutton was the author of "The Cursed Peach Orchard," published under the heading "Student Lore" in the *New York Folklore Quarterly* (17:4) for winter 1961. Perhaps the 1940 U.S. census will reveal more concerning these NYC friends of HPL. I am indebted to David E. Schultz for special assistance on Mayte E. Sutton and her daughter Margaret Morgan.

42. HPL's letters to Lee McBride White, Jr. (1915–1989) were published in the *Lovecraft Annual* 1 (2007), with editorial annotations and a biographical sketch of White by S. T. Joshi.

43. HPL made the acquaintance of artist and author Eola P. Willis (b. 1856 Decatur GA; d. 1952 Charleston SC) on one of his visits to Charleston SC. She was the author of *The Charleston Stage in the XVIIIth Century: With Social Settings of the Time* (Columbia, SC: State Co., 1924; rpt. New York: S. Blom, 1966). She was also the author of *A Pretty Mocking of the Life* (New York: Godey, 1893) and *Isle of Palms, Charleston, S.C.* (Charleston, SC: Lucas & Richardson, c. 1910–19); St. Julien Grimké was her coauthor for the second title. Her article on "The Dramatic Careers of Poe's Parents" appeared in the *Bookman* in 1926. No work by Eola Willis appears in *Lovecraft's Library*.

44. In the 1925 KS state census, Natalie Wooley, age 20, born KS, was recorded in the Kansas City KS household of her husband George H. Wooley, age 24, born MO, a sheep driver in the stockyards. In the 1930 U.S. census, their household was recorded in Kansas City MO on 8 April 1930. George H. Wooley, age 29, born MO of IL-born father and German-born mother, was working as a teamster for a grading company. His wife, Natalie, age 25, was born KS of a KS-born father

note: Marion Bonner,[45] and Miss Staples,[46] two elderly women fond of cats, have letters on the subject, likely amusing. Write c/o AEP Gamwell, she'll locate them in Providence

Entries in HPs 1937 diary[47]

[The "death diary" entries as transcribed by Barlow are published in the locations indicated in note 47 and are not reprinted here.]

---

and a MO-born mother. Also in their household that year was a son George A. Wooley, age 6, born MO. Natalie Wooley was well-known as a poet in the amateur journalism hobby in the 1930s. Records on Ancestry.com associate her with Natalie Ashburn (SSN 573-07-2921), born 11 November 1904, who died in April 1973 in Houston TX. TX death records recorded Natalie Ashburn's marital status as single. Refer to *An H. P. Lovecraft Encyclopedia* for additional information regarding Natalie Wooley.

45. Marion F. Bonner (b. 6 September 1883, Providence RI; d. 13 May 1952, Providence RI), daughter of Robert and Marion Bonner, spent her working career in the periodicals department of the Providence Public Library. In the 1930 U.S. census, she was a boarder in the rooming house at 55 Waterman Street. By 1947, she resided at 167 Evergreen. Her final Providence address (recorded in the 1952 city directory) was 303 Benefit Street. Her letters from HPL are in the Lovecraft Collection at Brown University. Refer to *An H. P. Lovecraft Encyclopedia* for additional information regarding Marion Bonner.

46. Evelyn M. Staples (b. 1 October 1860, Barrington, RI; d. 10 June 1938, St. John, New Brunswick, Canada) was the daughter of Henry Staples, a paper merchant, and his wife Mary H. Staples. Providence historian Judge William R. Staples (1798–1868), the author of *Annals of Providence* (1843), was her paternal grandfather. She began her career as a primary school teacher in her home town of Barrington RI, but was teaching in Providence by 1900. She boarded at 47 Camp Street in 1900, 118 Lexington Avenue in 1910, and 34 Mawney Street in 1920, and was teaching at the Charles Street School no later than 1910. By 1930, she was residing at 55 Waterman Street, in the same rooming house as Marion F. Bonner. She continued to be listed at 55 Waterman Street in City Directories through 1938. Evelyn Staples died during a visit to her niece in St. John, New Brunswick, Canada. No HPL letters to Miss Staples are known to survive. Like Marion Bonner, her fellow resident at 55 Waterman Street, Miss Staples was the owner of some of the cats belonging to the Kappa Alpha Tau feline fraternity whose headquarters was located atop the shed adjoining HPL's last home at 66 College Street.

47. For the diary entries transcribed by Barlow (the so-called "death diary") see CE 5.241–42. These transcribed entries were earlier published in Everts, *The Death of a Gentleman* (1987), 25–28.

Works Cited

Everts, R. Alain. *The Death of a Gentleman: The Last Days of Howard Phillips Lovecraft*. Madison WI: The Strange Company, 1987.

Joshi, S. T. *I Am Providence: The Life and Times of H. P. Lovecraft*. New York: Hippocampus Press, 2010. 2 vols.

———. *Lovecraft's Library: A Catalogue*. 3rd rev. ed. New York: Hippocampus Press, 2012.

Joshi, S. T., and David E. *An H. P. Lovecraft Encyclopedia*. 2001. New York: Hippocampus Press, 2004.

———————————

Briefly Noted

Stephen Jones has edited a large omnibus of Lovecraft's tales, *Eldritch Tales: A Miscellany of the Macabre* (Gollancz, 2011), as a companion to his earlier compilation, *Necronomicon: The Best Weird Tales of H. P. Lovecraft* (Gollancz, 2008). The volume includes a mix of lesser stories (including such juvenilia as "The Alchemist"), some revisions, the poetry cycle *Fungi from Yuggoth* and a few other poems, and the essay "Supernatural Horror in Literature." Some of the texts appear to be derived from S. T. Joshi's various corrected editions published by Arkham House. Also included is Jones's illuminating essay "Lovecraft in Britain," first published as a pamphlet in 2007.

The Case for "How the Enemy Came to Thlunrana" and *The Case of Charles Dexter Ward*

Peter Levi

H. P. Lovecraft's time as an obscure author has long since passed, as his lasting influence is acknowledged by such publications as the Library of America's 2005 collection of his work. He is now regarded as one of the most influential horror writers of the twentieth century. Even before the cumulative effect of these accolades, the study of Lovecraft goes back to the earliest fandom. Given that, one may wonder what is left to be said about his work. David E. Schultz memorably wrote to me in 2005, "Does everything HPL, or any writer for that matter, may have written need to be 'influenced' by someone else?" I think, beyond interpreting a work in modern context, what is left is the "mental furniture" (to borrow a phrase from Tolkien scholar Tom Shippey) that went into those works—that is to say, elements in the author's life and reading that impacted his or her writing.

The Case of Charles Dexter Ward, one of Lovecraft's seminal works, is a story with some as yet unexplored mental furniture. The object of this article is not a radical rereading of *Ward*, nor is it meant to challenge the analysis of S. T. Joshi, Barton St. Armand, and other scholars. I agree with Joshi about the message of the story, that "the pursuit of knowledge [is] intrinsically good. Sometimes, however, that pursuit simply leads to unfortunate and unforeseen consequences" (*IAP* 669). Previous works have explored the autobiographical, historical, and literary inspirations for the story—particularly Walter de la Mare's *The Return* (*IAP* 667)—and my intention here is to supplement the literary discussion.

Through my study, I believe that Lord Dunsany's "How the Enemy Came to Thlunrana" should be considered a part of the imaginative firmament from which Lovecraft's story sprang. His admiration of Lord Dunsany is well known, beginning in 1919 (*IAP* 335). His exposure to this particular tale, first published in *Fifty-one Tales* in 1915, was among his early readings (*IAP* 337). The impact of Dunsany on Lovecraft's writing has received a great deal of study (e.g., *IAP* 352–54), but the connection of "How the Enemy Came to Thlunrana" to *The Case of Charles Dexter Ward* has not been previously explored.

First and foremost, both stories are concerned with wizards. In *Ward*, Joseph Curwen is part of a trio of Salem wizards—Simon Orne and Edward Hutchinson are the others (*MM* 149)—who have followed Borellus's hints about "essential salts" (*MM* 122) in the hope of ruling the world. "It will be ripe in a yeare's time to have up ye Legions from Underneath, and then there are no Boundes to what shal be oures" (*MM* 197), says Hutchinson late in the novel. In Dunsany's brief tale, Thlunrana is the "chief cathedral of wizardry" and is the terror of the valley in which it sits. The identities of the Thlunrani wizards are unknown; they hide their appearances, but conspire by their work to maintain their power.

Secondly, foreshadowing is an important element in both stories, used to heighten and build reader anticipation. The internal narrative of *Ward* continually includes hints about its ending (e.g., *MM* 108) as well as the plans of Curwen and his cohorts. "*To Him Who Shal Come After, & How He May Gett Beyonde Time & ye Spheres*" (*MM* 155) tells the reader that Curwen foresaw his potential destruction and took steps to secure an heir to bring him back. "Thlunrana" contains similar hints, including its title. A doom will come upon the Thlunrani wizards, but they do not know who or what: "It had been prophesied of old and foreseen from the ancient days that its enemy would come upon Thlunrana. And the date of its doom was known and the gate by which it would enter, yet none had prophesied of the enemy who he was save that he was of the gods though he dwelt with men." Both Lovecraft and Dunsany illustrate that foreknowledge is useless without the wisdom to use it, with the Thlunrani wizards taking no precautions to avoid their fate and Joseph Curwen arrogantly believing he can replace his descendent despite his unassimilated nature in the future: "'You were a fool, Curwen, to fancy that a mere visual identity would be enough'" (*MM* 233).

More peripherally, Lovecraft's Curwen has a building with high and narrow windows that are lighted strangely at night, meant to evoke fear in the reader. "Then, too, there was something very obnoxious about a certain great stone building with only high narrow slits for windows" (*MM* 119); and "a great shaft of light shooting into the sky from some aperture in the roof of that cryptical stone building with the high, excessively narrow windows" (*MM* 139). This echoes Dunsany: "So narrow and high were the windows and so strange when lighted at night that they seemed to regard men with the demoniac leer of something that had a secret in the dark."

These similarities do not indicate that Lovecraft has simply lifted Dunsany's concepts and inserted them into the narrative. Instead, these elements have been turned to his own uses, so whereas Dunsany's Thlunrana is defeated by a mixture of bravery—the coming of "the man from the black-thatched cottage by the five pine-trees"—and laughter, "for laughter was the enemy that was doomed to come against Thlunrana," Lovecraft's Curwen is defeated by the hero Dr. Willett who outsmarts him and dispels him (*MM* 233–34), but at the cost of Ward's life and Willett's well-being (*MM* 230). While Dunsany's Thlunrana is gone forever, there is nothing in Lovecraft that suggests similar horrors could not arise elsewhere through similar agencies.

Despite the differences outlined above, it's clear that "How the Enemy Came to Thlunrana" influenced *The Case of Charles Dexter Ward*—from their concern with wizards, foreshadowing, and echoed descriptions, Dunsany's story makes up a part of the mental furniture whereby Lovecraft composed the tale.

Works Cited

Dunsany, Lord. "How the Enemy Came to Thlunrana." In *Fifty-one Tales*. Boston: Little, Brown, 1915. 85–88.

Joshi, S. T. *I Am Providence: The Life and Times of H. P. Lovecraft.* New York: Hippocampus Press, 2010. 2 vols.

Misperceptions of Malignity: Narrative Form and the Threat to America's Modernity in "The Shadow over Innsmouth"

Anna Klein

"The Shadow over Innsmouth" is a quintessential example of Lovecraft fiction. It is steeped in New England antiquarian folk-lore and well entrenched in his mythos of the fictional Miskatonic region. It has a familiar Lovecraftian narrative construction of a young genealogist on a journey for ancestral data which leads to his subsequent discovery of occluded New England colonial history with a strong impact on the present. This young genealogist's discoveries of his ancestry and his connection to a potent early New England patriarch causes an internal crisis that leads to the subsequent destruction of the identity of the narrator as he had been understood by the reader. The "Innsmouth" novella is told through a typical Lovecraftian first-person narrative, where the material is filtered solely through the perspective of a narrator and the deconstruction of this narrative filter is of pivotal importance to understanding the story told in "Innsmouth."

Lovecraft frames "Innsmouth" from the point of view of a survived experience, where the novella opens at the story's chronological end point, whence the narrator returns to the beginning of the chronological sequence to 'explain' how events have ended up at the point at which the reader has entered the tale. This frame establishes the outcome of the story as a foregone conclusion. While in truth no reader ever truly has control of how events in a work of fiction will turn out, a more typical narrative bears the illusion that the conclusion has not yet been reached and that as the story continues, any number of possible outcomes may yet be attained. With a narrative frame where the end point is set out at the beginning, readers have no hope of a changed outcome. Instead, they can apparently only hope to understand how that outcome has come to pass. This narrative frame, beginning with a single, foregone end point, might initially seem to foreclose narrative possibilities; however, it instead presents readers with a complex narrative structure where the narrator's motivations can be seen to gloss the retelling, and where the apparent discrepancy between the narrator's state of mind at the beginning and end of the novel, despite being ostensibly the same point in time, is the starting point for delving into the several narratives that can be deconstructed from "The Shadow over Innsmouth," and the insight it offers into early twentieth-century American anxiety around decay.

The critics' responses to "Innsmouth" typically put great emphasis on the Deep Ones and their interbreeding with the Innsmouth townsfolk, extrapolating this in terms of racial theory and citing excerpts of Lovecraft's personal letters that express racism to support these extrapolations. S. T. Joshi, in his annotations to the story, describes it as "a warning on the dangers of miscegenation" and "may be considered an expansion on the subtilization of the plot of 'Facts Concerning the Late Arthur Jermyn and His Family'" (*Call of Cthulhu* 410). In comparing it to other stories of the period, such as those by Irvin S. Cobb and Robert W. Chambers, Joshi elaborates on the scale concerned in "Innsmouth" where the other authors were "dealing with a single case of hybridism, not an entire community or civilization; it is only the latter that creates the sense of worldwide menace that we find in Lovecraft's tale" (*Call of Cthulhu* 410). Victoria Nelson interprets the story in an evolutionary sense, describing the fate of the human-Deep One hybrid offspring as "a kind of profane immortality . . . achieved by moving down the evolutionary scale" (118). Conversely, folklorist Timothy Evans views the story as a much more general rendering of "miscegenation and the loss of tradition (or rather, the replacement of New England traditions with alien traditions)" as well as "a narrative of the loss of a New England homeland" (124). There appears to be a prevailing sense of threat to and loss of traditions and identity across the critics' readings. My interpretation in this article will work with these readings in examining how the narrative structure of the novella conveys the narrator's distress at perceived threat to his identity but also how this distress is misleading, and based on a misperception of malignity.

"The Shadow over Innsmouth" is framed as an account of the events which lead to "strange and secret investigation of certain conditions in the ancient Massachusetts seaport of Innsmouth" (*DH* 303), as written by the character who "fled frantically out of Innsmouth in the early morning hours of July 16, 1927" and whose "frightened appeals for government inquiry and action brought on the whole reported episode" (*DH* 304). The novella opens at a point following that at which the events detailed in the narrative have transpired, thus the outcomes are already determined at the outset of the story. This is particularly important to note in "Innsmouth," as the knowledge that the narrator reveals at the end—that he is the great-great-grandson of Obed Marsh and his Deep One wife—causes an apparent discrepancy between the state of mind the narrator is in at the start of the novella and the state of mind the he is in at the end of it. The narrator already knows at the start of the novella that he is descended from Obed Marsh and Innsmouth, and its conclusion is a rapturous acceptance of his Deep One heritage. This presents something of a puzzle to the reader: if the narrator knew this when he started 'writing' "Innsmouth," why was the entire narrative framed from a perspective of fear and disgust?

This is not a mistake on Lovecraft's part, nor is it a detail of continuity sacrificed for the sake of narrative tension; it is in fact a vital part of the relation of the text to the narrative frame. The narrator claims that "the mere telling helps me to restore confidence in my own faculties" (*DH* 305), which indicates that his aim in writing the account is to reinforce a version of events that is conducive to "confidence in [his] own faculties," that is, protecting his human identity over his Deep One heritage. However, knowing what we know of the story's outcome, the narrator's position at the start of the story can only be impossibly divided or there is a clear missing link in the tale. If the former is the case, it would mean that the narrator is simultaneously attempting to reassert his humanity whilst being happy to become a Deep One. If the latter is the case, it would indicate that there is a clear missing link in how the situation at the start of the novella becomes the situation at the end.

At the opening of the novella, the narrator already knows—but the reader does not—that he is descended from Obed Marsh and a Deep One. As he reveals to the reader at the end of the novella, he is already experiencing the positive dreams of life as a Deep One under the sea when he began to write the account. These dreams fill the narrator, as he says, with "nameless horror the moment I awoke. But during the dreams they did not horrify me at all—I was one with them" (*DH* 366). At the end of the story, it is revealed that at the outset of the novella, he was faced with two choices: to reject his heritage and thus not change into a Deep One by committing suicide, or to accept it and become a Deep One. This point is only obliquely indicated at the outset, when he tells us, "I have carried away impressions which are yet to drive me to drastic measures" (*DH* 304), and is then elucidated at the end "So far I have not shot myself . . . I bought an automatic and almost took the step" (*DH* 367). The position of choice the narrator is in at the start of the story is, thus, only revealed at the end and this means that writing the account has assisted the narrator "in making up [his] mind regarding a certain terrible step which lies ahead of [him]" (*DH* 305). The reader is unaware at the start of narrative that the narrator is in a position of choice, then, and that the writing of the account is his attempt to deny his ancestry and reassert his humanity. The narrative simultaneously attempts to convince the reader, and the narrator himself, that his experiences in Innsmouth were those of an outsider under threat, and not that of a lost descendent being reclaimed by the town.

The narrator's lack of name in the novella is indicative of this identity crisis. Though Lovecraft's surviving notes indicate that he was called Robert Olmstead, neither his first nor last name are ever mentioned in the story. His ancestral connection to Obed Marsh and his Deep One wife is through the maternal line, thus even though we learn that his mother's family is Williamson (*DH* 362), the narrator never reveals her married name, allowing him to keep his complete anonymity. The lack of identity of "Innsmouth"'s narrator—especially in a story about genealogy which is littered with other ancestral names—is reflective of the narrator's state of mind at the point he is telling the story. His identity is in a state of denial from the beginning. He states that his "contact with this affair has been closer than that of any other layman" (*DH* 304), though he already knows he is not simply a "layman" but part of Innsmouth's heritage. He cannot give his name without affirming his identity—and affirming his identity would lead to a state of crisis, as it would mean acknowledging the ancestral connection to Innsmouth that he is attempting to deny. By the end of the novella, his earthly identity no longer matters as he has made the decision to adopt his Deep One identity. The narrator's namelessness is an important part of the denial that frames the whole narrative.

The narrative of "Innsmouth" is contained primarily within the pseudo-scholarly framework based in the Miskatonic mythos. Newburyport, Ipswich, and Rowley are locations within the story that exist in the Massachusetts of the real world while others, namely Innsmouth itself, Arkham, and the Manuxet River, are fictional and exist only as part of Lovecraft's mythos. The first chapter of the novella in particular spends some time establishing the scholarly credibility of the Innsmouth legend. The narrator relays its civic history from the Essex County records (*DH* 310), as well as citing references "to the strange jewellery vaguely associated with Innsmouth," of which there were "specimens in the museum of Miskatonic University at Arkham, and in the display room of the Newburyport Historical Society" (*DH* 310). Lovecraft here weaves the fiction of Innsmouth together with real world fact, since the Newburyport Historical Society is a real institution in a real town.

The town of Innsmouth itself is presented in the form of an antiquarian's travelogue, predominantly in the novella's chapters two and four. Timothy Evans describes "The Shadow over Innsmouth" as Lovecraft's "ultimate transformation of travelogue into horror story" (115). The narrator's running commentary comprises largely of comments such as "it was a town of wide extent and dense construction" (*DH* 316) and describing the architecture in an antiquarian's tone, noting observable architectural features such as "some large square Georgian houses, too, with hipped roofs, cupolas, and railed 'widow's walks'" and "a fairly well-preserved brick structure" (*DH* 316). The antiquarian detail functions as a coping mechanism on the part of the narrator, for whom the extensive reliance on objective, observable, physical detail and reported history serves to construct a barrier between the reader and the narrator's hidden crisis. It allows the narrator to construct a version of Innsmouth that is visual and historically engaging yet does not betray the narrator's own relationship with it.

For the narrator to successfully maintain his humanity and deny his Deep One heritage, his account of his experience in Innsmouth must frame his experience as that of an outsider. Much of the early part of "Innsmouth" is devoted to establishing the threat that Innsmouth poses to outsiders. The ticketing agent who first tells the narrator about Innsmouth tells him that "you can bet that prying strangers ain't welcome around Innsmouth. I've heard personally of more'n one business or government man that's disappeared there" (*DH* 309) and that he "wouldn't advise" (*DH* 308) the narrator to stay overnight. Others in Newburyport whom the narrator consults about Innsmouth, including the Y.M.C.A. clerk and the librarian, express an "obscure suspiciousness, as if there were something amiss with anyone too much interested in Innsmouth" (*DH* 310). A sense of expectation for hostility is further built by the warnings from the grocery boy who works at the Innsmouth branch of the First National chain store. The grocery boy "hail[s] from Arkham" and is thus an outsider who "did not like the place, its fishy smell, or its furtive people" (*DH* 320). He emphatically warns the narrator that "certain spots were almost forbidden territory . . . one must not, for example, linger much around the Marsh refinery, or around any of the still used churches, or around the pillared Order of Dagon Hall at New Church Green," and that "it would be well not to make oneself too conspicuous in such neighbourhoods . . . some strangers had even disappeared" (*DH* 320). These warnings, based on outsiders' perceptions of Innsmouth, are conveyed by the narrator to the reader in order to raise the readers' expectations of a hostile reception. Because the reader has heard extensively that there is danger present in Innsmouth, they will be more likely to accept the narrator's gloss of perceived danger even when it runs counter to the actual events described.

Zadok Allen's panicked warning also raises the tension, when he implores the narrator to *"git aout o' here!* Get aout o' here! *They seen us*—git aout fer your life! Dun't wait fer nothin'—*they know naow*— Run fer it—quick—*aout o' this taown*—" (*DH* 340). But it was not necessarily being seen talking to Allen that was the cause of such alarm, for even though the grocery boy mentions "it was not always safe to be seen questioning him" (*DH* 322), he also makes it clear that other outsiders speak to him and carry the stories out of Innsmouth when he says that "nobody ever believed [Zadok Allen] . . . it was probably from him that some of the wildest popular whispers and delusions were derived" (*DH* 322). Being seen speaking to Zadok is therefore clearly not an instant death sentence. It pays to note that Zadok's wording is that *"they* know naow" (*DH* 340; my emphasis), which indicates that the danger stems from something "they" know—such as that the narrator is a descendent of Obed Marsh—rather than the cause for alarm being forbidden knowledge on the part of the narrator.

In addition to the continuous and detailed antiquarian travelogue that the narrator provides, there are several other distraction measures that Lovecraft has him employ in the narrative. One of these is the abundance of reported speech. The majority of the first chapter is taken up with the narrator's reporting of what the ticket agent (*DH* 305–9) and the head of the Newburyport Historical Society (*DH* 311–13) say about Innsmouth. The first half of the second chapter is taken up with the relating of the conversation with the grocery boy (*DH* 320–23), while much of chapter three is relating the lengthy tale told by Zadok Allen (*DH* 329–40). Once again, the copious reporting of other people's opinions and thoughts serves as a containment measure for preventing the narrator from having to speak when it may betray his own feelings, and it allows him to reinforce his image as an outsider by his implicit agreement with the accounts which he reports.

The narrator builds on this perceived threat to outsiders—and therefore to himself—by creating an atmosphere of pursuit. Time is an issue for the narrator, as he cannot risk missing the only bus out of Innsmouth at 8.00 P.M., and the narrative is punctuated by his attention to the passing hours, beginning with the "hoarse strokes . . . tolling the hour of eleven" (*DH* 318) as he first arrives in Innsmouth. Following his first explorations, he notes "the cracked stroke of three sound[ing] from a belfry on [his] left" (*DH* 326). After this, his determination to leave the town increases as does his reporting of the time as he notes that only "about four hours remained for conversation" (*DH* 328) when he tracked down Zadok Allen, then while they talk he anxiously watches the time. When his attention is absorbed by the story, he loses track of the time and is startled to note that "the hour grown perilously late—[his] watch said 7:15, and the Arkham bus left Town Square at eight" (*DH* 341). The use of the word "perilously" indicates a sense of danger that the increasing number of temporal references have created. Together, these references give the reader the mistaken impression that the narrator is in some way in threatened, as he would be if he were a normal human being. The constant referrals to his map of Innsmouth similarly create a sense of constant movement, as well as provide a nonstop narrative that is, like the antiquarian travelogue, filled with detail yet avoids betraying any emotional connection on the part of the narrator. His time in Innsmouth is constantly narrated as his series of movements, such as: "Accordingly I kept north along Main to Martin, then turning inland, crossing Federal Street safely north of the Green, and entering the decayed patrician neighbourhood of northern Broad, Washington, Lafayette, and Adams Streets" (*DH* 325) and "I chose Marsh Street instead of State for my approach to Town Square. Near the corner of Fall street I began to see scattered groups of furtive whisperers" (*DH* 341). The narrator's escape from Innsmouth in the fourth chapter, in which he is actually pursued, retroactively reinforces the feeling that he was under threat all along.

But the narrative also shows, counter to the warnings and sense of threat that the narrator encourages, that outsiders are not actually murdered out of hand in Innsmouth. The grocery boy inhabits Innsmouth with no harm coming to him, as is presumably the case with the family from Ipswich with whom he boards (*DH* 320). He also mentions that "one never came to know the natives personally no matter how long one might live in Innsmouth" (*DH* 322), which indicates that there are even outsiders who dwell at length in

Innsmouth who survive unharmed. Zadok Allen, despite his knowledge of the town's secrets, is also allowed to dwell there unharmed. Though he is partially protected by certain oaths of Dagon he had taken, he is not shown as reviled by the townsfolk since the first time the narrator encounters him, he is "talking with a pair of unkempt but not abnormal-looking firemen" (DH 326).

There are other instances of visitors leaving Innsmouth unharmed, the ticket agent speaks of at least one "factory inspector who stopped at the Gilman a couple of years ago" (DH 308). A possible interpretation of the missing visitors is provided by the ticket agent's suggestion to the narrator that people "try to cover up any Innsmouth blood they have in 'em" (DH 306). This suggests that visitors who go missing in Innsmouth may secretly be of Innsmouth descent and are returning to their heritage. The ticket agent mentions one visitor "who went crazy and is out at Danvers now" (DH 309). A similar situation is echoed at the end of the novella by the narrator's cousin who is in the "permanent seclusion of a sanitarium" (DH 364), having apparently suffered a mental illness that is revealed to be the Innsmouth look. It is plausible to interpret that the visitor who ended up "crazy" could also be of Innsmouth descent and the visitors that go missing are simply inducted into their heritage.

On a closer reading of the early sections of the story, there is in fact little hostility shown toward the narrator in the narrative when reading beneath his gloss, although the townspeople do show a considerable amount of interest in him. The first Innsmouth native he encounters, Joe Sargent, looks at him "curiously" (DH 314) and he elicits similar reactions from other locals, such as when "furtive, shambling creatures stare[d] cryptically" in his direction, while others "eyed [him] coldly and curiously" (DH 326). Later at the hotel, "it seemed as if many bulging, watery, unwinking eyes looked oddly at [the narrator] as [he] claimed [his] valise in the lobby" (DH 341) and additionally receives more "strange glances" (DH 342). The recurring descriptors indicate curiosity and puzzlement—the Innsmouth residents are clearly disconcerted and uncertain what to make of the narrator. It has been established that he is far from the only non-native to exist in town, therefore their interest must be drawn by something else, possibly his physical resemblance to Obed Marsh. This physical resemblance is striking enough to be mentioned twice, once by Zadok Allen who notices that the narrator has "kind o' got them sharp-readin' eyes like Obed had" (*DH* 330) and once by the curator of the Arkham Historical Society who notes the narrator has "true Marsh eyes" (*DH* 363). The Innsmouth residents also exhibit small acts of friendliness towards the narrator, such as a shopkeeper who "was quite civil in his way" (*DH* 327). The narrator explains this sort of thing away as "being perhaps used to the custom of such convivial strangers . . . as were occasionally in town" (*DH* 327). Later, when the bus ostensibly breaks down, the proprietors "make the price easy" (*DH* 342) for him at the hotel. The incident at the Gilman House, when the narrator flees, is also not nearly as sinister as at first glance. Even the narrator admits that when his door was tried, he leapt to conclusions and admits that "it never once occurred to [him] that the fumbling might be a mere mistake . . . malign purpose was all [he] could think of" (*DH* 345). Though the intruders try to enter his room, it is also worth noting that upon finding their way barred, "a firm knock came at my outer door . . . then the knocking was repeated" (*DH* 347). Innsmouth thus exhibits no actual malice toward the narrator, only outward curiosity and even mild geniality, although this is all overshadowed by the narrator's reports of his panic, his suggestions of pursuit, and the many anecdotes from others of the potential danger in Innsmouth.

If there is no creature or creatures of malign intent stalking the narrator because of what he has discovered about the town's secrets, what is it about him that stirs the interest of the townspeople? Are readers really to believe that one overly inquisitive visitor warrants a full-scale chase, involving even the current Marsh patriarch? The Deep Ones are shown in the narrative to have a strong sense of family. Because of their long lives, Zadok Allen reports, it wasn't uncommon for "folks as had took to the water gen'rally come back a good deal to visit, so's a man ud often be a-talkin' to his own five-times-great-grandfather" (*DH* 332) and when the narrator starts to dream of his Deep One heritage, they prominently feature both his grandmother and his great-great grandmother (*DH* 366–67), who explain to him his destiny. It is also indicated by Zadok Allen that there are certain laws against harming those that are part Deep One or belong to the Order of Dagon when he says "they'd a kilt me long ago fer' what I know, only I'd took the fust an' secon' Oaths o' Dagon offen Obed, so was pertected" (DH 338). Even though the narrator is responsible for launching a government inquiry into Innsmouth which resulted in many deaths in the town, his Deep One family still welcomes him, and while he "must do a penance" they also assure him that it "would not be heavy" (DH 367). This also further indicates they are aware of who he is and what his actions were. The actions of the people of Innsmouth were more likely to have been motivated by familial allegiance, and the surprise at recovering not just any missing scion of the town, but one from Obed Marsh himself.

The differences in perception between being an outsider to Innsmouth and being 'in' on the secret is important to note here. It is not being argued here that the Deep Ones are misunderstood by outsiders and that they are really good people. Rather, I am arguing that a close reading of the text can support the interpretation that the people of Innsmouth bear no ill will toward the narrator. It is the narrator that needs his experience to be interpreted as that of an inquisitive outsider threatening Innsmouth's secrets, as otherwise he would betray his ancestral connection to Obed Marsh and the Deep Ones, as well as his growing sympathy toward it. The significant difference between the viewpoints of being 'in' or 'out' of Innsmouth's secret is most clearly illustrated by a passage from the end of the novella: "Then the other shapes began to appear, filling me with nameless horror the moment I awoke. But during the dreams they did not horrify me at all—I was one with them" (DH 366). With his human mind, he finds the idea horrifying but his Deep One half feels a sense of unity and later, even "wonder and glory" (DH 367). The natives of Innsmouth and their Deep One brethren have great joy in their existence, therefore their actions towards the narrator would not been from a stance of malice, but of welcoming him to their—and soon to be his—ways. The misconception that there is malignity abroad in Innsmouth thus comes from two sources: the wilful desire of the narrator to misrepresent his experience to corroborate his sense of human identity by portraying himself as a hunted outsider, and this is secondly compounded by the idea that the intent of the Deep Ones was malign, which is contrary to the Deep Ones' own perception of their existence and ways, as it is to the narrator's after he accepts his identity.

The aversion to Innsmouth is not unique to the narrator, as readers learn that "nobody around [Newburyport] or in Arkham or Ipswich will have anything to do with 'em" (*DH* 308). Any connection to Innsmouth is seen as shameful and those who live in the towns around Innsmouth "try to cover up any Innsmouth blood they have in 'em" (*DH* 306). The hamlet is "very sparsely treated" in the county's official records, "as if [the people] formed a discredit to the county" (*DH* 310). The outside world breaks off its connection to Innsmouth, as indicated by the lack of travel to and from the hamlet, to the extent that there is "no railroad now . . . the branch line from Rowley was given up years ago" (*DH* 306). This fear of Innsmouth extends to a national level too, and this is significant, as we will see. When the narrator alerts the authorities about the monsters that live in Innsmouth, they react violently with "a vast series of raids and arrests" followed by the "deliberate burning and dynamiting . . . of an enormous number of . . . supposedly empty houses along the abandoned waterfront" (*DH* 303) and even the torpedoing of Devil's Reef. The levels of distress caused by the existence of Innsmouth were so great that the Federal government ignored its own justice system, as "no trials, or even definite charges, were reported" (*DH* 303). Even the "many liberal organizations" that complained of these actions "became surprisingly passive and reticent" after what they learned in "long confidential discussions" and "trips to certain camps and prisons" (*DH* 304). Everyone that comes into contact with Innsmouth, from the narrator to the neighbouring townspeople to national level government, is shown to react with abhorrence and a desire to live as free of Innsmouth as possible, either by ignoring it completely or by destroying it. Innsmouth strikes a chord of abhorrence in the nation itself then, as represented by the government practices described above.

This abhorrence, I propose, is connected with the early twentieth-century American attitudes toward economic decline and fear national decay. Paul Buhle proposes that Lovecraft writes "at an historic moment when European intellectuals recognised and even embraced decay, while Americans rarely deigned to admit its presence in their own culture" (203). Jani Scandura and Michael Thurston describe American modernity as "touting [America's] eternal youth . . . encrypting its own history in a narrative of perpetual process and present. America was always 'becoming' and therefore always new—renewed" (5–6). Backgrounding this focus on newness, however, was the fact that between 1880 and 1924, America was radically altered due to the "influx of 25 million immigrants to the United States between 1880 and 1924" (Scandura and Thurston 7). If something is always new, renewed and eternally young then there is no decay, just as Buhle observes, and it is this rejected concept of decay that is at the heart of the fear surrounding Innsmouth. This theme of decay is conveyed primarily through Lovecraft's descriptions of the hamlet's urban landscape. Timothy Evans notes that in Lovecraft, tradition is "embodied primarily by architecture" and that in the instance of Innsmouth "decayed colonial houses and churches prefigure the protagonist's discovery of the decay and corruption of the people who live in them" (124, 118). The town is described from the outset as the "ancient town of decay and desolation" (DH 313), and this is reinforced by the descriptions of the cityscape that is comprised of "dismal buildings" (DH 317), where the "vast huddle of sagging gambrel roofs . . . conveyed with offensive clearness the idea of wormy decay" (DH 316). As the narrator explores the town, he observes on all sides the "gaping windows of deserted hovels" which "leaned at perilous and incredible angles through the sinking of part of the foundations" (DH 324). The extent to which the town's buildings are given over to "cobwebs and memories and the conqueror worm" (DH 324) frightens the narrator, as does the "squalid sea of decaying roofs" (DH 347). The prevalence of imagery relating to collapsing roofs and "the decaying remains of three once beautiful Georgian steeples" (DH 320) gives a further sense of decline, the decay of these icons of architectural high points corresponds to a fall from the heights of prosperity. When faced with this evidence of decay that contravenes America's "eternal youth" (Scandura and Thurston 5) and leaves America's "assumed destiny evidently exposed like all other social and biological system to the process of decline, decay and replacement" (Buhle 199), the narrator reacts in a manner reminiscent of what is suggested by Scandura and Thurston, in an elaborate and desperate encryption of his experience in Innsmouth, and his personal history.

The decay of Innsmouth conveys its failure of economic prosperity, and as Evans indicates, "the physical description is based on Lovecraft's explorations of Newburyport and other economically depressed communities on the north shore of Massachusetts Bay" (115). Innsmouth was once a prosperous place and "a seat of great marine prosperity in the early nineteenth century" (DH 310), according to the county records. The ticket agent remembers the days when Innsmouth was "almost a city—quite a port before the War of 1812" (DH 306). The decline hit when trade began "fallin' off, mills losin' business—even the new ones" (DH 329), which was made worse by the failure of several maritime ventures; and once Obed Marsh's "trade was doin' very poor . . . it hit the whole of Innsmouth, too, because in seafarint days what profited the master of a ship gen'lly profited the crew proportionate" (DH 333). This economic depression has lasted to the date of the narrator's visit, as he notes that Innsmouth is "oddly free from the noise of industry" (DH 324) and that there is a mere "dozen shops in current operation" to serve as "the civic centre of Innsmouth" (DH 320). The empty buildings, the unnatural lack of industry, the "loafers" (DH 342) in the streets and the generally sluggish economy indicated by the unwelcoming shops and discouragement of visitors, paints Innsmouth as a place of intense poverty and economic stasis. There is no growth in the town, buildings do not go up or out, instead they recede or crumble. There is civic and industrial stagnation, and advancing decay which was inspired by Lovecraft's experience of genuine communities of the sort.

Innsmouth's stagnation and decay extends to the surrounding landscape. Innsmouth is surrounded by "wide salt marshes, desolate and unpeopled" (DH 304), which does not only limit trading access to the town and isolate it by keeping "neighbours off . . . on the landward side" (DH 304) but also precludes viable farmland. What was once a "fertile and thickly settled countryside" was reduced to "dead stumps and crumbling foundation-walls" (DH 315).

These marshes are shown as having a double history. The change from populated farmland to desolate marshes happened at the time of the "Innsmouth epidemic of 1846" (*DH* 315), which is what the incident with the Deep Ones coming on land to free Obed Marsh and kill his enemies is known as to the outside world. There are two stories told about the change, one that attributes it to "a dark connexion with hidden forces of evil" (*DH* 315) while the other is an economic one stating that the change in the land "was caused by the unwise cutting of woodlands near the shore, which robbed the soil of the best protection and opened the way for waves of wind-blown sand" (*DH* 315). This double history shows the way in which "unwise" economic decisions leading to economic hardship can enter popular perception or myth as "hidden forces of evil." In Innsmouth, economic decline and hidden forces are inextricably linked. It is important to note the almost certainly deliberate pun: that the *marshes* (or is that the *Marshes?*) are responsible for Innsmouth's isolation, decay and economic decline. Here, the Marsh family almost supernaturally becomes one with the land, as the land changes not only to serve their purpose in protecting Innsmouth from outside interference, but also to share a name with them. The image here is significant, where the marshes' and Marshes' influence have created civic and economic destruction, due to injudicious economic choices, here spoken synonymously with "hidden forces of evil."

The economic decline of Innsmouth which led to its decay is as problematic as the resulting decay. "The project of New World conquest," writes Buhle, "contained both a Utopian search for geographic infinitude and a . . . desire to escape the contradictions of class society by establishing the ultimate self made class society" (198). This self made class society was made possible economic liberation from the confines of the old world, as "the colonial American on the edge of the forest can aspire to the individual liberty of self and property unknown in the Old world save to the very rich" (198). In Innsmouth, there is neither the land from which one can make their fortune, nor is there any economic opportunity left. Innsmouth uncomfortably undermines the "project of New World conquest" (Buhle 198) and "the signs of modern life—jazz, skyscrapers, automobiles . . . Fordist mass production, corporate capitalism, the Hollywood studio system," which were "born or seemed to be most at home" (Scandura and Thurston 4) in America. Scandura and Thurston put forward that during the 1930s, the time when "Innsmouth" was written, America's "progressive modernity' had to be "preserved . . . from the taint of depression—and the Depression—that embroiled American culture" (6). Innsmouth represents extreme economic decline that undermined the dreams that underpinned its colonisation, as well as its concept of itself as an eternally young culture of material prosperity. The narrator, the people of nearby towns, and the even the Federal government, through their attempts to ignore or destroy Innsmouth, acted in preserving against the depression and decay it threatened to reveal.

But where does that then leave the end of "The Shadow over Innsmouth"? What is signified by the narrator's abrupt acceptance of the undermining of his traditions and sense of modernity, to leave his humanity and "in that lair of the Deep Ones . . . dwell amidst wonder and glory forever" (DH 367)? Evans provides one possible reading that it is "acknowledging the presence of conflicting emotions in the face of change" and that even in the face of mourning "the loss of New England traditions" it is "acknowledging a future in which hybrid people and cultural forms may be recognised as the norm" (125) in a sense where hybrid does not translate to literal fish people but rather the combination of decay and of what is perceived as New England tradition. Buhle's theory of decay suggests that "the end of this social world we know means the dawning of an age almost unimaginable and somehow linked to that older existence so long ago left behind" (199), which echoes the fate of the hybrid offspring of Deep Ones and humans who revert to a water form and return to ancient cities under the sea. But whether this change is implied to be positive or negative is sketchier, and Evans concedes in his article that "there has been considerable debate about whether the end of this story is meant to dramatize a corruption of the narrator, or whether it constitutes a humanizing of the Deep Ones" (125). The answer perhaps is purposefully ambivalent, just as the complex layers of perspective in the narrative suggest that the interpretation of Innsmouth depends entirely on whether one identifies as aware of the secrets of Innsmouth and thus a part of it, or if one remains outside of it. To those outside, it is a threatening, frightening, and almost certainly malign prospect. To those within, such as the narrator allows himself to be, the prospect of such a change is "a kind of exaltation" (*DH* 367).

Works Cited

Buhle, Paul. "Dystopia as Utopia: Howard Phillips Lovecraft and the Unknown Content of American Horror Literature." In *H. P. Lovecraft: Four Decades of Criticism*, ed. S. T. Joshi. Athens: Ohio University Press, 1980.

Evans, Timothy H. "A Last Defense Against the Dark: Folklore, Horror and the Uses of Tradition in the Works of H. P. Lovecraft." *Journal of Folklore Research* 42.1 (2005): 99–136.

Lovecraft, H. P. *The Call of Cthulhu and Other Weird Stories*. Ed. S. T. Joshi. New York: Penguin, 1999.

Nelson, Victoria. *The Secret Life of Puppets*. Cambridge, MA: Harvard University Press, 2001.

Scandura, Jani and Thurston, Michael. "Introduction: America and the Phantom Modern." In *Modernism, Inc: Body, Memory, Capital*, ed. Jani Scandura and Michael Thurston. New York: New York University Press, 2001.

Elementary, My Dear Lovecraft: H. P. Lovecraft and Sherlock Holmes

Gavin Callaghan

> The point under discussion was, how far any singular gift in an individual was due to his ancestry and how far to his early training.
> —Sir Arthur Conan Doyle, "The Greek Interpreter,"
> *Memoirs of Sherlock Holmes*

I. Upon Well-Trodden Ground

H. P. Lovecraft's debt to the Sherlock Holmes mysteries of Sir Arthur Conan Doyle has been dealt with by Peter Cannon, Debora D'Agati, Philip A. Shreffler, and others,[1] so much so that one might think little more of value could be said on the matter. And while Peter Cannon grants Martin J. Swanson the honor of being, in the early 1960s, "the first student of both the Canon and the Cthulhu Mythos to draw parallels between Holmes and Lovecraft" ("The Return of H. P. Lovecraft" 217), one thinks that the first (admittedly non-scholarly) connection between the two occurred the moment Sherlockians such as August Derleth and Vincent Starrett took interest in Lovecraft's works, followed shortly thereafter by Edmund Wilson's denunciation of both and their followers in November 1945. While researching an essay on the relation between Lovecraft's ostensibly cosmic idea of "the unnamable" and Victorian issues of social probity, I found myself reading the entirety of the

---

1. Fictional team-ups between the Lovecraftian and Sherlockian worlds are becoming something of an industry, as in the role-playing game supplement *Cthulhu by Gaslight*, Michael Reeves and John Pelan's anthology *Shadows over Baker Street: New Tales of Terror* (2003), and Peter Cannon's satirical *Pulptime* (1984) and the story "The Rummy Affair of Young Charlie," in *Forever Azathoth* (2012).

Doyle's Sherlock Holmes canon. I found that the parallels between Lovecraft's weird fiction and Doyle's mysteries go much deeper, and reach much farther, than previous studies had touched upon. The commonalities between the writers do not stop with the well-known parallels between *The Hound of the Baskervilles* and "The Hound," or with Lovecraft's lifelong mirroring of Holmes's eccentricities; rather, they are only the beginning.

Several parallels I wish to draw between Lovecraft's and Doyle's works were anticipated in Philip A. Shreffler's essay "Watson's Weird Tales: Horror in the Sherlockian Canon," which makes a convincing case that the Holmes tales basically are "horror stories" (7) (a fact realized as early as 1978 by the author of *Sherlock Holmes vs. Dracula; or, The Adventure of the Sanguinary Count*, and which Shreffler traces partially to their mutual use of the trappings of Gothic Romanticism).[2] But whereas H. P. Lovecraft's similarities to Doyle may be due to their parallel use of elements of Gothic horror, I maintain that something else also is at work, something that goes far beyond and yet is also rooted in Doyle's influence upon the young Lovecraft: the horrific sadism of the Holmes stories enabling the youth to begin to express and formulate his own version of the unnamable, and, like a latter-day Watson, to reveal some of the familial horrors and anxieties that beset him. Indeed, much like Lovecraft's peculiar usage of the classical myths and pulp magazines of his childhood in his weird fiction, or his fevered reaction to the paternal themes evident in Sherwood Anderson's *Winesburg, Ohio*,[3] Lovecraft seems to have been particularly influenced by the specifically *paternal* aspects of Conan Doyle's Holmes stories.

II. Some Initial Parallels

Holmes's observation to Watson in *The Sign of Four* (1890), "How small we feel with our petty ambitions and strivings in the presence

---

2. These Gothic elements often include, as Shreffler points out, "dark castles, secret passages, haunted forests, stormy nights, and, almost always, ultimately revealed crime or sin" (9)—nearly all of which are found in HPL's "The Outsider."

3. See my essays "H. P. Lovecraft and the Munsey Pulps," "Secrets Behind the Locked Door: H. P. Lovecraft and the Theseus Myth," and "H. P. Lovecraft and Sherwood Anderson" (all forthcoming).

of the great elemental forces of Nature!", and his declaration that "the chief proof of man's real greatness lies in his perception of his own smallness" (Doyle 1.121), capture Lovecraft's cosmic viewpoint in a nutshell. The idea of the *insignificance of the human* will likewise be reflected in what Peter Cannon has noted regarding the lack of "compelling characters" in Lovecraft's fiction ("You Have Been in Providence, I Perceive" 46). It would indeed be ironic if it was *Holmes's own theory of human insignificance* that influenced Lovecraft in his decision to eschew not only realistic or compelling characters, but also the opportunity to create a heroic, recurring Holmes-like figure in his own tales. Holmes repeatedly berates Watson that he would rather solve his mysteries in anonymity. For him, the *work* is everything—*he* is nothing. Dr. Watson may have ignored Holmes's fictional advice, but *Lovecraft*, it appears, took it to heart.

Deborah D'Agati rightly contrasts Doyle's heroic stories, in which evil is usually caught or punished in the end, with Lovecraft's more macabre vision, in which the heroes are often reduced to madness or death (54–60 passim), the oft-derided but little-understood *heroic* aspects of Lovecraft's weird fiction—as represented by the notorious good vs. evil plots of "The Shunned House," "The Horror at Red Hook," "The Dunwich Horror," and *The Case of Charles Dexter Ward* (which, as Peter Cannon has observed, have caused some embarrassment to certain Lovecraft critics [*H. P. Lovecraft* 135])—would also seem to preserve something of Lovecraft's original Holmesian influence, and Holmes's strict ethos of order, probity, and justice. Indeed, Cannon goes so far as to link Dr. Armitage in "The Dunwich Horror" to "the archetypal fictional detective at mystery's end" (*H. P. Lovecraft* 88–89.) In "Red Hook," too, we even see Lovecraft attempting (unsuccessfully) to make the corrupt Robert Suydam detective Malone's "arch-fiend and adversary" (*D* 57), in a relationship somewhat akin to that between Moriarty and Holmes, both Moriarty and Suydam being cultured, educated men, who go in for crime.

Doyle's description in "The Five Orange Pips" of hostile weather as being symbolic of forces hostile to civilization refers, for example, to "the presence of those great elemental forces, which shriek at mankind though the bars of his civilization, like untamed beasts in a cage" (1.218), anticipating the familiar rhetoric

of the supposed "snarling chaos" that Lovecraft saw as lurking "behind life" (*D* 199), and which Lovecraft, following his own peculiar bent, would largely identify with sadistic and incestuous
processes of sexuality. John Radford, psychologist and Holmes
scholar, observed in a televised interview, using terms equally suggestive of Lovecraft's own largely unconscious inspirations:

> In many of the [Holmes] stories, the weather plays a significant
> role. It's treated almost as a kind of impersonal force, uncontrol-
> lable, and one might say this represents the underworld that
> Holmes is battling against. But one might go further, I suggest,
> and say that in a way it's analogous to what Freud described as
> the Id, the uncontrollable, unknown part of the personality.

Note the similarity between Doyle's conception of a criminal *underworld* and Lovecraft's picture of a corrupt, malevolent underworld in the subterranean inner earth—a connection that Peter
Cannon briefly alludes to in "The Rummy Affair of Young Charlie," in which he draws a humorous parallel between the subterranean bank robbery planned in Doyle's "The Red-Headed League"
(1891) and the largely psychological horrors in "The Rats in the
Walls," which proceed, as Cannon wryly avers, *"from beneath"*
(*Scream for Jeeves* 129).

Note, too, a similarity between Holmes and Watson's mutual
interest in the strange, the *outré*, and the bizarre, an interest held by
Lovecraft's narrators. Holmes observes in "The Red-Headed
League": "'I know, my dear Watson, that you share my love of all
that is bizarre and outside the conventions and humdrum routine of
everyday life'" (1.176). It is his longing for "bizarre" effects that leads
Holmes to indulge, like Lovecraft's narrators in "Celephaïs," "Hypnos," and "Dagon," in drugs during fallow periods, and to complain
despairingly in *The Sign of Four*: "'Crime is commonplace, existence
is commonplace, and no qualities save those which are commonplace have any function upon earth'" (1.93). Compare this with
Lovecraft's narrator in "The Lurking Fear," who possesses a "love of
the grotesque and the terrible which has made my career a series of
quests for strange horrors in literature and in life" (*D* 179) (not to
mention Lovecraft himself, and his own interest in depicting *viola-
tions of natural law* in his fiction). Lovecraft's narrator even chooses

as his confidant a man named Arthur Monroe, "whose education, taste, intelligence, and temperament all seemed to mark him as one not bound to conventional ideas and experiences" (*D* 185)—language that parallels the *sharing* of a common interest in the bizarre that binds Holmes and Watson. In Lovecraft's "The Tomb," too, Jervas Dudley laments, in language much like that of Holmes, "the unfortunate fact that the bulk of humanity is too limited in its mental vision to weigh with patience and intelligence those isolated phenomena, seen and felt only by a psychologically sensitive few, which lie outside its common experience" (*D* 3), although unlike Holmes, he does so from within an insane asylum. As late as 1935, Lovecraft's hero Robert Blake will be represented as living an endless "quest for scenes and effects of a bizarre, spectral sort" (*DH* 93), and although I had at first been inclined to view this aspect of Blake as a satire by Lovecraft on the aesthetic vagaries of the decadents, Blake may have been a decadent by way of the Sherlock Holmes stories, which, as Samuel Rosenberg has observed, seem to have been imbued by Doyle with certain decadent characteristics.[4]

Like Lovecraft, who sought strange effects, whether architectural or atmospheric, in the places around him, and who famously described life as "a hideous thing" (*D* 73), whose "shocking revelations" (*D* 72) would blast the mind unfortunate enough to correlate them, Holmes seeks strangeness in *life itself*, which, with its "'strange effects and extraordinary combinations,'" as Holmes declares in "The Red-Headed League," "'is always far more daring than any effort of the imagination'" (Doyle 1.176). Elsewhere, in the introduction to "A Case of Identity" (1891)—in a passage that Samuel Rosenberg claims (109) inspired a passage in Modernist writer James Joyce's *Finnegans Wake*—Holmes expands upon this theme in startlingly Lovecraftian terms:

> "Life is infinitely stranger than anything which the mind of man could invent. We would not dare to conceive the things which

---

4. According to Rosenberg, *The Sign of Four*, "The Red-Headed League" and other stories contain symbolic or satirical references to such decadents as Oscar Wilde and Robert Ross (Rosenberg 127–41 *passim*). Rosenberg does not mention it, but Thaddeus Sholto in the former story seems to be named after Sholto Douglas, one of the brothers of Wilde's lover, Sir Alfred Douglas.

are really mere commonplaces of existence. If we could fly out of that window hand in hand, hover over this great city, gently remove the roofs, and peep in at the queer things which are going on, the strange coincidences, the plannings, the cross-purposes, the wonderful chains of events, working through generations, and leading to the most *outré* results, it would make all fiction with its conventionalities and foreseen conclusions seem most stale and unprofitable." (Doyle 1.190–91)

In this passage, we glimpse Lovecraft's various multi-generational sagas of bestiality and cannibalism, and his lifelong fascination with the idea of "Living things—usually insane or idiotic members of the family—concealed in garrets or secret rooms of old houses"—things that, as he writes, "have been literal realities in rural New England" (*SL* 2.139).

Peter Cannon dealt with the clear parallels between Holmes's disquisition on the sinister aspects of rural English homes in "The Adventure of the Copper Beeches" and Lovecraft's description of the sinister aspects of backwoods Massachusetts dwellings in "The Picture in the House."[5] (Philip A. Shreffler also cited this passage from "Copper Beeches" in the service of his *Holmes-as-Horror Fiction* thesis ["Watson's Weird Tales" 7].) Clearly, Doyle provided Lovecraft with a *way* of looking at reality, a way that extended beyond the commonplace into the bizarre, the sinister, and the cosmic, although Lovecraft's "cosmic" was as tinged, and undermined, by the mundane and sadistic as Doyle's more unapologetically earthly mysteries.

III. Women and Whisperers

Critics have remarked upon the well-known dislike of both Sherlock Holmes and H. P. Lovecraft for women. Cannon calls it an indifference to women ("You Have Been in Providence, I Perceive" 46). Although Holmes observes tactfully in "The Lion's Mane" [1926], "Women have seldom been an attraction to me, for my brain has always governed my heart" [Doyle 2.1088], one senses that he is rather more honest about his true feelings when,

---

5. See Cannon, "You Have Been in Providence, I Perceive" 45–46; Cannon, "Parallel Passages" passim; and Cannon, "The Return of Sherlock Holmes" 219.

in *The Valley of Fear* [1915], he is struck by what he crassly calls the marked "absence of the usual feminine ululation" [1.801] at the scene of the apparent death of Ivy Douglas's husband.

As with Lovecraft's weird fiction, in which women play a large, if corruptive, role (as villainesses, witches, and demonic goddesses), this dislike does not in any way suggest *absence*. In fact, Doyle's stories, just as Lovecraft's, are fairly fraught with feminine entanglements, usually in the form of newly emancipated women—what Holmes perceptively calls "'One of the most dangerous classes in the world, [. . .] the drifting and friendless woman'" (1.942). Described as "a stray chicken in a world of foxes" (1.943), very often her inherited wealth and beauty is stolen or misappropriated by a dominant male or father for nefarious purposes (viz. *The Sign of Four*, "The Speckled Band" [1892], "A Case of Identity," "The Adventure of the Copper Beeches"), or by a genuine suitor for the same reason ("The Adventure of the Noble Bachelor" [1892] and "The Adventure of the Illustrious Client" [magazine publication 1924; book publication 1927].) The father in "The Speckled Band" (which Lovecraft famously, if cryptically, alludes to during the deranged father's monologue at the end of "The Rats in the Walls" [*DH* 45]) is particularly heinous, a brute who attempts to kill two of his daughters, and who allows his estate to be overrun with baboons, giant cats, and other creatures, symbolic of that animalistic degeneracy so familiar in Lovecraft's later weird fiction. In "The Thing on the Doorstep" (1933), the father steals not his daughter's wealth or inheritance, but her *body itself*. Asenath is described as "his trusting, weak-willed, half-human child," who was "at his mercy" (*DH* 289).

In "A Case of Identity" (1892), Doyle adds the implicitly *incestuous* idea of a woman, Mary Sutherland, being tricked by her *disguised father* into believing she has a suitor. The "suitor" vanishes (after swearing Mary to a vow of eternal loyalty), thus enabling Mary's father to retain the use of Mary's substantial annual income. The interesting thing with regard to "A Case of Identity," however, is the extent to which the father's disguise anticipates the later disguise of the alien-Akeley (who is perhaps Nyarlathotep himself) in Lovecraft's "The Whisperer in Darkness" (1930):

Doyle: "A Case of Identity"	Lovecraft: "The Whisperer in Darkness"
Mary's "suitor," Hosmer Angel, is "'a very shy man',," who would "'rather walk with me in the evening than in the daylight, for he said he hated to be conspicuous'" (Doyle 1.194).	The alien-Akeley sits in the "shadowy depths" (*DH* 252) of the room, his features described as "the white blur of a man's face and hands" (*DH* 252).
"'Even his voice was gentle. He'd had the quinsy and swollen glands when he was young, he told me, and it had left him with a weak throat, and a hesitating, whispering fashion of speech'" (1.194).	The alien-Akeley is a "figure who had tried to speak," but was restrained by an asthmatic "hacking whisper" (*DH* 252).
Mary's father "'masked [his] face with a moustache and a pair of bushy whiskers, [and] sunk that clear voice into an insinuating whisper'" (1.200).	Wilmarth observes "It was a hard whisper to catch at first, since the grey moustache concealed all movements of the lips" (*DH* 252).
At first Angel refuses to receive letters from Mary—even typewritten ones, since "'when they were typewritten he always felt that the machine had come between us'" (1.194); later, Angel corresponds with Mary as part of his deception, but all his letters, even the signature, are typewritten (1.197)—a fact Holmes uses to solve the mystery of the suitor's true identity, since, as Angel observes, "'a typewriter has really quite as much individuality as a man's handwriting'" (1.199).	The alien-Akeley uses a typewriter to correspond with Wilmarth, after the real Henry Akeley is done away with, to disguise the change in handwriting; an expedient also used by Charles Dexter Ward's usurper, Joseph Curwen.

Given the *paternal* nature of so many of Lovecraft's horrors, the apparent origin of his "Whisperer" imagery in a story about overt parental/paternal control (and implicit incest) is very suggestive of Lovecraft's overriding paternal concerns, and of the effect that Doyle's story must have had upon the young Lovecraft.

One can see a prefiguring of the ending of "The Whisperer in Darkness" (and also "Medusa's Coil" and "Facts concerning the Late Arthur Jermyn and His Family") in Doyle's eerie "The Yellow Face" (1893), a story with strong paternal (and, in this case, racial) themes. The marriage of loving husband Grant Munro and his seemingly loving wife Effie is rent after a mysterious family moves into a nearby house, and a malevolent face appears at the window. As the husband tells Holmes, "'I was some little way off, so that I could not make out the features, [but] there was something unnatural and inhuman about the face'" (Doyle 1.354). Even more disturbingly, the husband notices his wife leaving their bedroom in the dead of night, later emerging from the neighboring house and then refusing to give him any word of explanation.

Like Delapore in "The Rats in the Walls," the wife in this instance is a wealthy American from the southern United States, who came to England after a tragic death: in Delapore's case, the death of his son in World War I, which leaves him "bereaved and aimless" (*DH* 28). In Doyle's case, the death of Effie's lawyer-husband and their child apparently is from yellow fever: "This sickened her of America, and she came to live with a maiden aunt at Pinner, in Middlesex" (Doyle 1.353). Upon hearing the account of the mysterious lodger next door and the repulsive face, Holmes theorizes that the woman's husband is not dead but actually stalking her or blackmailing her from the cottage. As Holmes suggests—in terms that would resonate with the experiences of the young Lovecraft, whose father had contracted a disease and was confined:

> "The facts, as I read them, are something like this: This woman was married in America. Her husband developed some hateful qualities, or shall we say he contracted some loathsome disease and became a leper or an imbecile? She flies from him at first, returns to England, changes her name, and starts her life, as she thinks afresh . . ." (Doyle 1.359)

In the unexpected conclusion to Doyle's tale, Holmes, Watson, and the husband decide to brave the supposed blackmailer and barge into the house, making their way into the upstairs room, where instead of a husbandly monster they find a little girl wearing a sinister mask:

> The face which she turned towards us was of the strangest livid tint, and the features were absolutely devoid of any expression. An instant later the mystery was explained. Holmes, with a laugh, passed his hand behind the child's ear, a mask peeled off from her countenance, and there was a little coal black negress, with all her

white teeth flashing in amusement at our amazed faces. I burst out laughing out of sympathy with her merriment . . . (1.361)

We learn that Effie's first husband—a gentlemanly black man named John Hebron (of whom Effie says, "'a nobler man never walked the earth'" [1.361])—did indeed die of yellow fever, but their *daughter* did not, and the wife, unwilling to abandon her child, had her move in next door, but was fearful of telling her new husband. Peter Cannon observes that Doyle was "a fair-minded man who often championed the underdog regardless of color" ("The Adventure of the Three Anglo-American Authors" 144), an assertion ably proven by this story, which ends happily, with Grant lifting the little child and kissing her, "and then, still carrying her, he held his other hand out to his wife and turned towards the door" (1.362). A more dissimilar denouement than that of Lovecraft's "Medusa's Coil," in which Dennis de Russy stamps his wife to death after the revelation of her true identity, leaving his bloody bootprint on her naked back and her blood splattered all over the walls, can hardly be imagined. It is strange that the youthful Lovecraft, given his admitted love for the Holmes stories, was not swayed from his unswerving racial views by the tale. It is possible, however, that the story affected him in terms of fictional imagery. We can perhaps see here the prefiguring of many later themes in Lovecraft's weird fiction, whether the unmasking of the alien whisperer in Henry Akeley's study or the mysterious birth of "'Lavinny's black brat'" (*DH* 162) in "The Dunwich Horror."

IV. Apes, Cannibals, and Rats

Philip A. Shreffler cites Doyle's description of the apelike body of the murdered Enoch Drebber in *A Study in Scarlet* (1888) as an example of the "gruesome, repulsive, and horrifying" (8) in the Holmes Canon, as part in his *Holmes-as-Horror Fiction* thesis. Shreffler does not mention it, but one also notes a connection between Doyle's description of the apelike Drebber's "low forehead, blunt nose, and prognathous jaw," which "gave the dead man a singularly simious and ape-like appearance" (Doyle 1.29), and Lovecraft's similarly apelike and prognathous-jawed ghouls. This horrific image will haunt Dr. Watson during the night. Doyle adds that the man's face *was so horrible that he deserved to be killed*—an idea Robert Louis Stevenson contemporaneously applied to the indescribably unnatural Mr. Hyde in *The Strange Case of Dr. Jekyll and Mr. Hyde* (1886), and which Lovecraft applied to various unnatural entities in his own weird fiction.[6] As Doyle writes:

> Every time I closed my eyes I saw before me the distorted, baboon-like countenance of the murdered man. So sinister was the impression which that face had produced upon me that I found it difficult to feel anything but gratitude for him who had removed its owner from the world. If ever human features bespoke vice of a most malignant type, they were certainly those . . . (1.36)

Lovecraft's hints at cosmic alienage and otherworldly loathsomeness can be seen to have an ultimately visceral, mundane, and bestial basis.

In "The Adventure of the Six Napoleons" (1904), the Italian murderer and thief Beppo is pictured as a "sharp-featured simian man, with thick eyebrows and a very peculiar projection of the lower part of the face, like the muzzle of a baboon" (Doyle 2.586). The thief's physical skills mirror his appearance, for he moves as "swift and active as an ape" (2.592). This mirrors the apelike athleticism of Arthur Jermyn's family, known for "incredible agility" and "feats of strength and climbing" (*D* 75). As they remand Beppo to the police station, Watson makes the mistake of moving his hand too close to the chained prisoner, so that at once Beppo "snapped at it like a hungry wolf" (Doyle 2.592), prefiguring the cannibalistic (often lycanthropic) orientation of Lovecraft's various weird monsters, from the wolfish Jacques Roulet in "The Shunned House" to the wolfish Ephriam Waite in "The Thing on the Doorstep," not to mention such ostensibly cosmic entities as eternally hungry Azathoth and ravening Cthulhu.

---

6. Joseph Curwen "and all with him must die" (*MM* 136); Ephraim Waite ought to "be extirpated from the face of the earth" (*DH* 298); "only generous clothing" enables Wilbur Whateley "to walk on earth unchallenged or uneradicated" (*DH* 174); the "peculiarly abominable quality" of the "swarthy cult-fiends on the *Alert* [. . .] made their destruction seem almost a duty" (*DH* 149–50).

V. Killer Fathers and Fangs in the Neck

Peter Cannon has cited parallel passages in Doyle's sinister "The Adventure of the Copper Beeches" and Lovecraft's "The Picture in the House," but those few passages do not constitute the total number of parallels between "Copper Beeches" and Lovecraft's later writings. Along with *The Hound of the Baskervilles*, "Copper Beeches" had perhaps the strongest influence of all the Holmes mysteries on Lovecraft's weird fiction. The ending of "The Rats in the Walls," where Delapore speaks of how "they found me in the blackness after three hours; found me crouching in the blackness over the plump, half-eaten body of Capt. Norrys, with my own cat leaping and tearing at my throat" (*DH* 45), preserves several aspects of Doyle's earlier story.

For instance, the villain of "Copper Beeches" is a *fat*, repulsive sadist named Jephro Rucastle, who holds his daughter prisoner, and who, at the end of the tale, is attacked and bitten *in the throat* by a gigantic, *starving* mastiff, which Rucastle keeps locked up in a shed and which patrols the grounds at night—all elements to be duplicated or elaborated upon by Lovecraft. As Doyle writes:

> There was the huge *famished brute*, its black muzzle buried *in Rucastle's throat*, while he writhed and screamed upon the ground. Running up, I blew its brains out, and it fell over with its keen white teeth still meeting in the *great creases of his* [Rucastle's] *neck*. With much labour we separated them and carried him, living but horribly mangled, into the house." (1.331; my emphases)

Note the interesting transpositions between Doyle's story and Lovecraft's later recension: the hunger of the "famished" *dog* is transferred by Lovecraft to the cannibalistic *father*, Delapore; the plump sadist Rucastle ("a prodigiously stout man," with "a great heavy chin which rolled down in fold upon fold over his throat" [1.318]) resembles fat Captain Norrys, Delapore's victim; the dog itself is transformed into a vengeful cat. Two other things remain the same in both versions: the extreme *sadism of the father* and the location of the avenging animal's vengeance—*the throat of the sadistic father*. (Lovecraft also connects throat-imagery with paternal themes in "Arthur Jermyn," in which Jermyn's bestial father, Sir Alfred Jermyn, bites "fiendishly" at a gorilla's "hairy throat" [D 77].)[7]

Lovecraft's sinister "quadruped things" (DH 42) in "The Rats in the Walls," much like the starving guard dog in "Copper Beeches," are kept in a perpetual "delirium of hunger" (1.318) in their prehistoric pens—"starving things" (DH 44) that are finally devoured by the "ravenous rodent army" that, denied its habitual source of food after the murder of the Delapore family, "burst forth from the priory in that historic orgy of devastation which the peasants will never forget" (DH 44).

It is notable that Doyle deals with the issue of paternal depravity throughout "Copper Beeches," particularly in the idea of the transmission of innate depravity *from father to son.* Although Doyle's concerns are more psychiatric and pathological in nature than Lovecraft's evolutionary and macabre visions, one can discern a parallel between Violet Hunter's unknowing description of the sadistic habits of the male offspring of the portly Jephro Rucastle and Lovecraft's picture of Delapore's regressive resumption of the sadistic habits of his cannibalistic forefathers:

> "His whole life appears to be spent in an alternation between savage fits of passion and gloomy intervals of sulking. Giving pain to any creature weaker than himself seems to be his one idea of amusement, and he shows quite remarkable talent in planning the capture of mice, little birds, and insects. But I would rather not talk about the creature, Mr. Holmes, and, indeed, he has little to do with my story." (Doyle 1.324)

As Holmes confides to Watson, "'The most serious point in the case is the disposition of the child'" (1.329):

> "My dear Watson, you as a medical man are continually gaining light as to the tendencies of a child by the study of the parents. Don't you see that the converse is equally valid. I have frequently

---

7. HPL may have been influenced in this throat-imagery by Cotton Mather's *Wonders of the Invisible World* (1692), in which Mather tells of a witness against accused witch Susanna Martin, who was awakened at night by "the likeness of a *Cat,* which flew upon him" from his window and which "took fast hold of his Throat" (Mather 116). (One notes that witch Susanna Martin invokes the epithet *"She-Devil"* [116] in this account, used later by HPL [DH 294–96].)

gained my first real insight into the character of parents by studying their children. This child's disposition is abnormally cruel,
merely for cruelty's sake, and whether he derives this from his
smiling father, as I should suspect, or from his mother, it bodes
evil for the poor girl who is in their power." (1.329–30)

This idea of a child's possession by his ancestors (particularly *male*
ancestors) informs much of the Lovecraftian canon, from "The
Tomb" to "The Thing on the Doorstep."

Doyle revisits the issue of father-son depravity in "The Reigate
Puzzle" (1894), in which a father and son prove to be murderers, the
son being described in particularly bestial terms as having "dropped
all that jaunty, dashing style which had characterized him," so that
"the ferocity of a dangerous wild beast gleamed in his dark eyes and
distorted his handsome features" (1.406). Indeed, a surprised Watson
suddenly comes upon the father and son together, as they attempt to
murder the detective: "bending over the prostrate figure of Sherlock
Holmes, the younger clutching his throat with both hands, while the
elder seemed to be twisting one of his wrists" (1.406).

"The Rats in the Walls" may have been influenced by the paternal
themes in Doyle's "The Five Orange Pips" (1892), the story of a young
man named James Openshaw, the victim of vengeful Ku Klux Klan
terrorism at his estate in England. In both stories, a *male inheritance*
forms the basic impetus for the tale, with young Openshaw (as in
Lovecraft's "The Alchemist") inheriting a murderous *curse*—in this
case, at the hands of the KKK, which kills Openshaw's uncle and father. The uncle was once a high-ranking member of the KKK in the
U.S., but he later fled to England, bringing with him with a book detailing the activities of the KKK that implicated various prominent
Southern gentlemen in their crimes. As an unknowing Openshaw describes the activities of his Uncle Elias:

"When Lee laid down his arms my uncle returned to his plantation, where he remained for three of four years. About 1869 or
1870 he came back to Europe and took a small estate in Sussex,
near Horsham. He had made a very considerable fortune in the
States, and his reason for leaving them was his aversion to the negroes, and his dislike of the Republican policy in extending the
franchise to them." (Doyle 1,219)

Specific details differ between the two stories: Delapore's plantation is burned by Federal soldiers (*DH* 27), for instance; and Delapore later moves north to where his mother is from, and where despite his Confederate ties he goes so far as to become a "solid Yankee" businessman (*DH* 27). But the broader outlines of both stories—a wealthy American of previous residence in the South, with marked Confederate ties, travels to England after the American Civil War and, breaking his ties with his former life, purchases an estate—are very similar. Doyle actually *adds* the element of racism—an element that Lovecraft's obviously racist story merely sublimates to a deeper level of the narrative.

"The Five Orange Pips"	"The Silver Key"
Openshaw's *uncle* Elias shows him "an old rusty key, which must have belonged to the *attic*" (my emphasis), and "a small brass box, like a cashbox" (Doyle 1.220).	Randolph Carter's "Uncle Chris" is prevented from telling him "something odd once about an old unopened box with a key in it" (*MM* 417)—a box located in Carter's *attic*.
	"The Rats in the Walls"
Elias did his "duty well" (1.221) in "war time" and "had borne the repute of a brave soldier."	Delapore's father "was in the army, defending Richmond" (*DH* 27).
Elias destroys the "contents" (1.221) of the "brass box" out of fear of possible reprisals by the KKK, before Openshaw or his father can examine them and learn their meaning.	The "hereditary envelope" (*DH* 28) of the Delapores, which contains the secrets of a "tradition handed down" (*DH* 27) from father to son, is destroyed in a fire, so that "Neither I nor my father ever knew what" (*DH* 28) it "had contained."

It is interesting, too—not to mention typical—that Lovecraft applies the blame for the destruction of familial or paternal knowledge, not from self-destruction out of fear of the KKK, as in Doyle's version, but from an "incendiary outrage" at the hands of boisterous "Federal soldiers" (*DH* 27).

VI. Lovecraft and "The Musgrave Ritual"

One notes some suggestions of "The Rats in the Walls" (and other Lovecraft stories) in Doyle's earlier, classic mystery, "The Musgrave Ritual" (1893):

"The Musgrave Ritual"	"The Rats in the Walls"
Protagonist Reginald Musgrave is "'a scion of one of the very oldest families in the kingdom" (Doyle 1.388), whose "'Manor House of Hurlstone is perhaps the oldest inhabited building in the country. Something of his birth-place seemed to cling to the man, and I never looked at his pale, keen face [. . .] without associating him with gray archways and mullioned windows and all the venerable wreckage of a feudal keep'" (Doyle 1.388).	Lovecraft emphasizes the *great age* of Delapore's ancestors, and of Exham Priory where they resided, said to display evidences of Gothic, Saxon, Romanesque, "Roman, and even Druidic or native Cymric" (*DH* 27) architecture in its design.
"Over the low, heavy-lintelled door, in the centre of the old part" (1.393) of Hurlstone house, "is chiselled the date, 1607, but experts agreed that the beams and the stonework are really much older than this" (1.393).	Lovecraft cleverly juxtaposes "familiar English graffiti [. . .], some as recent as 1610" (*DH* 43), with the bones and debris from a cannibalistic cult existing from "three hundred, or a thousand, or two thousand, or ten thousand years ago" (*DH* 43). In both cases, a 17th-century date serves to convey great age, through its contrast and apparent coexistence with the far older remains around it.
Sherlock Holmes descends into the Hurlstone "'cellar'" (1.394), going down "'a winding stone stair'" (1.395) into the basement, where he finds "'a large and heavy flagstone with a rusted iron ring in the centre'" (1.392).	Delapore descends into the steps into the basement of Exham Priory, where he finds "a nearly square opening in the tiled floor" (*DH* 41) of the ancient Roman basement beneath the castle.
It takes both Holmes and a constable to raise the stone, after which "'A black hole yawned beneath into which we all peered,'" described as "'A small chamber about seven feet deep and four feet square'" (1.395). There, they see both "'a squat, brass-bound wooden box, [. . .], with this curious old-fashioned key projecting from the lock'" (cf. "The Silver Key"), and a dead man, who lies with "'his forehead sunk upon the edge of the box and his two arms thrown out on each side of it'" (1.395).	The steps within the hole lead down into a realm of death: "For yards about the steps extended an insane tangle of human bones" (*DH* 42), etc.

The man beneath the cellar proves to be a butler, who was killed and left behind by a hysterical, temperamental Welsh servant girl, who is "'fiery and passionate'" (1.392).	Delapore observes how "Temperament rather than ancestry was evidently the basis of this cult'" (DH 30) among his ancestors, since "Lady Margaret Trevor from Cornwall" (DH 30) became "the daemon heroine of a particularly horrible old ballad not yet extinct near the Welsh border" (DH 30). It takes little imagination to see a connection between Doyle's murderous Welsh girl and the butler in the cellar, and Lovecraft's "daemon heroine," Asenath Waite, who, as her husband complains, was "'seizing my body and putting me in that corpse of hers buried in the cellar'" (DH 302).
The box held by the butler proves to contain the lost and now tarnished, deteriorated crown of King Charles I, which his successor never claimed. Holmes explains: "'It is likely that the Musgrave who held the secret died in the interval, and by some oversight left this guide to his descendant without explaining the meaning of it. From that day to this it has been handed down from father to son, until at last it came within reach of a man who tore its secret out of it and lost his life in the venture" (1.397).	The "hereditary envelope" (DH 28) of the Delapores, which contains the secrets of a "tradition handed down" (DH 27) from father to son, is destroyed in a fire, so that "Neither I nor my father ever knew what" (DH 28) it had contained. Eventually, however, Delapore also tears out the secret . . . and loses his sanity, if not his life, in the venture!

The fact that Lovecraft seized upon the idea of a secret passed "from father to son" in a mystery story, for the purposes of his own bizarre, cannibalistically and bacchanalian-obsessed weird fiction, is suggestive of the paternal ideas and sadistic dynamics that underlay his fictional processes. Another writer influenced by Doyle, for instance, might seize upon the idea of the wild-eyed Welsh girl, and her penchant for betrayal; yet another might be influenced by the idea of the intricate cipher, or the boyhood friendship between Musgrave and Holmes. For Lovecraft, however, it is the mainly the mechanisms of paternal heredity and tradition that—along with Doyle's atmosphere of great age and the English Restoration period—draws Lovecraft's attention. Lovecraft, however, will also *invert* some of the paternal aspects of "The Musgrave Ritual"; and while the odd doings in Doyle's story only begin after the Reginald Musgrave's father is "'carried off'" (Doyle 1.388) by death, Delapore's return to his ancestral manor only occurs after the death of his *son*.

VII. Lovecraft and *The Hound of the Baskervilles*

The influence of Doyle's classic mystery *The Hound of the Baskervilles* (1902) on H. P. Lovecraft is well known.[8] Most discussion has focused merely upon the more obvious aspects of Lovecraft's short story "The Hound," and not "The Rats in the Walls" and other stories that show traces of the baleful hound's influence:

The Hound of the Baskervilles	"The Rats in the Walls"
The amiable Dr. Mortimer discovers a "prehistoric skull" (Doyle 2.714) in a Neolithic barrow on the moor, one of many megalithic and prehistoric sites on the Dartmoor downs near Baskerville Hall. (Mortimer makes a specialty of cranial phrenology and is uniquely qualified to "'tell the skull of a negro from that of an Esquimau'" [2.686]—one of Mortimer's first comments to Holmes is praise for the shape of Holmes's "'parietal fissure'" [2.672]!)	Delapore discovers "human or semi-human bones" (*DH* 41), including "skulls" denoting "nothing short of utter idiocy, cretinism, or primitive semi-apedom" (*DH* 41), in the subterranean grotto beneath Exham Priory (whose name recalls the title of Doyle's "The Adventure of the Priory School" [1904]).
Doyle refers to "great stones" upon the moor, "set by certain forgotten peoples in the days of old" (2.675), often formed into "gray circular rings" that Watson mistakes for "'sheep-pens'" (2.708). Mortimer reveals them to have once been "'the homes of our worthy ancestors. Prehistoric man lived thickly on the moor, and as no one in particular has lived there since, we find all his little arrangements exactly as he left them. These are his wigwams with the roofs off'" (2.709).	The subterranean grotto is filled with prehistoric "stone pens" (*DH* 42), in which human and sub-human victims were kept during generations of sadistic cannibalism and inbreeding during the primeval era—Lovecraft thereby making *explicit* an implicit connection between sheep's pens and human dwellings which Doyle's narrative had doubtlessly suggested to Lovecraft's young (and apparently morbid) mind.

---

8. See Swanson 36; Shreffler (1977) 81; Blackmore; Joshi 285.

Watson describes these structures to Holmes as "'the graves and the huge monoliths which are supposed to have marked [the] temples'" of primitive man, observing: "'As you look at the gray stone huts [. . .] you leave your own age behind you,'" and expect to see "'a skin-clad, *hairy* man crawl out from the *low* door…'" (2.712; my emphasis).	Cf. the temple and altar in the cellar of Exham Priory, whose rites are connected with, as Lovecraft wrote in a letter to F. B. Long, "a sadistic cult" perhaps prevalent among "exceedingly *low, hairy* Negroes existing perhaps 400,000 years ago" (*SL* 1:258; my emphasis).
Doyle draws an implicit connection between the towers of Baskerville Hall itself and the prehistoric burrows that surround it: "the two thin towers of Baskerville Hall" being "the only signs of human life which I could see, save only those prehistoric huts which lay thickly upon the slopes of the hills" (2.730).	Lovecraft subsumes such outlying stone circles and pens directly *beneath Exham Priory itself,* thereby unifying both civilized architecture and its prehistoric antecedents into *a single structure.* For Lovecraft, there ultimately is no difference between these differing stages of human habitation.

Although the Neolithic standing stones in Doyle's story bear little relation to the mystery of the hound itself, being used chiefly for atmosphere (Holmes secretly makes his shelter in a "stone hut upon the moor," for a time, where "'the old folk used to live'" [Doyle 2.732]), Lovecraft takes the extreme leap of directly connecting things like the Delapores' sadism and the Delapores' curse with a *prehistoric* heritage—thereby making a connection between *modern murder* and *prehistoric animalism* which Doyle, in his original version, had only fitfully suggested. For example, Doyle directly connects the "terrible animal face" of the escaped criminal hiding out on the moor, whose bestial visage is "seamed and scored with vile passions," with "one of those old savages" who once "dwelt in the burrows on the hillsides" (2.725). Lovecraft, of course, goes even farther back, far beyond the Neolithic, long before Doyle's "skin-clad, hairy man" ever existed, extending the Delapore-curse back into pre-hominid period. In Doyle's pointed juxtaposition of prehistoric primitivism and modern sadism, too, one can also discern a prefiguration of the landscape of Lovecraft's "The Lurking Fear," in which the deserted/decayed Martense Mansion is surrounded all sides by the subterranean mounds and burrows of the devolved Martense family. Lovecraft again makes explicit Doyle's implicit connection between the animalistic and the baser human passions. Clearly, the influence of Doyle, Sherlock Holmes, and *The Hound of the Basker-villes* runs deep in Lovecraft's weird fiction.

Just as in "The Musgrave Ritual," which dealt with a (frustrated) ancestral tradition, here too there is a "'certain legend which runs in the Baskerville family,'" contained in a paternal statement passing "in a direct line from Hugo Baskerville," and thence from father to father ("I had the story from my father, who also had it from his" [2.673]), before being formally recorded in a written statement in 1742. Indeed, Doyle underlines the particularly *paternal* nature of this statement, Hugo Baskerville leaving this warning "to his sons Rodger and John, with instructions that they say nothing thereof to their sister Elizabeth" (2.676). And, just as in Lovecraft's narrative, the family tradition involves base and sadistic practices—what the Baskerville legend calls "the fruits of the past," and those "foul passions whereby our family has suffered so grievously" (2.674)—language, again, that is certain to have struck a resonance with the youthful Lovecraft, smarting as he was from the stigma of his father's clouded demise.

The Hound of the Baskervilles	"The Rats in the Walls"
The first Hugo Baskerville is "wild, profane, and godless" (Doyle 2.674), possessing "a certain wanton and cruel humour, which made his name a byword through the West" (2.674).	The Delapore ancestors are "a race of hereditary daemons beside whom Gilles de Retz and the Marquis de Sade would seem the veriest tyros" (*DH* 30).
The tale begins with the death of Sir Charles Baskerville, who "made large sums of money in South African speculation" (2.676). He is "the scion of an old country family which has fallen on evil days," and who attempts to "restore the fallen grandeur of his line." Sir Charles's efforts, however, succeed only in reviving the ghost of the familial Hound.	The protagonist is "a retired manufacturer no longer young" (*DH* 28), who resolves "to divert my remaining years" in the restoration of his ancestral Exham Priory in England. His efforts succeed only in reviving the evil sadism/cannibalism of his family line.
	"The Alchemist"
The Baskerville Hound has "plagued the family so sorely ever since" (2.675), with "many of the family" (2.675) being "unhappy in their deaths, which have been sudden, bloody, and mysterious."	"All the Comtes of my line had met their end" (*D* 330) at an "early age."

Just as in "The Adventure of the Copper Beeches," Doyle combines *paternal themes* with images of *animal fangs in the father's throat*. He writes of "a foul thing, a great, black beast, shaped like a hound," seen "standing over Hugo, and plucking at his throat" (2.675). Lovecraft, as we have seen, oddly transfers this description in "The Rats in the Walls" to Delapore, whose avenging cat is seen "tearing at my throat" (*DH* 45) in an apparent frenzy somehow aroused by his cannibalistic actions. The *implicit* identification made by Doyle, between the sadistic crimes of the bestial Hugo Baskerville and the equally bestial Hound that kills him, is, in the person of Delapore, completed: *beast* and *man* have become one. Later, when the evil Stapledon looses the real Hound upon the kindly heir Sir Henry, Doyle likewise speaks of seeing "the beast spring upon its victim, hurl him to the ground, and worry at his throat" (2.757), although in this case Holmes is on hand to empty his revolver into the creature.

In both stories we see a contrast between the *outward benevolence* of the last remaining scion of an ancestral family and the *evil reputation* (and resurgent evil) of that family. Doyle resolves that contrast in the dichotomy between the likable and affable Sir Henry Baskerville on the one hand and his murderous cousin "Stapledon" on the other. Stapledon proves to be the son of the equally disreputable Rodger Baskerville, who "fled with a sinister reputation to South America" (2.761) (much in the same way, one thinks, that young Randolph Delapore of Carfax would go "among the negroes" [*DH* 31]), Stapledon having inherited all the sadistic and cunning blood of his ignoble forebears. Indeed, much as in Lovecraft's *The Case of Charles Dexter Ward*—in which young Ward's resemblance to his vampiric ancestor Joseph Curwen is proven by a hidden portrait that Ward discovers—the secret identity and motives of Stapledon as an heir to the Baskervilles are first suggested to Holmes by a portrait of the evil Hugo Baskerville hanging in Baskerville Hall. As Holmes observes, in curiously mystical terms for a supposed materialist and skeptic: "'Yes, it is an interesting instance of a throwback, which appears to be both physical *and* spiritual. A study of family portraits is enough to convert a man to the doctrine of reincarnation'" (2.750). It does not take much to connect this idea with young Ward's later usurpation by his vampiric ancestor, or Delapore's behavioral reversions. But whereas Doyle merely *suggests* such an idea, in an aside by Holmes at the conclusion to the tale, Lovecraft makes it the main kernel/impetus of his weird stories.

VIII. Servants and Peasants

Peter Cannon has noted certain parallels in the depiction of servants in Lovecraft's and Doyle's fiction, adducing the example of the sinister Innsmouthian servants in "The Thing on the Doorstep" in this regard ("The Adventure of the Three Anglo-American Authors" 143) But he does not specifically note the clear parallel *in language* between Doyle's description of the servant couple in his sinister "The Adventure of the Copper Beeches" and Lovecraft's description of the aged Innsmouthian pair:

"The Adventure of the Copper Beeches"	"The Thing on the Doorstep"
The servants consist of "a man and his wife" (Doyle 1.324), the former "a rough, uncouth man, with grizzled hair and whiskers, and *a perpetual smell of drink*" (1.324; my emphasis). The servant's wife is "a very tall and strong woman with a sour face" (1.324). The two form "a most unpleasant couple."	The servants include an "aged couple" (*DH* 283), and "a swarthy wench who had marked anomalies of feature and seemed *to exude a perpetual odour of fish*" (*DH* 283; my emphasis). The fishy servant is called a "repulsive wench" (*DH* 285).

Aside from the obvious parallel in the words "perpetual odour" used by Lovecraft and "perpetual smell" by Doyle, one notes the degree to which the fishy odor in Lovecraft's recension perhaps functions as an *analogue* for the smell of alcohol in Doyle's earlier account, with the native Innsmouthians, indeed, described in "The Shadow over Innsmouth" as perpetual alcoholics (*DH* 321). Doyle, however, reveals the female servant in "Copper Beeches," Mrs. Toller, to be benevolent in the end.

Lovecraft, just as Doyle, uses the word "peasants" in his fiction. Doyle refers to the rustic Dartmoor inhabitants as peasants throughout *The Hound of the Baskervilles*[9]—language that Lovecraft duplicates in "The Rats in the Walls" (*DH* 44) and "The Hound" (where he writes of "the peasantry" [*D* 173]). No class bias is discernible in Doyle's usage, which simply and accurately refers to the largely agrarian residents of outlying non-industrial districts during the period. Lovecraft's usage savors of aristocratic affectation.

IX. A Shadow and a Fear

Fans sometimes dislike Doyle's longer stories because of their glaring lack of Holmes during long stretches of the narrative. A reading of Doyle's brilliant novel *The Valley of Fear* (1915) reveals some interesting parallels with one of Lovecraft's longer narratives, "The Shadow over Innsmouth":

The Valley of Fear	"The Shadow Over Innsmouth"
Both titles feature the juxtaposition of a geographical feature and a signifier of danger. Fear:Shadow; Valley:Innsmouth.	
A formerly benign Masonic order, "The Eminent Order of Freemen," is transformed in the isolated Vermissa Valley mining region into an anti-capitalist, revolutionary, and criminal extortion organization called "The Scowrers," responsible for countless murders, beatings, robberies, and assassinations.	A "former Masonic Hall" (*DH* 318) has been "given over to a degraded cult" under the name of the "Esoteric Order of Dagon."
The Scowrers make their headquarters in McGinty's Saloon and often return home, after a night of carousing, much the worse for wear. The Scowrers are defeated by a Pinkerton agent sent to town to infiltrate their organization from within.	Cf. the omnipresent alcoholic torpor in Innsmouth, whose citizens are, "judging from the quantities of bootleg liquor they consumed" (*DH* 321), spending much "of the daylight hours in an alcoholic stupor."
The supposed criminal McMurdo's *true identity* is Birdy Edwards, a renowned Pinkerton agent.	Innsmouth is saved by a series of "raids and arrests" on the part of the Federal government (*DH* 303). Lovecraft reveals his protagonist's *true identity*, through a secret maternal relationship of the corrupt Captain Marsh to the Innsmouth hybrids.

9. Doyle II:708, 727, 746, 760, 762.

X. Other Parallels

I list further parallels below, tenuous as some may be, for whatever they may be worth. The compilation is by no means exhaustive. (I do not, for instance, note all parallel uses of the word "jaunty" by both Doyle and Lovecraft.) Some are from Doyle's later works, which could not have had as large an impact on the nascent imagination of H. P. Lovecraft as the stories he read while younger.

Foremost among the later tales may be Doyle's macabre "The Adventure of the Devil's Foot" (magazine publication 1910; book publication 1917), in which Doyle refers throughout to what he calls "'The Cornish Horror'" (Doyle 2.955, 956)—language that presents an immediate parallel with Lovecraft's "The Dunwich Horror" (1928). Indeed, the exotic African poison used in the tale, which reduces its victims either to death or to insanity ("gibbering like two great apes" [2.959]), proves to be a root "shaped like a foot, half human, half-goat-like" (2.969)—language that suggests something of Lovecraft's "The Unnamable" (1923), whose monster leaves behind foot marks resembling "split hooves and vaguely anthropoid paws" (D 204), as well as the "almost goatish" (DH 162) appearance of Wilbur Whateley in "The Dunwich Horror." As with the numerous "tall stone pillars" (DH 156) and other prehistoric monuments that dot the countryside in "The Dunwich Horror," the drama of Doyle's Cornish Horror plays out amid a landscape of "strange monuments of stone" and "various earthworks which hinted at prehistoric strife"—all relics "of some vanished race which had passed utterly away" (2.955).

Philip A. Shreffler has noted the Lovecraftian aspects of Doyle's famous passage describing the action of the African poison on Holmes and Watson: its scent induces hallucinations in the two men of a menacing black cloud, within which "lurked all that was vaguely horrible, all that was monstrous and inconceivably wicked in the universe," hinting at "the advent of some unspeakable dweller upon the threshold, whose very shadow would blast my soul" (2.965). As Shreffler observes, this passage could "as easily [. . .] have been written by H. P. Lovecraft as by John H. Watson" and that the story "would have found itself very much at home in the pages of Weird Tales, the publication in which Lovecraft and so many other authors of terrifying tales saw their work in print" ("Watson's Weird Tales" 6).

"A Scandal in Bohemia" (1891)	"Medusa's Coil"
Irene Adler "'turned all the men's heads down in that part'" of town (Doyle 1.168).	Marceline de Russy's "dance around the stone pillars at Auteuil" in France, "used to make those goggle-eyed yaps stare!" (*HM* 181).
"The Naval Treaty" (1894) "A slight noise" in the night, heard by a convalescent, akin to "the sound which a mouse makes when it is gnawing a plank" (1.461), proves to be that of a burglar outside the window.	Cf. the rat noises heard in "The Rats in the Walls" and other stories.
The Sign of Four The malevolent hordes of the Indian Mutiny are like "'a swarm of bees'" (1.146), and 'The city of Agra swarms "with fanatics and fierce devil-worshippers of all sorts'" (1.146).	Cf. Lovecraft's numerous references to "swarms" (*DH* 336, 363, *D* 256, etc.), and also the reappearance of "serious native unrest" (*DH* 132) in India in "The Call of Cthulhu."
"The Adventure of Wisteria Lodge" (magazine pub. 1908; book pub. 1917) A "retired brewer called Melville" (2.871) plays a vaguely peripheral role in the story, serving solely to introduce another peripheral character to the murder victim.	"Celephaïs" Cf. Lovecraft's "notably fat and especially offensive millionaire brewer" (*D* 89), who usurps the social position of the aristocratic Kuranes.
A former dictator, calling himself Henderson, the master of High Gable, is rumored by his servants to have "sold his soul to the devil in exchange for money" (2.883).	**"The Shadow Over Innsmouth"** Cf. rumors surrounding Captain Obed Marsh, regarding the source of Innsmouth's gold (*DH* 306).
Garcia's grotesque, voodoo-worshipping servant, is a "half-breed whom he [Garcia] had picked up in his travels" (2.872).	Cf. the numerous "half-breed" or "hybrid" servants in "The Thing on the Doorstep" and *The Case of Charles Dexter Ward*.
This "huge and hideous" (2.880) mulatto servant, with "yellowish features of pronounced negroid type" (2.880), later displays pronounced cannibalistic tendencies, biting at a constable and nearly chewing off his thumb (2.881).	**"Herbert West—Reanimator"** Cf. Buck Robinson, whose black features are accentuated by Lovecraft, and who is later observed devouring the *hand* of a young child (*D* 148).
Holmes quotes from *Voodooism and the Negroid Religions* (2.887), reciting a passage describing "human sacrifices followed by cannibalism."	Cf. Lovecraft's citing of voodoo rites in "The Rats in the Walls" (*DH* 31) and "The Call of Cthulhu" (*DH* 133).

"The Adventure of the Creeping Man" (magazine pub. 1923; book pub. 1927) Professor Presbury devolves into the form of an ape.	**"The Dunwich Horror"** Wilbur Whateley walks with a "gorilla-like lope" (*DH* 171).
Presbury is subject to the attacks of his once loyal dog, "which ramped and raged in front of him" (2.1081), with Presbury "crouching frog-like upon the ground and goading to a wilder exhibition of passion the maddened hound" (2.1081).	Wilbur Whateley is attacked by the "savage watchdog on the college campus" (*DH* 173). The Innsmouth residents, too, display frog-like characteristics.
"The Man with the Twisted Lip" (1892) Murderous things happen on moonless nights in a sinister building near the corner of Paul's Wharf. "'Between the wharf and the bedroom window is a narrow strip, which is dry at low tide but is covered at high tide with at least four and a half feet of water'" (1.235).	**"The Shadow over Innsmouth"** Cf. the sinister Devil's Reef off the coast of Innsmouth, where a narrow strip of land is visible at low tide, and where Captain Obed Marsh was seen to consort with the Deep Ones.
"The Crooked Man" (1894) Investigating the murder of an army Colonel, Holmes discovers "'tracings of the footmarks of some small animal'" (1.416) on a curtain in the room, prints that prove to be from "'Neither dog nor cat nor monkey nor any creature that we are familiar with. I have tried to reconstruct it from the measurements . . .'" Attempting to deduce what the creature is, Holmes decides that it is carnivorous, and "'probably some creature of the weasel and stoat tribe—and yet it is larger than any of these that I have seen'" (1.416).	**"Dreams in the Witch House"** Student Walter Gilman catches glimpses of a "darting little furry object" (*MM* 266), "no larger than a good-sized rat" (*MM* 266) that combines aspects of a human with that of a rodent. *Animal prints* also form one of the clues as to the creature: Gilman sees "some curious muddy rat-tracks leading out of a fresh [rat] hole and back into it again" (*MM* 287).[10]

10. Others have suggested a connection between HPL's Brown Jenkin and a real mongoose that apparently haunted the Isle of Man (Cannon, *H. P. Lovecraft* 137). I have suggested a connection with HPL's reading of the various witch accounts cited by Dr. Margaret A. Murray, in which similar ratlike familiars often are described (see my essay "Triumvirate of Trouble: Blacks, Jews, and Women in the Fiction of H. P. Lovecraft" [forthcoming].)

"The Adventure of the Illustrious Client" A wronged woman of the street splashes acid in the face of the evil murderous womanizer Baron Gruner. Gruner, in agony, denounces her as a "'she-devil'" (2.998).	"The Thing on the Doorstep" Asenath Waite is described as a "she-devil" (*DH* 294–96).[11]
"The Adventure of the Sussex Vampire" (magazine pub. 1924; book pub. 1927) A South American poison— "curare or some other devilish drug" (2.1043)—is used to poison an infant.	"The Silver Key" (1926) Randolph Carter describes "a South American acquaintance" (*MM* 413) who provides him with "a very curious liquid to take him to oblivion without suffering" (*MM* 413).

XI. The Unnamable and Some Conclusions

Philip A. Shreffler's contention that "a substantial number of the Holmes adventures may be classified as horror stories" ("Watson's Weird Tales" 7) rests primarily on the numerous instances of sadism in the tales—what Shreffler calls a fascination with "gore" (9) evident in the Canon, which is often completely "independent of any supernaturalism at all" (7), and which Shreffler contrasts with a Victorian age and society that, however incongruously, "valued delicacy and manners" (8) above all else. In this, however, the Holmes Canon is not unique, and directly mirrors such contemporary works as Stevenson's *Dr. Jekyll and Mr. Hyde*, Arthur Machen's horror stories, and the often provocative writings of the decadents, all of which were in turn influenced by the lurid and sensationalist journalism of the period—what Holmes, in "The Adventure of the Red Circle" (magazine pub. 1911; book pub.1917) calls "a chorus of groans, cries, and bleatings!" emanating from the "agony columns of the various London journals" (Doyle 2.904). As Thomas Boyle observes in his study of Victorian journalism, *Black Swine in the Sewers of Hampstead*, the tenor of the mid-Victorian newspaper was "sensational to say the least" (3), and "certainly not supportive of an image of domestic tranquility" (3) such as is usually associated with the period, being filled with lurid accounts of murders, suicides, crimes, and accidents of the most horrible sort.

Holmes often regards Watson's detective stories as being the

---

11. See note 7.

true version of events (despite Watson's occasional embellish-
ments)—as in "The Adventure of the Retired Colourman" (1927),
in which Holmes, reading a newspaper account that incorrectly
credits the official police force, rather than himself, with solving the
case, tells Watson, "'You can file it in our archives. Some day the
true story will be told'" (Doyle 2.1122). As in Lovecraft's *At the
Mountains of Madness*, the *true* account is not found in either the
newspapers or the official record, but rather in Watson's and Dyer's
later literary efforts, in which much is still left unsaid. Indeed, much
like Lovecraft's Dyer and Danforth, who "had to adopt an actual
rule of strict censorship" (*MM* 28) in what they told, in the interest
of "the public's general peace of mind" (*MM* 33), so too will Holmes
and Watson conceal far more than they reveal with regard to events
of both public importance and personal privacy.

Doyle's contemporaries were very much aware of Dr. Watson's
paradoxical role as both revealer and censor: a paradox shared by
Lovecraft's Dyer and other narrators. As a friend of decadent artist
Fred Holland Day wrote to Day in 1909: "I told Bro. [Herbert]
Copeland you should have had a Dr. Watson to place the chronicles
of No. 9 [Pinckney Street] in enduring print. He thought, sometimes the truth is better left unsaid. Nevertheless, the walls, doubtless if they could speak, could tell some interesting tales" (Jussim
194). In "The Adventure of Charles Augustus Milverton," for example—a narrative steeped in much the same atmosphere of
blackmail and scandal that immerses Stevenson's *Dr. Jekyll and Mr.
Hyde* and Machen's *The Great God Pan*—Watson tells us how, "For
a long time, even with the utmost discretion and reticence, it would
have been impossible to make the facts public," although now,
"with due suppression the story may be told in such a fashion as to
injure no one" (Doyle 2.572). The story may thus be told, but certain
aspects of it still remain unnamable. (The fact that whatever suppression in which Watson engages would in reality never be sufficient actually to conceal the true identity of the woman who
figures in the narrative, must be ignored by the casual reader.)

In Doyle's "The Adventure of the Empty House," meanwhile,
Watson observes that he had been "barred by a positive prohibition
from his [Holmes's] own lips" from sharing his knowledge with the
public—a prohibition "which was only withdrawn upon the third

of last month" (2.483). In Lovecraft's "The Whisperer in Darkness," too, Wilmarth will encounter a similar such prohibition from Akeley, speaking of "Akeley's imperative command to tell no one of the matter before us. If I seem to disobey that command now, it is only because I think at this stage a warning [. . .] is more conducive to public safety than silence would be" (*DH* 224).

Perhaps realizing the implicit contradiction between Watson's reputation for trustworthiness on the one hand and his simultaneous trade as an author on the other, Doyle repeatedly stresses the propriety of both Holmes and Watson. Watson, Holmes tells us, is "the very soul of discretion" (Doyle 2.1072); while Watson himself reassures us, regarding those cases "which involve the secrets of private families," "I need not say that such a breech of confidence is unthinkable, and that these records will be separated and destroyed now that my friend has time to turn his energies to the matter" (2.1055)—burned just the way Thurber burns the offending photograph in Lovecraft's "Pickman's Model" (*DH* 25), or just as the raiding party on the vampiric Joseph Curwen's farm "destroyed each scrap which bore the least allusion to the matter" (*MM* 146), or just as the narrator in Lovecraft's "Cool Air" "drew a match and burned" a "stickily smeared paper" "to a crisp" (*DH* 207), which told the truth about Dr. Muñoz's true medical condition, or the way the fellow members of Jermyn's Royal Anthropological Institute burn "the thing" they find in a box, later refusing to "admit that Arthur Jermyn ever existed" (*D* 82). In "Hypnos," too, even "a wish which he dared not utter with his tongue" (*D* 166) is dangerous enough to be burned.

The strong similarities between the mutual reticences of Dr. Watson and Lovecraft's narrators helps to illuminate a common point of misunderstanding with regard to Lovecraft's concept of The Unnamable, since the fact that Lovecraft's Dyer vainly wishes, as he tells us, to "let hints stand for actual fact and ineluctable deduction" (*MM* 36) means that the deductions *are* there for him to make. Science is not rendered *mute* by The Unnamable in Lovecraft's works, as so many of his readers seem to believe; rather, *Man* is rendered mute due to what Science *reveals about* The Unnamable, and Man's reaction thereto—a reaction grounded in essentially Victorian social proprieties and ineluctable taboos.

This strong intermixture of sadism and probity, of secrecy and revelation in Doyle's mysteries, often with regard to sinister male or paternal figures, suggests what aspects of the Sherlock Holmes mysteries the young H. P. Lovecraft would have found interesting. Indeed, this same mix of sadism, gore, and reticence would go on to be characteristic of most of Lovecraft's (ostensibly cosmic) horror stories. The same crimes and passions that underlie most of the cases investigated by the cold and steely Holmes would likewise form the animating motive underlying Lovecraft's bacchanalian and ecstatic Cthulhu Cult.

Lovecraft was not the only writer to be influenced by Doyle's mysteries. James Joyce mentions Sherlock Holmes and Doyle's other writings in *Finnegans Wake,* and Samuel Rosenberg even traces the basic plot of Joyce's *Ulysses* to the plot of *A Study in Scarlet* (107). T. S. Eliot, meanwhile, quotes directly from Doyle's "The Musgrave Ritual" in his play *The Murder in the Cathedral* and mentions the "Baskerville Hound" in his poem "Lines to Ralph Hodgson Esquire." Both writers used the narrative of Holmes to make sophisticated commentaries involving their own polemical views of the world. Lovecraft is part of this tradition.

Acknowledgments

Special thanks to Steven Rothman of the *Baker Street Journal,* to *Intellisearch* at the Toronto Public Library, and to S. T. Joshi for providing invaluable research materials that aided in the completion of this essay.

Works Cited

Blackmore, Leigh. "Sherlock Holmes Meets Cthulhu: A. C. Doyle & H. P. Lovecraft." Black Mausoleum. <http://members. optusnet. com.au/lvxnox/articles.html>, accessed 2 December 2011.

Boyle, Thomas. *Black Swine in the Sewers of Hampstead: Beneath the Surface of Victorian Sensationalism.* New York: Viking, 1989.

Cannon, Peter. "The Adventure of the Three Anglo-American Authors: Some Reflections on Conan Doyle, P. G. Wodehouse, and H. P. Lovecraft." 1994. Included in *The Lovecraft Papers.* New York: Guild America Books, n.d. 133–50.

————. *H. P. Lovecraft*. Twayne's United States Authors Series. Boston: G. K. Hall, 1989.

————. "Parallel Passages in 'The Adventures of the Copper Beeches' and 'The Picture in the House.'" *Lovecraft Studies* No. 1 (Fall 1979): 3–6.

————. "The Return of Sherlock Holmes and H. P. Lovecraft." *Baker Street Journal* No. 34 (1984): 217–20.

Cannon, Peter. "Scream for Jeeves." 1994. Included in *The Lovecraft Papers*. New York: Guild America Books, n.d. 77–132.

————. "You Have Been in Providence, I Perceive." *Nyctalops* No. 14 (March 1978): 45–46.

D'Agati, Deborah. "The Problem with Solving: Implications for Sherlock Holmes and Lovecraft Narrators." *Lovecraft Studies* Nos. 42–43 (Autumn 2001): 54–60.

Doyle, Sir Arthur Conan. *The Complete Sherlock Holmes*. Garden City, NY: Doubleday, n.d. 2 vols.

Joshi, S. T. *H. P. Lovecraft: A Life*. West Warwick, RI: Necronomicon Press, 1996.

Jussim, Estelle. *Slave to Beauty: The Eccentric Life and Controversial Career of F. Holland Day, Photographer, Publisher, Aesthete*. Boston: David R. Godine, 1981.

Mather, Cotton. *On Witchcraft: Being The Wonders of the Invisible World*. New York: Dorset Press, 1991.

Radford, John. Interview: "Sherlock Holmes—The Great Detective." *A&E Biography*. Produced and Directed by Peter Swain. A Satellite Documentary Production. A&E, 1995.

Rosenberg, Samuel. *Naked Is the Best Disguise: The Death and Resurrection of Sherlock Holmes*. Indianapolis: Bobbs-Merrill, 1974.

Shreffler, Philip A. *The H. P. Lovecraft Companion*. Westport, CT: Greenwood Press, 1977.

————. "Watson's Weird Tales: Horror in the Sherlockian Canon." *Baker Street Journal* 56, No. 2 (Summer 2006): 6–16.

Swanson, Martin J. "Sherlock Holmes and H. P. Lovecraft." *NOW* 4, No. 1 (Winter 1963): 35–37.

Review

H. P. LOVECRAFT. *The Annotated Revisions and Collaborations of H. P. Lovecraft*. Edited by S. T. Joshi. Welches, OR: Arcane Wisdom (Bloodletting Press). Volume I: *Medusa's Coil and Others* (2011), 475 pp. Volume II: *The Crawling Chaos and Others* (2012), 350 pp. Limited edition hardcovers signed by the editor and numbered on a custom signature sheet featuring artwork by Zach McCain. Reviewed by Steven J. Mariconda.

This is a beautifully edited, illustrated, and produced two-volume set. The publisher promotes it as including "the best" of Lovecraft's revisions and collaborations. This is a bit like promoting "the best of the worst." While if there is little to recommend here on the merits of the stories themselves, there are at least several powerful items, plus the critical apparatus, that combine to make the set worth owning. S. T. Joshi again breaks new ground by providing a brief overview of each story, determining the definitive texts, outlining the details of the writing and Lovecraft's likely contribution, and annotating the material. Many of the never-before-published annotations, in particular, shed new light on these works and the author's creative process.

For the Lovecraft scholar, the revisions and collaborations represent a vexing question: why are they so bad? Lovecraft only wrote about fifty or sixty stories, and after enjoying these amazing creations we naturally go looking for more. Several generations of hopeful Lovecraft addicts have eagerly sought these stories out, in the hope of a further fix of the intoxicating elixir distilled into "The Call of Cthulhu" or "The Colour out of Space." What they have found is less like an elixir and more like an emetic. Even after reading and studying Lovecraft for many years, one comes away from these stories appalled and confused regarding how it all went to so horribly wrong. No matter how you approach this body of work, the bulk of it remains dross, with which we would be better off without. There are a few gems mixed in, but precious few.

Joshi's excellent introduction and notes go a long way toward sorting a lot of the confusion regarding this material. He unwinds all the details and makes the facts of who, what, and where easy to understand. And he also confronts the second big question regarding the revisions—what the hell was Lovecraft thinking? Lovecraft, who never had a nine-to-five job, apparently decided he could make an income by providing revisory services to struggling writers. Fair enough. However, it seems he only helped writers who were really, really struggling. And he only helped writers who were writing weird fiction—really, really bad weird fiction. And he only helped writers who had no means to pay him.

Re-reading these stories after a long period of time, it may be affirmed that none of the co-authors represented had any talent. At least one, Zealia Bishop, appears to have been borderline illiterate. Taking pen in hand, this is all she could choke out: "There is an Indian mound near here, which is haunted by a headless ghost. Sometimes it is a woman." Not exactly Zola or Proust, or even Seabury Quinn. Lovecraft conceived the notion that he would spin this out into the 30,000-word novella "The Mound." And he somehow came up with a story that is better than some of his signed work (including the "The Dunwich Horror" [1928]). But perhaps there *was* a method to Lovecraft's madness: reverse psychology. Bishop later recalled: "The stories I sent him always came back so revised from their basic idea that I felt I was a complete failure as a writer." Well moused, lion.

Another perplexing issue: why were so many of Lovecraft's revision clients female? The roster sounds like a women's softball team, and despite Joshi's scorecard there remains a lingering suspicion they are the same person. After all, their stories all equally appalling, and their names sound pretty much interchangeable: Winifred Virginia Jackson, Winifred Virginia Jordan, Zealia Brown, Zealia Brown Reed, Zealia Reed Bishop, Anna Helen Crofts, Sonia Haft Greene, Elizabeth Neville Berkeley, and Hazel Heald. Why did Lovecraft not supply Heald, a valued client, with a middle name? Could he not have borrowed one from Ms.

Bishop? Joshi confides that Heald, a divorcée residing in Somerville, Mass., was romantically attracted to Lovecraft. Coming back from a trip to Quebec, Lovecraft told a friend "he was going to take a midnight bus to Providence after dinner in Somerville." Did Lovecraft ever actually get on that bus, and if he didn't, how long was Hazel held? Joshi wisely leaves this question to future scholars. One hopes the story "Midnight Bus to Providence," as by Hazel Winifred Neville, remains undiscovered in the pages of *Thrilling Love* magazine.

The tales are presented in chronological order of writing. The first volume contains eighteen items written up to 1930, plus four items to which Lovecraft contributed relatively less content. There are several stories worth reading here. The Winifred V. Jackson items are redolent of Edgar Allan Poe—the Poe of "The Colloquy of Monos and Una" and "Shadow—A Parable." "The Green Meadow" (1918/19) has an introduction in Lovecraft's realistic style, and a theme that anticipates "The Colour out of Space." "The Crawling Chaos" (1920/1921) has a compelling frisson, in part because of a nebulous connection with "Nyarlathotep" (1920). Both were written around the same time; the two items share little beyond the memorable phrase "the Crawling Chaos," certainly one of the most Lovecraftian of all Lovecraft's locutions. Pioneering Lovecraft scholar George Wetzel saw the two Jackson tales, plus "Poetry and the Gods" (with Anna Helen Crofts, 1920) as part of a "trilogy of quasi-Greek stories" that Lovecraft wrote. Wetzel's argument that the Cthulhu Mythos was influenced by Greek mythology is unconvincing, but he makes the interesting point that the stories in this cluster end with a kind of cosmic apocalypse that is a distinctively Lovecraftian trope.

"Under the Pyramids" (with Harry Houdini, 1924), long considered as part of the Lovecraft cannon proper, towers above the other items here as the Pyramids tower over the plateau of Giza. This story marks the apex of Lovecraft's early style—incandescent in the manner of Lafacadio Hearn's translations of Théophile Gautier and Gustave Flaubert:

> Mystery attracts mystery. Ever since the wide appearance of my name as a performer of unexplained feats, I have encountered

strange narratives and events which my calling has led people to link with my interests and activities. Some of these have been trivial and irrelevant, some deeply dramatic and absorbing, some productive of weird and perilous experiences, and some involving me in extensive scientific and historical research. Many of these matters I have told and shall continue to tell freely; but there is one of which I speak with great reluctance, and which I am now relating only after a session of grilling persuasion from the publishers of this magazine, who had heard vague rumours of it from other members of my family.

This is a classic Lovecraft opening paragraph. It looks back to "The Statement of Randolph Carter" (1919) and forward to "The Call of Cthulhu" (1926)—the first-person narrator suspended between reticence and revelation, the modulated periods, the many parallel constructions, and the suspended syntactical closure. The story is constructed with several sub-climaxes, featuring some energetic bursts of pure Lovecraftian prose:

Then the mental cataclysm came. It was horrible—hideous beyond all articulate description because it was all of the soul, with nothing of detail to describe. It was the ecstasy of nightmare and the summation of the fiendish. The suddenness of it was apocalyptic and daemoniac—one moment I was plunging agonisingly down that narrow well of million-toothed torture, yet the next moment I was soaring on bat-wings in the gulfs of hell; swinging free and swoopingly through illimitable miles of boundless, musty space; rising dizzily to measureless pinnacles of chilling ether, then diving gaspingly to sucking nadirs of ravenous, nauseous lower vacua. . . . Thank God for the mercy that shut out in oblivion those clawing Furies of consciousness which half unhinged my faculties, and tore Harpy-like at my spirit! That one respite, short as it was, gave me the strength and sanity to endure those still greater sublimations of cosmic panic that lurked and gibbered on the road ahead.

To bask in the white heat of Lovecraft's descriptions of "nighted, necropolitan Egypt" is enough justification to go out and purchase these volumes.

A more modest but no less interesting achievement is the last

story in the volume, written with Zealia Bishop in 1929–30. From
the low plateau of "The Mound" one can see the titanic peaks of
At the Mountains of Madness, written a year later. "The Mound" is
one of many stories here that really benefit from Joshi's new annotations. A member of Coronado's expedition of 1541, one
Zamacona y Nuñez, conducts an expedition to the mound region
of Oklahoma. There he hears tales of an underground realm of
great wealth beneath a mound, and finds an Indian who will lead
him there. Zamacona comes upon the civilization of Xinaian, established by creatures from outer space. These inhabitants possess
powers of telepathy and the dematerialization—an ability to dissolve themselves and nearby objects and reconstitute the atoms at
a distant location. Zamacona initially finds the civilization has declined both intellectually and morally from a much higher level
into decadence. He attempts to escape but suffers a horrible fate.
His written record of his adventures is unearthed in modern times
by an archeologist, who paraphrases his tale. The story is the first
of Lovecraft's tales to utilize an alien civilization as a metaphor for
dystopic Western civilization: "Daily life was organised in ceremonial patterns; with games, intoxication, torture of slaves, day-
dreaming, gastronomic and emotional orgies, religious exercises,
exotic experiments, and the like, as the principal occupations."
Very much like modern American, except for the artistic and philosophical discussions. There is a strange thread of sadism and violence in this story like nothing else in Lovecraft:

> As time progressed, [Zamacona] noticed an increasing tendency of
> the people to resort to dematerialisation as an amusement; so that
> the apartments and amphitheaters of Tsath became a veritable
> Witches' Sabbath of transmutations, age-adjustments, death-
> experiments, and projections. With the growth of boredom and
> restlessness, he saw, cruelty and subtlety and revolt were growing
> apace. There was more and more cosmic abnormality, more and
> more curious sadism, more and more ignorance and superstition,
> and more and more desire to escape out of physical life into a
> half-spectral state of electronic dispersal.

Note the closing, prescient allusion to Facebook.

The second volume, which contains thirteen items, continues

to appall and confuse. There are fewer thrills and more comedy, all of it unintentional. It becomes progressively impossible to decide at any given moment if Lovecraft is pulling the reader's leg. He *must* be kidding—how could he possibly plagiarize and parody himself so badly without knowing it? Take for example the speech of a black maid in "Medusa's Coil" (with Zealia Bishop, 1930):

> "'Iä! Iä! Shub-Niggurath! Ya-R'lyeh! N'gagi n'bulu bwana n'lolo! Ya, yo, pore Missy Tanit, pore Missy Isis! Marse Clooloo, come up outen de water an' git yo chile—she done daid! She done daid! De hair ain' got no missus no mo', Marse Clooloo. Ol' Sophy, she know! Ol' Sophy, she done got de black stone outen Big Zimbabwe in ol' Affriky! Ol' Sophy, she done dance in de moonshine roun' de crocodile-stone befo' de N'bangus cotch her and sell her to de ship folks! No mo' Tanit! No mo' Isis! No mo' witch-woman to keep de fire a-goin' in de big stone place! Ya, yo! N'gagi n'bulu bwana n'lolo! Iä! Shub-Niggurath! She daid! Ol' Sophy know!'"

"The Horror in the Museum" (with Hazel Heald, 1932) and "Out of the Aeons" (also with Heald, 1933), too, have the stench of "Marse Clooloo" hanging about them, but here it is as if the octopoid god has been pickled in formaldehyde. This must have been a truly difficult time for Lovecraft the writer, in between the composition of "The Dreams in the Witch House" and "The Thing on the Doorstep," both signed fictional misfires.

One actual boon for the uninitiated in the second volume is "The Night Ocean" (with R. H. Barlow, 1936), which has the feel of a prose poem and something the manner of Algernon Blackwood's *Incredible Adventures*. Also of note is "The Challenge from Beyond" (with C. L. Moore, A. Merritt, Robert E. Howard, and Frank Belknap Long, 1935), a round-robin tale where one author begins the story, and another author continues the story to a certain point, after which yet another author picks it up, and so on. Lovecraft fares well among his pulpish peers.

In terms of comic rather than cosmic appeal, one of the crown jewels in this volume is "The Diary of Alonzo Typer" (1935). The story was written with William Lumley (yet another illiterate, insolvent client). A diary is found in an old Dutch house in upstate

New York near the town of Chorazin. The diarist is an occultist investigating rumors of a haunting. He finds himself unable to leave the premises, trapped by a wall of brambles, and tormented by the spirits and the shadowy presence of something with very large paws. Again, one is unable to tell if Lovecraft is dryly mocking his own style or playing it straight: "I am conscious of several presences in this house. One in particular is decidedly hostile toward me—a malevolent will which is seeking to break down my own and overcome me. I must not countenance this for an instant, but must use all my forces to resist it." During his explorations of the house, he finds a locked door in the basement, the key, and the incantations to enter the mysterious realm of Yian-ho beyond the portal. The ending never fails to amuse, and is one of the most quoted passages in Lovecraft. So here it is again—classic Lovecraft—parody or not, none dare say: "Too late—cannot help self—black paws materialise—am dragged away toward the cellar. . . ."

www.ingramcontent.com/pod-product-compliance
Lightning Source LLC
Chambersburg PA
CBHW051820090426
42736CB00011B/1577